The Akhirah Expounded

By Gregory Heary

The Akhirah is an Arabic word referring to the eternal afterlife. The Akhirah is every person's ultimate destination regardless of their beliefs or deeds. As Islam is the prophetic religion and Muhammad pbuh is the final prophet, the revelation sent to Muhammad pbuh within the Quran and authentic hadith contains the most detailed information about the Akhirah known to mankind in the age of modern history. As a former Christian I can testify Christians and non-Muslims in general have virtually no textually based ideas or details regarding the afterlife and the whole entirety of the average non-Muslim's knowledge about the subject are based completely upon traditional myths, guess and conjecture. Thus in the Quran 2:111 it says: *And they say, "None shall enter Paradise unless he be a Jew or a Christian." These are their own desires. Say, "Produce your proof if you are truthful."* It is because of such gross ignorance, due directly to their lack of proof which leads to baseless claims founded upon personal whims, that they ultimately meet some of the worst of experiences in that afterlife because a lack of knowledge always leads to corruption in creed and deed. Then you have extremists who say *"So and So is in heaven"* or *"So and So is in hell"* without textual evidences for such claims which are proclaimed merely because of personal beliefs, desires, hopes, dreams and preferences. Therefore I feel it necessary to present the data regarding what is known about the afterlife so that nobody else makes baseless claims or clings to faulty creeds. Truly nobody in the modern era has any excuse to regard what comes after death as being unknown or debatable. It is known! It is proven! It's as simple as doing the research but because it is unseen today many confuse the unseen future for the unknown or unknowable. Such a position constitutes disbelief in that unseen reality by rejecting the known proofs concerning its details. You can't get credit from the Creator for believing in the unseen afterlife if you don't know anything about it. Nor if you believe false things concerning it. To hold a position of *"Well when I die then I'll find out the truth for sure."* is to disbelieve in the authentic data already available and is no different than believing falsehood about the Akhirah whatever falsehood that may be. As a gambler would say: *"You can't win unless you place your bet before the game is over."* Its more foolish to disbelieve in the Akhirah than it is to disbelieve in the weather forecast especially when the details about the Akhirah are more certain and reliable than the detailed weather forecasts. It's truly amazing that God is known by unanimous worldwide consensus to not have given us information regarding the future weather but the vast majority place more faith in mankind's predictions on the weather for the future than they do for the Akhirah which God has given us information about, of which some people enter on a daily basis to exist there forever. Due to the clarity and abundance of authentic prophetic textual information regarding the eternal afterlife, I will limit my commentary to the minimum aside from what is essential so the overall synopsis is coherent. The texts are clear. I am compiling some of the available data in a semi-chronological format, relying upon Quran with occasional Tafsir and reliable hadith (mainly from the six Sunan) to create this primer on the Akhirah. Lastly correct beliefs about the Akhirah should cause correct deeds in this life. So, improve.

Data about Death

Quran 2:28

How can you disbelieve in Allâh? Seeing that you were dead and He gave you life. Then He will give you death, then again will bring you to life (on the Day of Resurrection) and then unto Him you will return.

Quran 2:154

And say not of those who are killed in the Way of Allâh, "They are dead." Nay, they are living, but you perceive (it) not.

Narrated Jabir ibn Atik:

The Messenger of Allah came to visit Abdullah ibn Thabit who was ill. He found that he was dominated (by the divine decree). The Messenger of Allah called him loudly, but he did not respond.

He uttered the Qur'anic verse "We belong to Allah and to Him do we return" and he said: We have been dominated against you, AburRabi'. Then the women cried and wept, and Ibn Atik began to silence them. The Messenger of Allah said: Leave them, when the divine decree is made, no woman should weep.

They (the people) asked: What is necessary happening, Messenger of Allah? He replied: Death. His daughter said: I hope you will be a martyr, for you have completed your preparations for jihad. The Messenger of Allah said: Allah Most High gave him a reward according to his intentions. What do you consider martyrdom?

They said: Being killed in the cause of Allah.

The Messenger of Allah said: There are seven types of martyrdom in addition to being killed in Allah's cause: one who dies of plague is a martyr; one who is drowned is a martyr; one who dies of pleurisy is a martyr; one who dies of an internal complaint is a martyr; one who is burnt to death is a martyr; who one is killed by a building falling on him is a martyr; and a woman who dies while pregnant is a martyr.

Source: Sunan Abi Dawud 3111 Graded Sahih by Albani

Narrated Hasana' daughter of Mu'awiyah:

She reported on the authority of her paternal uncle: I asked the Prophet: Who are in Paradise? He replied: Prophets are in Paradise, martyrs are in Paradise, infants are in Paradise and children buried alive are in Paradise.

Source: Sunan Abi Dawud 2521 Graded Sahih by Albani

Ka'b ibn Malik reported: The Messenger of Allah, said,

"Verily, the souls of martyrs are in green birds, hanging from the fruit of Paradise, or the trees of Paradise."

Source: Sunan al-Tirmidhī 1641 Graded Sahih by Tirmidhi

It was narrated from Miqdam bin Ma'dikarib that the Messenger of Allah (ﷺ) said:

"The martyr has six things (in store) with Allah: He is forgiven from the first drop of his blood that is shed; he is shown his place in Paradise; he is spared the torment of the grave; he is kept safe from

the Great Fright; he is adorned with a garment of faith; he is married to (wives) from among the wide-eyed houris; and he is permitted to intercede for seventy of his relatives."

Source: Sunan ibn Majah English reference: Vol. 4, Book 24, Hadith 2799

Graded Hasan by Darussalam

It has been narrated on the authority of Masruq Who said:

We asked 'Abdullah about the Qur'anic verse:" Think not of those who are slain in Allah's way as dead. Nay, they are alive, finding their sustenance in the presence of their Lord.." (iii. 169). He said: We asked the meaning of the verse (from the Prophet) who said: The souls, of the martyrs live in the bodies of green birds who have their nests in chandeliers hung from the throne of the Almighty. They eat the fruits of Paradise from wherever they like and then nestle in these chandeliers. Once their Lord cast a glance at them and said: Do ye want anything? They said: What more shall we desire? We eat the fruit of Paradise from wherever we like. Their Lord asked them the same question thrice. When they saw that they will continue to be asked and not left (without answering the question). they said: O Lord, we wish that Thou mayest return our souls to our bodies so that we may be slain in Thy way once again. When He (Allah) saw that they had no need, they were left (to their joy in heaven).

Source: Sahih Muslim 1887

It was narrated from Kathir bin Murrah that the Messenger of Allah (ﷺ) said:

~ 7 ~

"There is no soul on Earth that dies, and is in a good position before Allah, that would like to come back to you, even if it had all this world, except the one who is killed (in the cause of Allah); he wishes that he could come back and be killed again."

Source: Sunan an-Nasa'i 3159 Graded Hasan by Darussalam

Quran 2:260

And (remember) when Ibrâhim (Abraham) said, "My Lord! Show me how You give life to the dead." He (Allâh) said: "Do you not believe?" He [Ibrâhim] said: "Yes (I believe), but to be stronger in Faith." He said: "Take four birds, then cause them to incline towards you (then slaughter them, cut them into pieces), and then put a portion of them on every hill, and call them, they will come to you in haste. And know that Allâh is All-Mighty, All-Wise."

Tafsir of the ayat by ibn kathir:

Ibrahim caught four birds, slaughtered them, removed the feathers, tore the birds to pieces and mixed the pieces together. He then placed parts of these mixed pieces on four or seven hills. Ibn `Abbas said, "Ibrahim kept the heads of these birds in his hand. Next, Allah commanded Ibrahim to call the birds to him, and he did as Allah commanded him. Ibrahim witnessed the feathers, blood and flesh of these birds fly to each other, and the parts flew each to their bodies, until every bird came back to life and came walking at a fast pace towards Ibrahim, so that the example that Ibrahim was witnessing would become more impressive. Each bird came to collect its head from Ibrahim's hand, and if he gave the bird another head the bird refused to accept it. When Ibrahim gave each bird its own head, the head was placed on its body by Allah's leave and power. "

Quran 2:259

Or like the one who passed by a town and it had tumbled over its roofs. He said: "Oh! How will Allâh ever bring it to life after its death?" So Allâh caused him to die for a hundred years, then raised him up (again). He said: "How long did you remain (dead)?" He (the man) said: "(Perhaps) I remained (dead) a day or part of a day". He said: "Nay, you have remained (dead) for a hundred years, look at your food and your drink, they show no change; and look at your donkey! And thus We have made of you a sign for the people. Look at the bones, how We bring them together and clothe them with flesh". When this was clearly shown to him, he said, "I know (now) that Allâh is Able to do all things."

Tafsir of the ayat by ibn kathir:

Ibn Abi Hatim recorded that `Ali bin Abi Talib said that the Ayah 2:259 meant `Uzayr. Ibn Jarir also reported it, and this explanation was also reported by Ibn Jarir and Ibn Abi Hatim from Ibn `Abbas, Al-Hasan, Qatadah, As-Suddi and Sulayman bin Buraydah. Mujahid bin Jabr said that the Ayah refers to a man from the Children of Israel, and the village was Jerusalem, after Nebuchadnezzar destroyed it and killed its people.

Allah's statement, (up to its roofs) indicates that the roofs and walls (of the village) fell to the ground. `Uzayr stood contemplating about what had happened to that city, after a great civilization used to inhabit it. He said, (Oh! How will Allah ever bring it to life after its death) because of the utter destruction he saw and the implausibility of its returning to what it used to be. Allah said, (So Allah caused him to die for a hundred years, then raised him up (again).)

The city was rebuilt seventy years after the man (`Uzayr) died, and its inhabitants increased and the Children of Israel moved back to it. When Allah resurrected `Uzayr after he died, the first organ that He resurrected were his eyes, so that he could witness what Allah does with him, how He brings life back to his body. When his resurrection was complete, Allah said to him, meaning through the angel, ("How long did you remain (dead)" He (the man) said: "(Perhaps) I remained (dead) a day or part of a day.")

The scholars said that since the man died in the early part of the day and Allah resurrected him in the latter part of the day, when he saw that the sun was still apparent, he thought that it was the sun of that very day. He said, ("Or part of a day. " He said: "Nay, you have remained (dead) for a hundred years, look at your food and your drink, they show no change.")

He had grapes, figs and juice, and he found them as he left them; neither did the juice spoil nor the figs become bitter nor the grapes rot. (And look at your donkey!), "How Allah brings it back to life while you are watching." (And thus We have made of you a sign for the people) that Resurrection

(wakes) you up again that a term appointed (your life period) be fulfilled, then (in the end) unto Him will be your return. Then He will inform you of that which you used to do. (60) He is the Irresistible, Supreme over His slaves, and He sends guardians (angels guarding and writing all of one's good and bad deeds) over you, until when death approaches one of you, Our Messengers (angel of death and his assistants) take his soul, and they never neglect their duty (61) Then they are returned to Allâh, their Maulâ [True Master (God), the Just Lord (to reward them)]. Surely, for Him is the judgement and He is the Swiftest in taking account

Quran 6:93-94

And who can be more unjust than he who invents a lie against Allâh, or says: "A revelation has come to me," whereas as no revelation has come to him in anything; and who says, "I will reveal the like of what Allâh has revealed." And if you could but see when the Zâlimûn (polytheists and wrong-doers) are in the agonies of death, while the angels are stretching forth their hands (saying): "Deliver your souls! This day you shall be recompensed with the torment of degradation because of what you used to utter against Allâh other than the truth. And you used to reject His Ayât (proofs, evidences, verses, lessons, signs, revelations etc.) with disrespect!" (93) And truly you have come unto Us alone (without wealth, companions or anything else) as We created you the first time. You have left behind you all that which We had bestowed on you. We see not with you your intercessors whom you claimed to be partners with Allâh. Now all relations between you and them have been cut off, and all that you used to claim has vanished from you. (94)

Quran 7:37

Who is more unjust than one who invents a lie against Allâh or rejects His Ayât (proofs, evidences, verses, lessons, signs, revelations)? For such their appointed portion (good things of this worldly life and their period of stay therein) will reach them from the Book (of Decrees) until, when Our Messengers (the angel of death and his assistants) come to them to take their souls, they (the angels) will say: "Where are those whom you used to invoke and worship besides Allâh," they will reply, "They have vanished and deserted us." And they will bear witness against themselves, that they were disbelievers.

Quran 16:28-29

"Those whose lives the angels take while they are doing wrong to themselves (by disbelief and by associating partners in worship with Allâh and by committing all kinds of crimes and evil deeds)." Then, they will make (false) submission (saying): "We used not to do any evil." (The angels will reply): "Yes! Truly, Allâh is All-Knower of what you used to do. (28) "So enter the gates of Hell, to abide therein, and indeed, what an evil abode will be for the arrogant."

Quran 16:32

Those whose lives the angels take while they are in a pious state (i.e. pure from all evil, and worshipping none but Allâh Alone) saying (to them): Salâmun 'Alaikum (peace be on you) enter you Paradise, because of that (the good) which you used to do (in the world)."

Quran 18:99

And on that Day [i.e. the Day Ya'jûj and Ma'jûj (Gog and Magog) will come out], We shall leave them to surge like waves on one another, and the Trumpet will be blown, and We shall collect them (the creatures) all together.

Quran 29:57

Everyone shall taste the death. Then unto Us you shall be returned.

Quran 32:11

Say: "The angel of death, who is set over you, will take your souls, Then you shall be brought to your Lord."

Quran 34:51-54

And if you could but see, when they will be terrified with no escape (for them), and they will be seized from a near place. (51) And they will say (in the Hereafter): "We do believe (now);" but how could they receive (Faith and the acceptance of their repentance by Allâh) from a place so far off (i.e. to return to the worldly life again). (52) Indeed they did disbelieve (in the Oneness of Allâh, Islâm, the Qur'ân and Muhammad) before (in this world), and they (used to) conjecture about the unseen [i.e. the Hereafter, Hell, Paradise, Resurrection and the Promise of Allâh (by saying) all that is untrue], from a far place. (53) And a barrier will be set between them and that which they desire [i.e. At-Taubah (turning to Allâh in repentance) and the accepting of Faith], as was done in the past with the people of their kind. Verily, they have been in grave doubt.

Quran 39:42

It is Allâh Who takes away the souls at the time of their death, and those that die not during their sleep. He keeps those (souls) for which He has ordained death and sends the rest for a term appointed. Verily, in this are signs for a people who think deeply.

Quran 41:30-32

Verily, those who say: "Our Lord is Allâh (Alone)," and then they stand firm, on them the angels will descend (at the time of their death) (saying): "Fear not, nor grieve! But receive the glad tidings of Paradise which you have been promised! (30) "We have been your friends in the life of this world and are (so) in the Hereafter. Therein you shall have (all) that your inner-selves desire, and therein you shall have (all) for which you ask. (31) "An entertainment from (Allâh), the Oft-Forgiving, Most Merciful."

Quran 47:25-28

Verily, those who have turned back as disbelievers after the guidance has been manifested to them — Shaitân (Satan) has beautified for them (their false hopes), and (Allâh) prolonged their term (age). (25) This is because they said to those who hate what Allâh has sent down: "We will obey you in part of the matter," but Allâh knows their secrets. (26) Then how (will it be) when the angels will take their souls at death, smiting their faces and their backs? (27) That is because they followed that which angered Allâh, and hated that which pleased Him. So He made their deeds fruitless.

Quran 50:19

And the stupor of death will come in truth: "This is what you have been avoiding!"

Quran 56:83-95

Then why do you not (intervene) when (the soul of a dying person) reaches the throat? (83) And you at the moment are looking on, (84) But We (i.e. Our angels who take the soul) are nearer to him than you, but you see not, (85) Then why do you not, if you are exempt from the reckoning and recompense (punishment) − (86) Bring back the soul (to its body), if you are truthful? (87) Then, if he (the dying person) be of the Muqarrabûn (those brought near to Allâh), (88) (There is for him) rest and provision, and a Garden of Delights (Paradise). (89) And if he (the dying person) be of those on the Right Hand, (90) Then there is safety and peace (from the Punishment of Allâh) for those on the Right Hand. (91) But if he (the dying person) be of the denying (of the Resurrection), the erring (away from the Right Path of Islâmic Monotheism), (92) Then for him is entertainment with boiling water. (93) And burning in Hell-fire. (94) Verily, this! This is an absolute Truth with certainty.

Quran 63:10-11

And spend (in charity) of that with which We have provided you, before death comes to one of you and he says: "My Lord! If only You would give me respite for a little while (i.e. return to the worldly life), then I should give Sadaqah (i.e. Zakât) of my wealth , and be among the righteous [i.e. perform Hajj (pilgrimage to Makkah)] and other good deeds. (10) And Allâh grants respite to none when his appointed time (death) comes. And Allâh is All-Aware of what you do.

Quran 75:26-30

Nay, when (the soul) reaches to the collar bone (i.e. up to the throat in its exit), (26) And it will be said: "Who can cure him (and save him from death)?" (27) And he (the dying person) will conclude that it was (the time) of parting (death); (28) And one leg will be joined with another leg (shrouded) (29) The drive will be, on that Day, to your Lord (Allâh)!

Quran 80:17-22

Be cursed (the disbelieving) man! How ungrateful he is! (17) From what thing did He create him? (18) From Nutfah (male and female semen drops) He created him, and then set him in due proportion; (19) Then He makes the Path easy for him; (20) Then He causes him to die, and puts him in his grave; (21) Then, when it is His Will, He will resurrect him (again).

Data about Life in the Grave

Upon the authority of al-Bara' ibn `Aazib who said:

We went out with the the Prophet to a burial of a man from the Ansar (original inhabitants of Madina) until we arrived at the grave, and he still had not been placed in the slot of the grave.

Then the Messenger of Allah sat down and we sat around him. You would have thought that birds were upon our heads from our silence, and in the hand of the Messenger of Allah was a stick which he was poking the ground with. [Then he started looking at the sky and looking at the earth and looking up down three times]. Then he said to us: "Ask Allah for refuge from the torment of the grave", he repeated this command two or three times. [Then he said O Allah I seek refuge in you from the torment of the grave][three times]. Then he said: "Verily, the believing servant, when leaving this life and journeying to the hereafter angels will descend upon him, their faces will be white as if they were suns, they will have with them a shroud (kafan) from the shroud of Paradise), and an embalmment (Hanout) from the embalmments of heaven. Then, they will sit within eye-shot of him.

Then the angel of death will come and sit at his head and will say "O you virtuous soul; come out to a forgiveness and a pleasure from your Lord ". So it will come out as a drop comes out of the mouth of a jug (with ease), then he will take it, not leaving it in his hand for longer that a blink of an eye until they (he and the other angels) have placed it in that shroud and that embalmment. And there will emanate from it a smell like that of the most sweet smelling musk on the face of the earth. Then they shall ascend with it, and they shall not pass with it by any group of angels but they will say: What is this good and sweet-smelling soul?. Then they shall say to them (he is) "such" the son of "such" choosing the best of the names he used to be called in this life. Until they reach the lowest sky, then they shall ask permission to enter, and they shall be granted entry, until they end at the seventh heaven sky, then Allah, exalted and high, shall say: "write the book of my servant in `illiyeen (1) [And what will expalin to you what Illiyeen is `illiyeen, there is a register fully inscribed to which bear witness those nearest to Allah (see 83:18)], and his book will be written in `illiyeen, and the shall be said "return him to the earth, for [I promised them] I have created them from it, and into it I shall return them, and from it I shall extract (resurrect) them a second time (20:55)". So [he is returned to earth and] his soul is returned to his body [he said and he will hear the footsteps of his friends who buried him when they leave him].

Then two [severe] angels shall come and [terrify him and] sit him up next to them and shall ask him: "Who is your Lord?". He shall reply "My Lord is Allah". Then they shall ask him: "What is your religion?". He shall answer them: "My religion is Islam". Then they shall ask him "Who is this man who was sent among you?". He will reply "He is the Messenger of Allah peace be upon him". Then they shall ask him "What have you done?". He shall reply: "I read the book of Allah, then I believed in it and accepted it". [The angel will terrify him and ask him "who is your Lord?", "what is *your religion?" "who is your prophet?", and this will be the last trial on earth for the believer, it is then when Allah says : "Allah will establish in strength those who believe with the word that stands firm in this world", so he will answer my Lord is Allah, my religion is Islam and my Prophet is Muhammad salla Allahu alaihi wa sallam. Then a caller will call from the sky: "My slave has spoken the truth, so spread out for him from the heaven, and clothe him from the heaven, and open a door for him from the heaven (within his grave)", so it's goodness and its smell will come unto him, then his grave will be expanded for him as far as he can see.*

Then a man will come to him. His face will be handsome, and his clothes will be handsome, and his smell will be sweet. Then he shall say unto him: I bring you glade tidings of that which will make you happy [Rejoice with a pleasure of Allah and delights that endure]. This is the day that you were promised (46:16). Then he will say [and may Allah give you glad tiding] "who are you?, for your face is the face of someone who comes with good news". He shall reply: "I am your good deeds, [by Allah, I did not know of you but that you were quick to the obedience of Allah and slow to His disobedience, so may Allah reward you good]". Then he shall say: "My Lord bring the hour so that I might return to my family and my wealth" [it will be said to him "be tranquil"].

He (Muhammed) said: { And the disbelieving [transgressor/wicked] servant}, if he is leaving this life and journeying to the hereafter then angels will descend upon him, their faces will be black, they have with them a coarse woolen fabric (sackcloth)[made of fire]. Then they will sit within eye-shot of him. Then the angel of death will come and sit at his head and will say "O you wicked soul; come out to a anger from your Lord and a

fury (from Him)". So it will be distributed (spread out) throughout
his body, then it will be ripped away as a skewer/spit is ripped out
of damp cotton [and in its way out it will tear and cut the nerves
and blood vessels] [and then he will be cursed by all the angels
between the earth and the sky and by all the angels in the sky, and
the gates of heaven are closed. There is no gate in the heaven but its
people supplicate that the wicked soul shall not be ascended to their
side], then he will take it (the soul), not leaving it in his hand for
longer than a blink of an eye until they have placed it in that
sackcloth. And there will emanate from it a stench like that of the
most evil smelling corpse on the face of the earth. Then they shall
ascend with it, and they shall not pass with it by a group of angels
but they will say: What is this wicked soul?. Then they shall say to
them (he is) "such" the son of "such" choosing the most hated of
the names he used to be called in this life. Until they reach the
lowest heaven(sky), then they shall ask permission to enter, and
they shall not be granted entry. Then the Messenger of Allah
recited "The doors of the sky are not opened to them, nor shall they
enter heaven until the camel passes through the eye of the needle"
(7:40)[which is impossible].

Then Allah, exalted and high, shall say: "write the book of my
servant in Sijjeen (2)(83:7) in the lowest earth". [Then will be said
"return my slave to the earth, for I promised them I have created
them from it, and into it I shall return them, and from it I shall
extract (resurrect) them a second time (20:55)"]. Then his soul
shall be taken away [from the sky] with a mighty hurl [until it is
cast into his body]. Then he (the Prophet) read: "and those who
associate partners with Allah, They are as one who falls from the
sky then is snatched by the birds or is cast by the wind into a very

~ 22 ~

low place (22:31)". Then his soul will be returned into his body, [he (the prophet) said : verily he will hear the footsteps of his friends who buried him when they leave him]. Then two harsh severe and fearsome angels shall come and [terrify him and] sit him up and shall ask him: "Who is your Lord?". He shall reply "Huh?, Huh (this is an expression of sorrow), I don't know". Then they shall ask him: "What is your religion?". He shall answer them: "Huh?, Huh?, I don't know". Then they shall ask him "Who is this man who was sent among you?". He will reply "Huh?, Huh?, I don't know [I heard people saying that!]". He (the Prophet) said "And then will be said to him don't ever know and don't ever recite!"

Then a caller will call from the sky: "My slave has spoken falsely, so spread out for him from the hell fire, and open a door for him from the hell fire (within his grave)", so its heat and hot wind will come unto him, then his grave will be contracted upon him until his limbs are caught up among one another. Then a man will come to him. His face will be ugly, and his clothes will be ugly, and his smell will be vile. Then he shall say unto him: I bring you tidings of that which will harm you. This is the day that you were promised (70:44). Then he will say [and you, may Allah give you bad tiding] "who are you?, for your face is the face of someone who comes with evil". He shall reply: "I am your evil deeds [by Allah, I did not know of you but that you were quick to the disobedience of Allah and slow to His obedience, so may Allah reward you bad, and then will be assigned to him a blind, deaf and mute person who holds in his hand a hammer, if a mountain is hit with it, it would disintegrate, and he will beat him with it until he becomes dust, and then Allah will render him to his initial form, and he will beat

him again, and he (the wicked) will cry of sorrow and pain a cry
that will be heard by all creatures except humans and jinn, and a
door of hell will be opened unto him within his grave and will
spread out for him sheets of hell fire]". Then he shall say: "My
Lord do not bring the hour".

The previous hadith was narrated by Ahmad Ibn Hanbal,
Abu Dawud, Ibn Majah, at-Tayalisi, and al-Hakim who said
it is according to the standards of Bukhari and Muslim. This
text is the text of Ahmad, the text between brackets is from
the other narrators and other narrations of Ahmad.

Narrated Samura bin Jundab:

Whenever the Prophet finished the (morning) prayer, he would
face us and ask, "Who amongst you had a dream last night?" So if
anyone had seen a dream he would narrate it. The Prophet would
say: "Ma sha'a-llah" (An Arabic maxim meaning literally, 'What
Allah wished,' and it indicates a good omen.) One day, he asked us
whether anyone of us had seen a dream. We replied in the negative.
The Prophet said, "But I had seen (a dream) last night that two
men came to me, caught hold of my hands, and took me to the
Sacred Land (Jerusalem). There, I saw a person sitting and another
standing with an iron hook in his hand pushing it inside the
mouth of the former till it reached the jawbone, and then tore off
one side of his cheek, and then did the same with the other side; in
the meantime the first side of his cheek became normal again and
then he repeated the same operation again. I said, 'What is this?'
They told me to proceed on and we went on till we came to a man
Lying flat on his back, and another man standing at his head
carrying a stone or a piece of rock, and crushing the head of the

Lying man, with that stone. Whenever he struck him, the stone rolled away. The man went to pick it up and by the time he returned to him, the crushed head had returned to its normal state and the man came back and struck him again (and so on). I said, 'Who is this?' They told me to proceed on; so we proceeded on and passed by a hole like an oven; with a narrow top and wide bottom, and the fire was kindling underneath that hole. Whenever the fire-flame went up, the people were lifted up to such an extent that they about to get out of it, and whenever the fire got quieter, the people went down into it, and there were naked men and women in it. I said, 'Who is this?' They told me to proceed on. So we proceeded on till we reached a river of blood and a man was in it, and another man was standing at its bank with stones in front of him, facing the man standing in the river. Whenever the man in the river wanted to come out, the other one threw a stone in his mouth and caused him to retreat to his original position; and so whenever he wanted to come out the other would throw a stone in his mouth, and he would retreat to his original position. I asked, 'What is this?' They told me to proceed on and we did so till we reached a well-flourished green garden having a huge tree and near its root was sitting an old man with some children. (I saw) Another man near the tree with fire in front of him and he was kindling it up. Then they (i.e. my two companions) made me climb up the tree and made me enter a house, better than which I have ever seen. In it were some old men and young men, women and children. Then they took me out of this house and made me climb up the tree and made me enter another house that was better and superior (to the first) containing old and young people. I said to them (i.e. my two companions), 'You have made me ramble all the night. Tell me all about that I have seen.' They said, 'Yes. As for the one whose cheek you saw being torn away, he was a liar and he used to tell lies, and the people would report those lies on his authority till they spread all over the world. So, he will be punished like that till the Day of Resurrection. The one whose head you saw being crushed is the one whom Allah had given the knowledge of Qur'an (i.e. knowing it by heart) but he used to sleep at night (i.e. he did not recite it then) and did not use to act upon it (i.e. upon its orders etc.) by day; and so this punishment will go on till the Day of Resurrection. And those you saw in the hole (like oven) were adulterers (those men and women who commit illegal sexual intercourse). And those you saw in the river of blood were those dealing in Riba (usury / interest). And the old man who was sitting at the base of the tree was Abraham and the little children around him were the offspring of the people. And the one who was kindling the fire was Malik, the gatekeeper of the Hell-fire. And the first house in which you have gone was the house of the common believers, and the second house was of the martyrs. I am Gabriel and this is Michael. Raise your head.' I raised my head and saw a thing like a cloud over me. They said, 'That is your place.' I said, 'Let me enter my place.' They said, 'You still have some life which you have not yet completed, and when you complete (that remaining portion of your life) you will then enter your place.' "

Source: Sahih al-Bukhari 1386

Abu Huraira reported:

When the soul of a believer would go out (of his body) it would be received by two angels who would take it to the sky. Hammad (one of the narrators in the chain of transmitters) mentioned the sweetness of its odour, (and further said) that the dwellers of the *sky say: Here comes the pious soul from the side of the earth Let there be blessings of Allah upon the body in which it resides. And it is carried (by the angels) to its Lord, the Exalted and Glorious. He would say: Take it to its destined end. And if he is a nonbeliever and as it (the soul) leaves the body-Hammad made a mention of its foul smell and of its being cursed-the dwellers of the sky say: There comes a dirty soul from the side of the earth, and it would be said: Take it to its destined end. Abu Huraira reported that Allah's Messenger put a thin cloth which was with him upon his nose while making a mention (of the foul smell) of the soul of a non-believer.*

Source: Sahih Muslim 2872

It was narrated from Abu Hurairah that the Prophet said:

"When the believer is dying, the angels of mercy come to him with white silk and say: 'Come out content and with the pleasure of Allah upon you to the mercy of Allah, fragrance and a Lord Who is not angry; So it comes out like the best fragrance of musk. They pass him from one to another until they bring him to the gate of heaven, where they say: '; How good is this fragrance that has come to you from the Earth! Then the souls of the believers come to him and they rejoice more over him than any one of you rejoices when his absent loved one comes to him. They ask him: 'What happened to so-and-so, what happened to so-and-so?' They say: 'Let him be, for he was in the hardship of the world. When he says, 'Did he not come here?' They say: 'He was taken to the pit (of Hell).' Come out discontent, subject of Divine wrath, to the punishment of Allah, the Mighty and Sublime; So it comes out like the foulest stench of a corpse. They bring him to the gates of the

Earth, where they say: 'How foul is this stench!' Then they bring him to the souls of the disbelievers."

Source: Sunan an-Nasa'i 1833 Graded Sahih by Darussalam

Abu Hurairah narrated that:

The Messenger of Allah said: "The believer's soul is suspended by his debt until it is settled for him."

Source: Jami` at-Tirmidhi 1078

Graded Hasan by Darussalam

It was narrated from Thawban, the freed slave of the Messenger of Allah (ﷺ), that the Messenger of Allah (ﷺ) said:

"Anyone whose soul leaves his body and he is free of three things, will enter Paradise: Arrogance, stealing from the spoils of war, and debt."

Source: Sunan ibn Majah

 English reference: Vol. 3, Book 15, Hadith 2412

Graded Sahih by Darussalam

It was narrated from Abu Hurairah that the Prophet (ﷺ) said:

"Angels come to the dying person, and if the man was righteous, they say: 'Come out, O good soul that was in a good body, come out praiseworthy and receive glad tidings of mercy and fragrance and a Lord Who is not angry.' And this is repeated until it comes

out, then it is taken up to heaven, and it is opened for it, and it is asked: 'Who is this?' They say: 'So-and-so.' It is said: 'Welcome to the good soul that was in a good body. Enter praiseworthy and receive the glad tidings of mercy and fragrance and a Lord Who is not angry.' And this is repeated until it is brought to the heaven above which is Allah. But if the man was evil, they say: 'Come out O evil soul that was in an evil body. Come out blameworthy, and receive the tidings of boiling water and the discharge of dirty wounds,' and other torments of similar kind, all together. And this is repeated until it comes out, then it is taken up to heaven and it is not opened for it. And it is asked: 'Who is this?' It is said: 'So-and-so.' And it is said: 'No welcome to the evil soul that was in an evil body. Go back blameworthy, for the gates of heaven will not be opened to you.' So it is sent back down from heaven, then it goes to the grave."

Source: Sunan ibn Majah

English reference: Vol. 5, Book 37, Hadith 4262

Graded Sahih by Darussalam

Narrated Anas bin Malik:

Allah's Messenger said, "When carried to his grave, a dead person is followed by three, two of which return (after his burial) and one remains with him: his relative, his property, and his deeds follow him; relatives and his property go back while his deeds remain with him."

Source: Sahih al-Bukhari 6514

Narrated Al-Bara' ibn Azib:

We went out with the Messenger of Allah accompanying the bier of a man of the Ansar. When we reached his grave, it was not yet dug. So the Messenger of Allah sat down and we also sat down around him as if birds were over our heads. He had in his hand a stick with which he was scratching the ground.

He then raised his head and said: Seek refuge with Allah from the punishment in the grave. He said it twice or thrice.

The version of Jabir adds here: He hears the beat of their sandals when they go back, and at that moment he is asked: O so and so! Who is your Lord, what is your religion, and who is your Prophet?

Hannad's version says: Two angels will come to him, make him sit up and ask him: Who is your Lord?

He will reply: My Lord is Allah. They will ask him: What is your religion? He will reply: My religion is Islam. They will ask him: What is your opinion about the man who was sent on a mission among you? He will reply: He is the Messenger of Allah . They will ask: Who made you aware of this? He will reply: I read Allah's Book, believed in it, and considered it true; which is verified by Allah's words: "Allah establishes those who believe with the word that stands firm in this world and the next."

The agreed version reads: Then a crier will call from Heaven: My servant has spoken the truth, so spread a bed for him from Paradise, clothe him from Paradise, and open a door for him into Paradise. So some of its air and perfume will come to him, and a space will be made for him as far as the eye can see.

He also mentioned the death of the infidel, saying: His spirit will be restored to his body, two angels will come to him, make him sit up and ask him: Who is your Lord?

He will reply: Alas, alas! I do not know. They will ask him: What is your religion? He will reply: Alas, alas! I do not know. They will ask: Who was the man who was sent on a mission among you? He will reply: Alas, alas! I do not know. Then a crier will call from Heaven: He has lied, so spread a bed for him from Hell, clothe him from Hell, and open for him a door into Hell. Then some of its heat and pestilential wind will come to him, and his grave will be compressed, so that his ribs will be crushed together.

Jabir's version adds: One who is blind and dumb will then be placed in charge of him, having a sledge-hammer such that if a mountain were struck with it, it would become dust. He will give him a blow with it which will be heard by everything between the east and the west except by men and jinn, and he will become dust. Then his spirit will be restored to him.

Source: Sunan Abi Dawud 4753 Graded Sahih by Albani

Anas bin Malik said:

"The Prophet of Allah said: 'When a person is placed in his grave and his companions depart from him, he hears the sound of their sandals. Then two angles came to him and make him sit up, and they say to him: What did you say about this man? As for the believer, he says: "I bear witness that he is the slave of Allah and His Messenger. Then it is said to him: Look at your place in Hell, Which Allah has replaced for you with a place in Paradise. The prophet said: 'And he sees them both."'

Source: Sunan an-Nasa'i 2050 Graded Sahih by Darussalam

It was narrated from Abu Hurairah that the Prophet (ﷺ) said:

"The dead person ends up in his grave, then the righteous man is made to sit up in his grave with no fear or panic. Then it is said to him: 'What religion did you follow?' He said: 'I was in Islam.' It is said to him: 'Who is this man?' He says: 'Muhammad the Messenger of Allah. He brought us clear signs from Allah and we believed him.' It is said to him: 'Have you seen Allah?' He says: 'No one is able to see Allah.' Then a window to Hell is opened for him, and he sees it, parts of it destroying others. Then it is said to him: 'Look at what Allah has saved you from.' Then a window to Paradise is opened to him, and he looks at its beauty and what is in it. It is said to him: 'This is your place.' And it is said to him: 'You had certain faith and you died in that state, and in that state you will be resurrected if Allah wills.' And the evil man is made to sit up in his grave with fear and panic. It is said to him: 'What religion did you follow?' He says: 'I do not know.' It is said to him: 'Who is this man?' He says: 'I heard the people saying something and I said it too.' Then a window to Paradise is opened to him, and he looks at its beauty and what is in it. It is said to him: 'Look at what Allah has diverted away from you.' Then a window to Hell is opened for him, and he sees it, parts of it destroying others, and it is said to him: 'This is your place. You were doubtful; in this state you died and in this state you will be resurrected, if Allah wills.'"

Source: Sunan ibn Majah

English reference : Vol. 5, Book 37, Hadith 4268

Graded Sahih by Darussalam

Anas bin Malik said:

The Messenger of Allah entered the garden of the palm trees of Banu al-Najjar. He heard a voice and was terrified. He asked: Who are the people buried in these graves? The people replied: Messenger of Allah! These are some people who died in the pre-Islamic times. He said: Seek refuge in Allah from the punishment of the fire, and the trial of Antichrist. They asked: Why is it that, Messenger of Allah? He said: When a man is placed in his grave, an angel comes to him and says to him: Whom did you worship? Allah then guides him and he says: I worshiped Allah. He is then asked: What was your opinion of this man? He replies: He is Allah's servant and His Apostle. He will not then be asked about anything else. He will then be taken to his abode in Hell and will be told: This was your abode in Hell, but Allah protected you and had mercy on you substituted for you an abode in Paradise for it. He will say: Leave me so that I may go and give glad tidings to my family. He will be told: Dwell. When an infidel is placed in his grave, an angel comes to him, reprimands him and asks him: Whom did you worship? He replies: I do not know. He will be told: You neither knew nor did you follow(the believers). He is then asked: What was your opinion on this man? He replies: I held the opinion that the other people held. He will then give him a blow between his ears with an iron hammer and will utter a shout which will be heard by all the creatures (near him) with the exception of men and jinn.

Source: Sunan Abi Dawud 4751 Graded Sahih by Albani

Narrated Anas:

The Prophet said, "When a human being is laid in his grave and his companions return and he even hears their foot steps, two angels come to him and make him sit and ask him: What did you use to say about this man, Muhammad ? He will say: I testify that he is Allah's slave and His Apostle. Then it will be said to him, 'Look at your place in the Hell-Fire. Allah has given you a place in Paradise instead of it.' " The Prophet added, "The dead person will see both his places. But a non-believer or a hypocrite will say to the angels, 'I do not know, but I used to say what the people used to say! It will be said to him, 'Neither did you know nor did you take the guidance (by reciting the Qur'an).' Then he will be hit with an iron hammer between his two ears, and he will cry and that cry will be heard by whatever approaches him except human beings and jinns."

Source: Sahih al-Bukhari 1338

Asma' reported:

The sun eclipsed during the lifetime of the Messenger of Allah. As I went to 'A'isha who was busy in prayer. I said: What is the matter with the people that they are praying (a special prayer)? She ('A'isha) pointed towards the sky with her head. I said: Is it (an unusual) sign? She said: Yes. The Messenger of Allah stood up for prayer for such a long time that I was about to faint. I caught hold of a waterskin lying by my side, and began to pour water over my head, or (began to sprinkle water) on my face. The Messenger of Allah then finished and the sun had brightened. The Messenger of Allah then addressed the people, (after) praising Allah and lauding Him, and then said: There was no such thing as I did not see earlier, but I saw it at this very place of mine. I even saw Paradise and Hell. It was also revealed to me that you would be tried in the graves, as you would he tried something like the turmoil of the Dajjal. Asma' said: I do not know which word he actually used (qariban or mithl), and each one of you would be brought and it would be said: What is your knowledge about this man? If the person is a believer, (Asma' said: I do not know whether it was the word al-Mu'min or al-Mu'qin) he would say: He is Muhammad and he is the Messenger of Allah. He brought to us the clear signs and right guidance. So we responded and obeyed him. (He would repeat this three times), and it would be said to him: You should go to sleep. We already knew that you are a believer in him. So the pious man would go to sleep. So far as the hypocrite or sceptic is concerned (Asma' said: I do not know which word was that: al-Munafiq (hypocrite) or al-Murtad (doubtful) he would say: I do not know. I only uttered whatever I heard people say.

Source: Sahih Muslim 905 a

It was narrated that Jabir said:

"The Messenger of Allah forbade plastering over graves."

Source: Sunan an-Nasa'i 2029 Graded Sahih by Darussalam

It was narrated that Jabir said:

"The Messenger of Allah forbade writing anything on graves."

Source: Sunan ibn Majah English reference : Vol. 1, Book 6, Hadith 1563 Graded Sahih by Darussalam

Jabir narrated:

"The Messenger of Allah prohibited plastering graves, writing on them, building over them, and treading on them."

Source: Jami at-Tirmidhi 1052 Graded Sahih by Darussalam

Narrated Masruq:

`Aisha said that a Jewess came to her and mentioned the punishment in the grave, saying to her, "May Allah protect you from the punishment of the grave." `Aisha then asked Allah's Messenger about the punishment of the grave. He said, "Yes, (there is) punishment in the grave." `Aisha added, "After that I never saw Allah's Messenger but seeking refuge with Allah from the punishment in the grave in every prayer he prayed."*

Source: Sahih Bukhari 1372

It was narrated that 'Umar said:

"I heard the Messenger of Allah say: 'The deceased is punished in his grave due to the wailing over him.'"

Source: Sunan an-Nasa'i 1853 Graded Sahih by Darussalam

Abu Hurairah narrated that:

The Messenger of Allah said: "When the deceased - or he said when one of you - is buried, two angels, black and blue eyed come to him. One of them is called Al-Munkar, and the other An-Nakir. They say: 'What did you used to say about this man?' So he says what he was saying (before death) 'He is Allah's slave and His Messenger. I testify that none has the right to be worshipped but

*Allah and that Muhammad is His slave and His Messenger.' So
they say: 'We knew that you would say this.' Then his grave is
expanded to seventy by seventy cubits, then it is illuminated for
him. Then it is said to him: 'Sleep.' So he said: 'Can I return to my
family to inform them?' They say: 'Sleep as a newlywed, whom
none awakens but the dearest of his family.' Until Allah resurrects
him from his resting place." "If he was a hypocrite he would say: 'I
heard people saying something, so I said the same; I do not know.'
So they said: 'We knew you would say that.' So the earth is told:
'Constrict him.' So it constricts around him, squeezing his ribs
together. He continues being punished like that until Allah
resurrects him from his resting place."*

Source: Jami` at-Tirmidhi 1071

Graded Hasan by Darussalam

Anas bin Malik reported Allah's Apostle having said:

*When the servant is placed in his grave, his companions retrace
their steps, and he hears the noise of their footsteps, two angels
come to him and make him sit and say to him: What you have to
say about this person (the Prophet)? If he is a believer, he would
say: I bear testimony to the fact that he is a servant of Allah and
His Messenger. Then it would be said to him: Look to your seat in
the Hellfire, for Allah has substituted (the seat of yours) with a seat
in Paradise. Allah's Messenger said: He would be shown both the
seats. Qatada said: It was mentioned to us that his grave (the grave
of a believer) expands to seventy cubits and is full with verdure
until the Day when they would be resurrected.*

Source: Sahih Muslim 2870 a

Narrated Al-Bara:

that regarding Allah's saying: Allah will keep firm those who believe, with the word that stands firm in this world and in the Hereafter (14:27). The Prophet said: "In the grave, when it is said to him: 'Who is your Lord? What is your religion? And who is your Prophet?'"

Source: Jami at-Tirmidhi

English reference : Vol. 5, Book 44, Hadith 3120

Graded Sahih by Darussalam

Anas (b. Malik) reported Allah's Messenger (ﷺ) as saying. None of you should make a request for death because of the trouble in which he is involved, but if there is no other help to it, then say:

O Allah, keep me alive as long as there is goodness in life for me and bring death to me when there is goodness in death for me.

Source: Sahih Muslim 2680 a

Narrated Abu Qatada bin Rib'i Al-Ansari:

A funeral procession passed by Allah's Messenger who said, "Relieved or relieving?" The people asked, "O Allah's Messenger! What is relieved and relieving?" He said, "A believer is relieved (by death) from the troubles and hardships of the world and leaves for the Mercy of Allah, while (the death of) a wicked person relieves the people, the land, the trees, (and) the animals from him."

Source: Sahih al-Bukhari 6512

Narrated Abu Huraira:

The Prophet said, "Allah will not accept the excuse of any person whose instant of death is delayed till he is sixty years of age."

Source: Sahih al-Bukhari 6419

Narrated Al-Mughira bin Shu`ba:

On the day of Ibrahim's death, the sun eclipsed and the people said that the eclipse was due to the death of Ibrahim (the son of the Prophet). Allah's Messenger said, "The sun and the moon are two signs amongst the signs of Allah. They do not eclipse because of someone's death or life. So when you see them, invoke Allah and pray till the eclipse is clear."

Source: Sahih al-Bukhari 1060

It was narrated from 'Aishah that the Messenger of Allah (ﷺ) said:

"Whoever loves to meet Allah, Allah loves to meet him, and whoever hates to meet Allah, Allah hates to meet him." It was said to him: "O Messenger of Allah, does hating to meet Allah mean hating to meet death? For all of us hate death." He said: "No. Rather that is only at the moment of death. But if he is given the glad tidings of the mercy and forgiveness of Allah, he loves to meet Allah and Allah loves to meet him; and if he is given the tidings of the punishment of Allah, he hates to meet Allah and Allah hates to meet him."

Source: Sunan ibn Majah English reference: Vol. 5, Book 37, Hadith 4264 Graded Sahih by Darussalam

It was narrated from 'Abdullah bin 'Amr that the Prophet (ﷺ) said:

"Allah accepts the repentance of His slave so long as the death rattle has not yet reached his throat."

Source: Sunan ibn Majah

English reference : Vol. 5, Book 37, Hadith 4253

Graded Hasan by Darussalam

Abu Sa'id and Abu Hurairah narrated that the messenger of Allah (ﷺ) said:

"Remind those who are on their death bed of the Shahadah "La' Ilaha illall-ah." (to say it, hoping it will be their last words)"

Source: Bulugh al-Maram 535 and 536

Ali narrated that the Messenger of Allah said:

'A slave (of Allah) shall not believe until he believes in four: The testimony of La Ilaha Illallah, and that I am the Messenger of Allah whom He sent with the Truth, and he believes in the death, and he believes in the Resurrection after death, and he believes in Qadar."

Source: Jami at-Tirmidhi

English reference : Vol. 4, Book 6, Hadith 2145

Graded Hasan by Darussalam

Al-Mughirah bin Shu'bah said:

I heard the Messenger of Allah saying, "He who allows (others) to wail over his death, will be punished for it on the Day of Resurrection."

Source: Al Bukhari and Muslim

It was narrated that Abu Hurairah said; "The Messenger of Allah said:

Whoever loves to meet Allah, Allah loves to meet him, and whoever hates to meet Allah, Allah hates to meet him." (One of the narrators) Shuraih said: 'I went to Aishan and said: O mother of the believers! I heard Abu Hurairah narrate from the Messenger of Allah a Hadith which, if that is the case, we are all doomed. She said: 'What is that?' He said: 'The Messenger of Allah said: Whoever loves to meet Allah, Allah loves to meet him, and whoever hates to meet Allah, Allah hates to meet him. But there is no one among us who does not hate death.' She said: 'The Messenger of Allah did say that, but it is not what you think. When the eyes begin to stare, the death rattle sounds in the chest and the flesh shiver, at that point, whoever loves to meet Allah, Allah loves to meet him, and whoever hates to meet Allah, Allah hates to meet him."'

Source: Sunan an-Nasa'i 1834 Graded Sahih by Darussalam

Hammam b. Munabbih said:

Abu Huraira narrated to us ahadith from Allah's Messenger and out of these one is that Allah's Messenger said: None amongst you should make a request for death, and do not call for it before it

comes, for when any one of you dies, he ceases (to do good) deeds
and the life of a believer is not prolonged but for goodness.

Source: Sahih Muslim 2682

Abu Hurairah narrated that the Messenger of Allah said:

*"Indeed a man, and a woman, perform deeds in obedience to Allah
for sixty years, then death presents itself to them, and they cause
such harm in the will that the Fire becomes warranted for them."
Then he recited: After payment of legacies he (or she) may have
bequeathed or debts, without causing harm. This is a
Commandment from Allah. up to His saying: That is the
magnificent success.*

Source: Jami at-Tirmidhi 2117 Graded Hasan by Darussalam

Fadalah bin 'Ubaid reported:

*The Messenger of Allah said, "The actions of every dead person
come to a halt with his death except the one who is on the frontier
in Allah's way (i.e., observing Ribat). This latter's deeds will be
made to go on increasing for him till the Day of Resurrection, and
he will be secure from the trials in the grave."*

Source: Sunan Tirmidhi (4/165) No. 1621 and Sunan Abu
Dawud (3/9) No. 2500

Graded Sahih by Darussalam

**Abdullah (b. Mas'ud) reported that Allah's Messenger (ﷺ)
who is the most truthful (of the human beings) and his
being truthful (is a fact) said:**

Verily your creation is on this wise. The constituents of one of you are collected for forty days in his mother's womb in the form of blood, after which it becomes a clot of blood in another period of forty days. Then it becomes a lump of flesh and forty days later Allah sends His angel to it with instructions concerning four things, so the angel writes down his livelihood, his death, his deeds, his fortune and misfortune. By Him, besides Whom there is no god, that one amongst you acts like the people deserving Paradise until between him and Paradise there remains but the distance of a cubit, when suddenly the writing of destiny overcomes him and he begins to act like the denizens of Hell and thus enters Hell, and another one acts in the way of the denizens of Hell, until there remains between him and Hell a distance of a cubit that the writing of destiny overcomes him and then he begins to act like the people of Paradise and enters Paradise.

Source: Sahih Muslim 2643 a

Narrated Abu Huraira:

Allah's Messenger said, "Allah said, 'I will declare war against him who shows hostility to a pious worshipper of Mine. And the most beloved things with which My slave comes nearer to Me, is what I have enjoined upon him; and My slave keeps on coming closer to Me through performing Nawafil (praying or extra deeds besides what is obligatory) till I love him, so I become his sense of hearing with which he hears, and his sense of sight with which he sees, and his hand with which he grips, and his leg with which he walks; and if he asks Me, I will give him, and if he asks My protection (Refuge), I will protect him; (i.e. give him My Refuge) and I do not hesitate to do anything as I hesitate to take the soul of the believer, for he hates death, and I hate to disappoint him."

Source: Sahih al-Bukhari 6502

Narrated Ibn `Abbas:

The Prophet once passed by two graves, and those two persons (in the graves) were being tortured. He said, "They are being tortured not for a great thing (to avoid). One of them never saved himself from being soiled with his urine, while the other was going about with calumnies (to make enmity between friends). He then took a green leaf of a date-palm tree split it into two pieces and fixed one on each grave. The people said, "O Allah's Messenger! Why have you done so?" He replied, "I hope that their punishment may be lessened till they (the leaf) become dry."

Source: Sahih al-Bukhari 1361

It was narrated that Abu Hurairah said:

"The Messenger of Allah said: 'Most of the torment of the grave is because of urine.'"

Source: Sunan ibn Majah

English reference : Vol. 1, Book 1, Hadith 348

Graded Hasan by Darussalam

It was narrated that 'Aishah said:

"Two of the old Jewish women of Al-Madinah came to me and said: 'The people of the graves are tormented in their graves.' But I did

not believe them, and I did not believe them, and I did not want to believe them. They left and the Messenger of Allah entered upon me, and I said: 'O Messenger of Allah, two of the old Jewish women of Al-Madinah said that the people of the graves are tormented in their graves.' He said: 'They spoke the truth. They are tormented in a manner that all the animals can hear.' And I never saw him offer any Salah but he sought refuge with Allah from the torment of the grave."

Source: Sunan an-Nasa'i 2067 Graded Sahih by Darussalam

Anas reported Allah's Apostle (ﷺ) as saying:

If you were not (to abandon) the burying of the dead (in the grave), I would have certainly supplicated Allah that He should make you listen to the torment of the grave.

Source: Sahih Muslim 2868

Hani' the freed slave of 'Uthman said:

When 'Uthman would stop at a grave he would cry until his beard was soaked (in tears). It was said to him: 'The Paradise and the Fire were mentioned and you did not cry, yet you cry because of this?' So he said: 'Indeed the Messenger of Allah said: "Indeed the grave is the first stage among the stages of the Hereafter. So if one is saved from it, then what comes after it is easier than it. And if one is not saved from it, then what comes after it is worse than it." And the Messenger of Allah said: "I have not seen any sight except that the grave is more horrible than it."

Source: Jami` at-Tirmidhi 2308

Graded Hasan by Darussalam

Narrated Ibn 'Umar from his father:

The Prophet said, "The deceased is tortured in his grave for the wailing done over him."

Narrated Shu'ba:

The deceased is tortured for the wailing of the living ones over him .

Source: Sahih al-Bukhari 1292

It was narrated that Abu Hurairah said:

"The Messenger of Allah said: 'If any one of you were to sit on a live coal until it burns his garment, that would be better for him than sitting on a grave."

Source: Sunan an-Nasa'i 2044 Graded Sahih by Darussalam

It was narrated from Jabir that the Prophet (ﷺ) said:

"When the deceased enters the grave, the sun is made to appear as if it is setting. He sits up, wipes his eyes and says: 'Let me pray.'"

Source: Sunan ibn Majah

English reference : Vol. 5, Book 37, Hadith 4272

Graded Sahih by Darussalam

Abdullah bin Amr narrated that:

The Messenger of Allah said: "No Muslim dies on the day of Friday, nor the night of Friday, except that Allah protects him from the trials of the grave."

Source: Jami` at-Tirmidhi 1074

Graded Hasan by Darussalam

It was narrated from Rashid bin Sa'd, that a man among the Companions of the Prophet said:

"O Messenger of Allah, why will the believers be tested in their graves except the martyr?" He said: "The flashing of the swords above his head is trial enough."

Source: Sunan an-Nasa'i 2053 Graded Sahih by Darussalam

Abu Ishaq As-Sabi'i said:

"Sulaiman bin Surad said to Khalid bin Urfutah - or, Khalid said to Sulaiman - 'Did you hear the Messenger of Allah saying: "Whoever is killed by his stomach then he will not be punished in the grave"?' One of them said to the other: "Yes."

Source: Jami` at-Tirmidhi 1064 Graded Sahih by Darussalam

Abu Hurairah said:

"He (meaning the Prophet) said: 'Seek refuge with Allah from five things: From the torment of Hell, the torment of the grave, the trials of life and death, and the tribulation of Al-Masihid-Dajjal.'"

Source: Sunan an-Nasa'i 5511 Graded Sahih by Darussalam

Narrated Muhammad bin Al-Munkadir:

"Salman Al-Farisi passed by Shurahbil bin As-Simt while he was in garrison in which he and his companions were suffering from difficulties. He said to him: 'Shall I narrate to you - O Ibn As-Simt - a Hadith I heard from the Messenger of Allah ?' He said: 'Of course.' He said: 'I heard the Messenger of Allah saying: "(Ribat) Guarding the frontier for a day in the cause of Allah is more virtuous" - and perhaps he said: "better, than fasting a month and standing (in prayer) for it. And whoever dies in it, he is protected from the trials of the grave, and his deeds (continuously) multiplied until the Day of Resurrection.

Source: Jami` at-Tirmidhi 1665 Graded Sahih by Darussalam

Narrated Ibn Shihab:

The funeral prayer should be offered for every child even if he were the son of a prostitute as he was born with a true faith of Islam (i.e. to worship none but Allah Alone). If his parents are Muslims, particularly the father, even if his mother were a non-Muslim, and if he after the delivery cries (even once) before his death (i.e. born alive) then the funeral prayer must be offered. And if the child does not cry after his delivery (i.e. born dead) then his funeral prayer should not be offered, and he will be considered as a miscarriage. Abu Huraira, narrated that the Prophet said, "Every child is born with a true faith (i.e. to worship none but Allah Alone) but his parents convert him to Judaism or to Christianity or to Magianism, as an animal delivers a perfect baby animal. Do you find it mutilated?" Then Abu Huraira recited the verses: 'The pure Allah's Islamic nature (true faith i.e. to worship none but Allah Alone), with which He has created human beings.' " (30.30).

Source: Sahih al-Bukhari 1358

It was narrated from 'Abdullah bin Mas'ud that the Prophet (ﷺ) said:

"If the appointed time of death of anyone of you is in a certain land, some need will cause him to go there, then when he reaches the furthest point that it is decreed he will reach, Allah takes (his soul). And on the Day of Resurrection the earth will say: 'My Lord, this is what You entrusted to me.'"

Source: Sunan ibn Majah

English reference : Vol. 5, Book 37, Hadith 4263

Graded Sahih by Darussalam

It was narrated from Bishr bin Suhaim that:

The Messenger of Allah delivered a sermon on the days of Tashriq (11th, 12th, and 13th of Dhul-Hijjah) and said: "No one will enter Paradise but a Muslim soul, and these days are the days of eating and drinking."

Source: Sunan ibn Majah

English reference: Vol. 1, Book 7, Hadith 1720

Graded Sahih by Darussalam

It has been narrated on the authority of 'Abd al-Rahman b. Shamasa al- Mahri who said:

I was in the company of Maslama b. Mukhallad, and 'Abdullah b. 'Amr b. 'As was with him. 'Abdullah said: The Hour shall some only when the worst type of people are left on the earth. They will be worse than the people of pre-Islamic days. They will get whatever they ask of Allah. While we were yet sitting when 'Uqba b. 'Amir came, and Maslama said to him: 'Uqba, listen to what 'Abdullah says. 'Uqba said: He knows better; so far as I am concerned, I heard the Messenger of Allah say: A group of people from my Umma will continue to fight in obedience to the Command of Allah, remaining dominant over their enemies. Those who will oppose them shall not do them any harm. They will remain in this condition until the Hour overtakes them. (At this) 'Abdullah said: Yes. Then Allah will raise a wind which will be fragrant like musk and whose touch will be like the touch of silk; (but) it will cause the death of all (faithful) persons, not leaving behind a single person with an iota of faith in his heart. Then only the worst of men will remain to be overwhelmed by the Hour.

Source: Sahih Muslim 1924

The last hadith in this section is a proof believers/Muslims will not exist before the end of the world. I have not included the signs of the hour in this book for this reason. Your personal Akhirah will likely start before the end of the world so for the majority of people it doesn't matter if they know what will happen before the end of the world because their end/Akhirah beginning, will have come before then. The only reason it is important to know about the end of the world is to preserve the knowledge for future generations who will experience it to benefit thereby. The reason for curiosity in end of the world is due to love for this world.

Data about the day of judgement

Quran 2:48

And fear a Day (of Judgement) when a person shall not avail another, nor will intercession be accepted from him nor will compensation be taken from him nor will they be helped.

Quran 2:85-86

After this, it is you who kill one another and drive out a party of you from their homes, assist (their enemies) against them, in sin and transgression. And if they come to you as captives, you ransom them, although their expulsion was forbidden to you. Then do you believe in a part of the Scripture and reject the rest? Then what is the recompense of those who do so among you, except disgrace in the life of this world, and on the Day of Resurrection they shall be consigned to the most grievous torment. And Allâh is not unaware of what you do. (85) Those are they who have bought the life of this world at the price of the Hereafter. Their torment shall not be lightened nor shall they be helped.

Quran 2:113

The Jews said that the Christians follow nothing (i.e. are not on the right religion); and the Christians said that the Jews follow nothing (i.e. are not on the right religion); though they both recite the Scripture. Like unto their word, said (the pagans) who know not. Allâh will judge between them on the Day of Resurrection about that wherein they have been differing.

Quran 2:123

And fear the Day (of Judgement) when no person shall avail another, nor shall compensation be accepted from him, nor shall intercession be of use to him, nor shall they be helped.

Quran 2:174-175

Verily, those who conceal what Allâh has sent down of the Book, and purchase a small gain therewith (of worldly things), they eat into their bellies nothing but fire. Allâh will not speak to them on the Day of Resurrection, nor purify them, and theirs will be a painful torment. (174) Those are they who have purchased error at the price of Guidance, and torment at the price of Forgiveness. So how bold they are (for evil deeds which will push them) to the Fire.

Quran 2:210

Do they then wait for anything other than that Allâh should come to them in the shadows of the clouds and the angels? (Then) the case would be already judged. And to Allâh return all matters (for decision).

Quran 2:212

Beautified is the life of this world for those who disbelieve, and they mock at those who believe. But those who obey Allâh's Orders and keep away from what He has forbidden, will be above them on the Day of Resurrection. And Allâh gives (of His Bounty, Blessings,

Favours, Honours, on the Day of Resurrection) to whom He wills without limit.

Quran 2:281

And be afraid of the Day when you shall be brought back to Allâh. Then every person shall be paid what he earned, and they shall not be dealt with unjustly.

Quran 3:9

Our Lord! Verily, it is You Who will gather mankind together on the Day about which there is no doubt. Verily, Allâh never breaks His Promise,

Quran 3:25

How (will it be) when We gather them together on the Day about which there is no doubt (i.e. the Day of Resurrection). And each person will be paid in full what he has earned? And they will not be dealt with unjustly.

Quran 3:30

On the Day when every person will be confronted with all the good he has done, and all the evil he has done, he will wish that there were a great distance between him and his evil. And Allâh warns you against Himself (His Punishment) and Allâh is full of Kindness to the (His) slaves.

Quran 3:77

Verily, those who purchase a small gain at the cost of Allâh's Covenant and their oaths, they shall have no portion in the

Hereafter (Paradise). Neither will Allâh speak to them, nor look at them on the Day of Resurrection, nor will He purify them, and they shall have a painful torment.

Quran 3:91

Verily, those who disbelieved, and died while they were disbelievers, the (whole) earth full of gold will not be accepted from anyone of them even if they offered it as a ransom. For them is a painful torment and they will have no helpers.

Quran 3:106-107

On the Day (i.e. the Day of Resurrection) when some faces will become white and some faces will become black; as for those whose faces will become black (to them will be said): "Did you reject Faith after accepting it? Then taste the torment (in Hell) for rejecting Faith." (106) And for those whose faces will become white, they will be in Allâh's Mercy (Paradise), therein they shall dwell forever.

Quran 3:180

And let not those who covetously withhold of that which Allâh has bestowed on them of His Bounty (Wealth) think that it is good for them (and so they do not pay the obligatory Zakât). Nay, it will be worse for them; the things which they covetously withheld shall be tied to their necks like a collar on the Day of Resurrection. And to Allâh belongs the heritage of the heavens and the earth; and Allâh is Well¬Acquainted with all that you do.

Quran 4:41-42

How (will it be) then, when We bring from each nation a witness and We bring you (O Muhammad) as a witness against these people? (41) On that day those who disbelieved and disobeyed the Messenger (Muhammad) will wish that they were buried in the earth, but they will never be able to hide a single fact from Allâh.

Quran 4:123

It will not be in accordance with your desires (Muslims), nor those of the people of the Scripture (Jews and Christians), whosoever works evil, will have the recompense thereof, and he will not find any protector or helper besides Allâh.

Quran 4:159

And there is none of the people of the Scripture (Jews and Christians), but must believe in him ['Īsā (Jesus), son of Maryam (Mary), as only a Messenger of Allâh and a human being], before his ['Īsā (Jesus) or a Jew's or a Christian's] death (at the time of the appearance of the angel of death). And on the Day of Resurrection, he ['Īsā (Jesus)] will be a witness against them

Quran 4:172-173

The Messiah will never be proud to reject to be a slave of Allâh, nor the angels who are near (to Allâh). And whosoever rejects His worship and is proud, then He will gather them all together unto Himself. So, as for those who believed (in the Oneness of Allâh - Islâmic Monotheism) and did deeds of righteousness, He will give their (due) rewards, and more out of His Bounty. But as for those who refused His worship and were proud, He will punish them with a painful torment . And they will not find for themselves besides Allâh any protector or helper.

Quran 5:18

And the Jews and the Christians say: "We are the children of Allâh and His loved ones." Say: "Why then does He punish you for your sins?" Nay, you are but human beings, of those He has created, He forgives whom He wills and He punishes whom He wills. And to Allâh belongs the dominion of the heavens and the earth and all that is between them, and to Him is the return (of all).

Quran 5:109-110

On the Day when Allâh will gather the Messengers together and say to them: "What was the response you received (from men to your teaching)? They will say: "We have no knowledge, verily, only You are the All¬Knower of all that is hidden (or unseen)." (109) (Remember) when Allâh will say (on the Day of Resurrection). "O 'Īsā (Jesus), son of Maryam (Mary)! Remember My Favour to you and to your mother when I supported you with Rûh-ul-Qudus [Jibrail (Gabriel)] so that you spoke to the people in the cradle and in maturity(after returning to earth); and when I taught you writing, Al¬Hikmah (the power of understanding), the Taurât (Torah) and the Injeel; and when you made out of the clay, a figure like that of a bird, by My Permission, and you breathed into it, and it became a bird by My Permission, and you healed those born blind, and the lepers by My Permission, and when you brought forth the dead by My Permission; and when I restrained the Children of Israel from you (when they resolved to kill you) as you came unto them with clear proofs, and the disbelievers among them said: 'This is nothing but evident magic.' "

Quran 5:116-119

And (remember) when Allâh will say (on the Day of Resurrection): "O 'Īsā (Jesus), son of Maryam (Mary)! Did you say unto men: 'Worship me and my mother as two gods besides Allâh?' " He will say: "Glory be to You! It was not for me to say what I had no right (to say). Had I said such a thing, You would surely have known it. You know what is in my inner-self though I do not know what is in Yours, truly, You, only You, are the All-Knower of all that is hidden (and unseen). (116) "Never did I say to them aught except what You (Allâh) did command me to say: 'Worship Allâh, my Lord and your Lord.' And I was a witness over them while I dwelt amongst them, but when You took me up, You were the Watcher over them, and You are a Witness to all things. (This is a great admonition and warning to the Christians of the whole world). (117) "If You punish them, they are Your slaves, and if You forgive them, verily You, only You are the All¬Mighty, the All¬Wise." (118) Allâh will say: "This is a Day on which the truthful will profit from their truth: theirs are Gardens under which rivers flow (in Paradise) - they shall abide therein forever. Allâh is pleased with them and they with Him. That is the great success (Paradise).

Quran 6:12

Say: "To whom belongs all that is in the heavens and the earth?" Say: "To Allâh. He has prescribed Mercy for Himself. Indeed He will gather you together on the Day of Resurrection, about which there is no doubt. Those who have lost themselves will not believe [in Allâh as being the only Ilâh (God), and Muhammad as being one of His Messengers, and in Resurrection].

Quran 6:15-16

*Say: "I fear, if I disobey my Lord, the torment of a Mighty Day."
(15) He Who is averted from (such a torment) on that Day, (Allâh)
has surely been Merciful to him. And that would be the obvious
success*

Quran 6:22-24

*And on the Day when We shall gather them all together, We shall
say to those who joined partners (in worship with Us): "Where are
your partners (false deities) whom you used to assert (as partners
in worship with Allâh)?" (22) There will then be (left) no Fitnah
(excuses or statements or arguments) for them but to say: "By
Allâh, our Lord, we were not those who joined others in worship
with Allâh." (23) Look! How they lie against themselves! But the
(lie) which they invented will disappear from them.*

Quran 6:29-30

*And they said: "There is no (other life) but our (present) life of this
world, and never shall we be resurrected (on the Day of
Resurrection)." (29) If you could but see when they will be held
(brought and made to stand) in front of their Lord! He will say: "Is
not this (Resurrection and the taking of the accounts) the truth?"
They will say: "Yes, by our Lord!" He will then say: "So taste you
the torment because you used not to believe."*

Quran 6:128

*And on the Day when He will gather them (all) together (and say):
"O you assembly of jinn! Many did you mislead of men," and their
Auliyâ' (friends and helpers) amongst men will say: "Our Lord!*

We benefited one from the other, but now we have reached our appointed term which You did appoint for us." He will say: "The Fire be your dwelling¬place, you will dwell therein forever, except as Allâh may will. Certainly your Lord is All¬Wise, All¬Knowing."

Quran 6:130

O you assembly of jinn and mankind! "Did not there come to you Messengers from amongst you, reciting unto you My Verses and warning you of the meeting of this Day of yours?" They will say: "We bear witness against ourselves." It was the life of this world that deceived them. And they will bear witness against themselves that they were disbelievers

Quran 7:6-7

Then surely, We shall question those (people) to whom it (the Book) was sent and verily, We shall question the Messengers. (6) Then surely, We shall narrate unto them (their whole story) with knowledge, and indeed We were not absent.

Quran 7:32

Say (O Muhammad): "Who has forbidden the adornment with clothes given by Allâh, which He has produced for His slaves, and At-Taiyyibât [all kinds of Halâl (lawful) things] of food?" Say: "They are, in the life of this world, for those who believe, (and) exclusively for them (believers) on the Day of Resurrection (the disbelievers will not share them)." Thus We explain the Ayât (Islâmic laws) in detail for people who have knowledge.

Quran 7:53

Await they just for the final fulfillment of the event? On the Day the event is finally fulfilled (i.e. the Day of Resurrection), those who neglected it before will say: "Verily, the Messengers of our Lord did come with the truth, now are there any intercessors for us that they might intercede on our behalf? Or could we be sent back (to the first life of the world) so that we might do (good) deeds other than those (evil) deeds which we used to do?" Verily, they have lost their ownselves (i.e. destroyed themselves) and that which they used to fabricate (invoking and worshipping others besides Allâh) has gone away from them.

Quran 7:187

They ask you about the Hour (Day of Resurrection): "When will be its appointed time?" Say: "The knowledge thereof is with my Lord (Alone). None can reveal its time but He. Heavy is its burden through the heavens and the earth. It shall not come upon you except all of a sudden." They ask you as if you have a good knowledge of it. Say: "The knowledge thereof is with Allâh (Alone) but most of mankind know not."

Quran 10:4

To Him is the return of all of you. The Promise of Allâh is true. It is He Who begins the creation and then will repeat it, that He may reward with justice those who believed (in the Oneness of Allâh – Islâmic Monotheism) and did deeds of righteousness. But those who disbelieved will have a drink of boiling fluids and painful torment because they used to disbelieve.

Quran 10:28-30

And the Day whereon We shall gather them all together, then We shall say to those who did set partners in worship with Us: "Stop at your place! You and your partners (whom you had worshipped in the worldly life)." then We shall separate them, and their (Allâh's so-called) partners shall say: "It was not us that you used to worship." (28) "So sufficient is Allâh for a witness between us and you, that We indeed knew nothing of your worship of us." (29) There! Every person will know (exactly) what he had earned before, and they will be brought back to Allâh, their rightful Maula (Lord), and their invented false deities will vanish from them.

Quran 10:48-54

And they say: "When will be this promise (the torment or the Day of Resurrection), - if you speak the truth?" (48) Say (O Muhammad): "I have no power over any harm or profit to myself except what Allâh may will. For every Ummah (a community or a nation), there is a term appointed; when their term comes, neither can they delay it nor can they advance it an hour (or a moment)." (49) Say: "Tell me, - if His torment should come to you by night or by day, - which portion thereof would the Mujrimûn (disbelievers, polytheists, sinners, criminals) hasten on ?" (50) Is it then, that when it has actually befallen, you will believe in it? What! Now (you believe)? And you used (aforetime) to hasten it on!" (51) Then it will be said to them who wronged themselves: "Taste you the everlasting torment! Are you recompensed (aught) save what you used to earn?" (52) And they ask you (O Muhammad) to inform them (saying): "Is it true (i.e. the torment and the establishment of the Hour; - the Day of Resurrection)?" Say: "Yes! By my Lord! It is the very truth! and you cannot escape it!" (53) And if every person who had wronged (by disbelieving in Allâh and by worshipping others besides Allâh), possessed all that is on earth, and sought to ransom himself therewith (it will not be accepted), and they would feel in their hearts regret when they see the torment, and they will be judged with justice, and no wrong will be done unto them.

Quran 11:18

And who does more wrong than he who invents a lie against Allâh. Such will be brought before their Lord, and the witnesses will say, "These are the ones who lied against their Lord!" No doubt! the curse of Allâh is on the Zâlimûn (polytheists, wrong-doers, oppressors)

Quran 11:60

And they were pursued by a curse in this world and (so they will be) on the Day of Resurrection. No doubt! Verily, 'Ad disbelieved in their Lord. So away with 'Ad, the people of Hûd

Quran 11:96-99

And indeed We sent Mûsa (Moses) with Our Ayât (proofs, evidences, verses, lessons, signs, revelations, etc.) and a manifest authority; (96) To Fir'aun (Pharaoh) and his chiefs, but they followed the command of Fir'aun (Pharaoh), and the command of Fir'aun (Pharaoh) was no right guide. (97) He will go ahead of his people on the Day of Resurrection, and will lead them into the Fire, and evil indeed is the place to which they are led. (98) They were pursued by a curse in this (deceiving life of this world) and (so they will be pursued by a curse) on the Day of Resurrection. Evil indeed is the gift gifted [i.e., the curse (in this world) pursued by another curse (in the Hereafter)].

Quran 11:103-105

Indeed in that (there) is a sure lesson for those who fear the torment of the Hereafter. That is a Day whereon mankind will be gathered together, and that is a Day when all (the dwellers of the heavens and the earth) will be present. (103) And We delay it only for a term (already) fixed. (104) On the Day when it comes, no person shall speak except by His (Allâh's) Leave. Some among them will be wretched and (others) blessed.

Quran 14:22

And Shaitân (Satan) will say when the matter has been decided: "Verily, Allâh promised you a promise of truth. And I too promised you, but I betrayed you. I had no authority over you except that I called you, so you responded to me. So blame me not, but blame yourselves. I cannot help you, nor can you help me. I deny your former act in associating me (Satan) as a partner with Allâh (by obeying me in the life of the world). Verily, there is a painful torment for the Zâlimûn (polytheists and wrong-doers)."

Quran 14:42-45

Consider not that Allâh is unaware of that which the Zâlimûn (polytheists, wrong-doers) do, but He gives them respite up to a Day when the eyes will stare in horror. (42) (They will be) hastening forward with necks outstretched, their heads raised up (towards the sky), their gaze returning not towards them and their hearts empty (from thinking because of extreme fear). (43) And

warn mankind of the Day when the torment will come unto them;
then the wrong-doers will say: "Our Lord! Respite us for a little
while, we will answer Your Call and follow the Messengers!" (It
will be said): "Had you not sworn aforetime that you would not
leave (the world for the Hereafter). (44) "And you dwelt in the
dwellings of men who wronged themselves, and it was clear to you
how We had dealt with them. And We put forth (many) parables
for you."

Quran 14:48-51

On the Day when the earth will be changed to another earth and so
will be the heavens, and they (all creatures) will appear before
Allâh, the One, the Irresistible. (48) And you will see the
Mujrimûn (criminals, disbelievers in the Oneness of Allâh —
Islâmic Monotheism, polytheists) that Day Muqarranûn (bound
together) in fetters. (49) Their garments will be of pitch, and fire
will cover their faces. (50) That Allâh may requite each person
according to what he has earned. Truly, Allâh is Swift at
reckoning.

Quran 16:27

Then, on the Day of Resurrection, He will disgrace them and will
say: "Where are My (so called) 'partners' concerning whom you
used to disagree and dispute (with the believers, by defying and
disobeying Allâh)?" Those who have been given the knowledge
(about the Torment of Allâh for the disbelievers) will say: "Verily!
Disgrace this Day and misery this Day are upon the disbelievers.

Quran 16:84-89

And (remember) the Day when We shall raise up from each nation a witness (their Messenger), then, those who have disbelieved will not be given leave (to put forward excuses), nor will they be allowed (to return to the world) to repent and ask for Allâh's Forgiveness (of their sins). (84) And when those who did wrong (the disbelievers) will see the torment, then it will not be lightened unto them, nor will they be given respite. (85) And when those who associated partners with Allâh see their (Allâh's so-called) partners, they will say: "Our Lord! These are our partners whom we used to invoke besides you." But they will throw back their word at them (and say): "Surely! You indeed are liars!" (86) And they will offer (their full) submission to Allâh (Alone) on that Day, and their invented false deities [all that they used to invoke besides Allâh, e.g. idols, saints, priests, monks, angels, jinn, Jibrael (Gabriel), Messengers] will vanish from them. (87) Those who disbelieved and hinder (men) from the Path of Allâh, for them We will add torment to the torment; because they used to spread corruption [by disobeying Allâh themselves, as well as ordering others (mankind) to do so]. (88) And (remember) the Day when We shall raise up from every nation a witness against them from amongst themselves. And We shall bring you (O Muhammad) as a witness against these. And We have sent down to you the Book (the Qur'an) as an exposition of everything, a guidance, a mercy, and glad tidings for those who have submitted themselves (to Allâh as Muslims).

Quran 16:111

(Remember) the Day when every person will come up pleading for himself, and every one will be paid in full for what he did (good or *evil, belief or disbelief in the life of this world) and they will not be dealt with unjustly.*

Quran 17:36

And follow not (i.e., say not, or do not or witness not) that of which you have no knowledge. Verily! The hearing, and the sight, and the heart, of each of those one will be questioned (by Allâh).

Quran 17:49-52

And they say: "When we are bones and fragments (destroyed), should we really be resurrected (to be) a new creation?" (49) Say (O Muhammad) "Be you stones or iron," (50) "Or some created thing that is yet greater (or harder) in your breasts (thoughts to be resurrected, even then you shall be resurrected)" Then, they will say: "Who shall bring us back (to life)?" Say: "He Who created you first!" Then, they will shake their heads at you and say: "When will that be ?" Say: "Perhaps it is near!" (51) On the Day when He will call you, and you will answer (His Call) with (words of) His Praise and Obedience, and you will think that you have stayed (in this world) but a little while!

Quran 17:71-72

(And remember) the Day when We shall call together all human beings with their (respective) Imâm [their Prophets, or their records of good and bad deeds, or their Books like the Qur'ân, the Taurât (Torah), the Injeel). So whosoever is given his record in his right hand, such will read their records, and they will not be dealt with unjustly in the least. (71) And whoever is blind in this world

(i.e., does not see Allâh's Signs and believes not in Him), will be blind in the Hereafter, and more astray from the Path.

Quran 17:97

And he whom Allâh guides, he is led aright; but he whom He sends astray for such you will find no Auliyâ' (helpers and protectors), besides Him, and We shall gather them together on the Day of Resurrection on their faces, blind, dumb and deaf, their abode will be Hell; whenever it abates, We shall increase for them the fierceness of the Fire

Quran 18:47-49

And (remember) the Day We shall cause the mountains to pass away (like clouds of dust), and you will see the earth as a levelled plain, and we shall gather them all together so as to leave not one of them behind. (47) And they will be set before your Lord in (lines as) rows, (and Allâh will say): "Now indeed, you have come to Us as We created you the first time. Nay, but you thought that We had appointed no meeting for you (with Us)." (48) And the Book (one's Record) will be placed (in the right hand for a believer in the Oneness of Allâh, and in the left hand for a disbeliever in the Oneness of Allâh), and you will see the Mujrimûn (criminals, polytheists, sinners), fearful of that which is (recorded) therein. They will say: "Woe to us! What sort of Book is this that leaves neither a small thing nor a big thing, but has recorded it with numbers!" And they will find all that they did, placed before them, and your Lord treats no one with injustice.

Quran 18:52-53

And (remember) the Day He will say: "Call those (so-called) partners of Mine whom you pretended." Then they will cry unto them, but they will not answer them, and We shall put Maubiq (barrier) between them. (52) And the Mujrimûn (criminals, polytheists, sinners), shall see the Fire and apprehend that they have to fall therein. And they will find no way of escape from there.

Quran 18:100-102

And on that Day We shall present Hell to the disbelievers, plain to view, – (100) (To) those whose eyes had been under a covering from My Reminder (this Qur'ân), and who could not bear to hear (it). (101) Do then those who disbelieved think that they can take My slaves [i.e., the angels, Allâh's Messengers, 'Īsā (Jesus), son of Maryam (Mary)] as Auliyâ' (lords, gods, protectors) besides Me? Verily, We have prepared Hell as an entertainment for the disbelievers (in the Oneness of Allâh Islâmic Monotheism).

Quran 18:103-105

Say (O Muhammad): "Shall We tell you the greatest losers in respect of (their) deeds? (103) "Those whose efforts have been wasted in this life while they thought that they were acquiring good by their deeds!(104)"They are those who deny the Ayât (proofs, evidences, verses, lessons, signs, revelations, etc.) of their Lord and the Meeting with Him (in the Hereafter). So their works are in vain, and on the Day of Resurrection, We shall assign not weight for them. (105)

Quran 19:38-40

How clearly will they (polytheists and disbelievers in the Oneness of Allâh) see and hear, the Day when they will appear before Us! But the Zalimûn (polytheists and wrong-doers) today are in plain error (38) And warn them (O Muhammad) of the Day of grief and regrets, when the case has been decided, while (now) they are in a state of carelessness, and they believe not (39) Verily! We will inherit the earth and whatsoever is thereon. And to Us they all shall be returned

Quran 19:85-87

The Day We shall gather the Muttaqûn (pious and righteous persons) unto the Most Gracious (Allâh), like a delegatation (presented before a king for honour). (85) And We shall drive the Mujrimûn (polytheists, sinners, criminals, disbelievers in the Oneness of Allâh) to Hell, in a thirsty state (like a thirsty herd driven down to water), (86) None shall have the power of intercession, but such a one as has received permission (or promise) from the Most Gracious (Allâh).

Quran 19:95

And everyone of them will come to Him alone on the Day of Resurrection (without any helper, or protector or defender).

Quran 20:100-112

Whoever turns away from it (this Qur'ân i.e. does not believe in it, nor acts on its orders), verily, they will bear a heavy burden (of sins) on the Day of Resurrection, (100) They will abide in that (state in the Fire of Hell), − and evil indeed will it be that load for them on the Day of Resurrection; (101) The Day when the

Trumpet will be blown (the second blowing): that Day, We shall gather the Mujrimûn (criminals, polytheists, sinners, disbelievers in the Oneness of Allâh) blue or blind eyed with thirst. (102) In whispers will they speak in a very low voice to each other (saying): "You stayed not longer than ten (days)." (103) We know very well what they will say, when the best among them in knowledge and wisdom will say: "You stayed no longer than a day!" (104) And they ask you concerning the mountains, say; "My Lord will blast them and scatter them as particles of dust. (105) "Then He shall leave them as a level smooth plain. (106) "You will see therein nothing crooked or curved." (107) On that Day mankind will follow strictly (the voice of) Allâh's caller, no crookedness (that is without going to the right or left of that voice) will they show him (Allâh's caller). And all voices will be humbled for the Most Gracious (Allâh), and nothing shall you hear but the low voice of their footsteps (108) On that day no intercession shall avail, except the one for whom the Most Gracious (Allâh) has given permission and whose word is acceptable to Him. (109) He (Allâh) knows what happens to them (His creatures) in this world, and what will happen to them (in the Hereafter), but they will never compass anything of His Knowledge. (110) And (all) faces shall be humbled before (Allâh), the Ever Living, the One Who sustains and protects all that exists. And he who carried (a burden of) wrongdoing (i.e. he who disbelieved in Allâh, ascribed partners to Him, and did deeds of His disobedience), will be indeed a complete failure (on that Day). (111) And he who works deeds of righteousness, while he is a believer (in Islâmic Monotheism) then he will have no fear of injustice, nor of any curtailment (of his reward).

Quran 20:124-127

"But whosoever turns away from My Reminder (i.e. neither believes in this Qur'ân nor acts on its teachings) verily, for him is a life of hardship, and We shall raise him up blind on the Day of Resurrection." (124) He will say:"O my Lord! Why have you raised me up blind, while I had sight (before)." (125) (Allâh) will say: "Like this, Our Ayât (proofs, evidences, verses, lessons, signs, revelations, etc.) came unto you, but you disregarded them (i.e. you left them, did not think deeply in them, and you turned away from them), and so this Day, you will be neglected (in the Hell-fire, away from Allâh's Mercy)." (126) And thus do We requite him who transgresses beyond bounds [i.e. commits the great sins and disobeys his Lord (Allâh) and believes not in His Messengers, and His revealed Books, like this Qur'ân.], and believes not in the Ayât (proofs, evidences, verses, lessons, revelations) of his Lord, and the torment of the Hereafter is far more severe and more lasting.

Quran 21:1

Draws near for mankind their reckoning, while they turn away in heedlessness.

Quran 21:97-105

And the true promise (Day of Resurrection) shall draw near (of fulfillment). Then (when mankind is resurrected from their graves), you shall see the eyes of the disbelievers fixedly staring in horror. (They will say): "Woe to us! We were indeed heedless of this; nay, but we were Zâlimûn (polytheists and wrong-doers)." (97) Certainly! You (disbelievers) and that which you are worshipping now besides Allâh, are (but) fuel for Hell! (Surely), you will enter it. (98) Had these (idols) been âlihah (gods), they would not have entered there (Hell), and all of them will abide therein. (99) Therein they will be breathing out with deep sighs and roaring, and therein they will hear not. (100) Verily those for whom the good has preceded from Us, they will be removed far therefrom (Hell). (101) They shall not hear the slightest sound of it (Hell), while they abide in that which their ownselves desire. (102) The greatest terror (on the Day of Resurrection) will not grieve them, and the angels will meet them, (with the greeting): "This is your Day which you were promised." (103) And (remember) the Day when We shall roll up the heaven like a scroll rolled up for books, As We began the first creation, We shall repeat it, (it is) a promise binding upon Us. Truly, We shall do it. (104) And indeed We have written in Az-Zabûr after (We have already written in) Al-Lauh Al-Mahfûz (the Book, that is in the heaven with Allâh), that My righteous slaves shall inherit the land (i.e. the land of Paradise).

Quran 22:1-2

O mankind! Fear your Lord and be dutiful to Him! Verily, the earthquake of the Hour (of Judgement) is a terrible thing. (1) The Day you shall see it, every nursing mother will forget her nursling, and every pregnant one will drop her load, and you shall see mankind as in a drunken state, yet they will not be drunken, but severe will be the Torment of Allâh.

Quran 22:5

O mankind! If you are in doubt about the Resurrection, then verily! We have created you (i.e. Adam) from dust, then from a Nutfah (mixed drops of male and female sexual discharge i.e. offspring of Adam), then from a clot (a piece of thick coagulated blood) then from a little lump of flesh, — some formed and some

*unformed (as in the case of miscarriage), that We may make (it)
clear to you (i.e. to show you Our Power and Ability to do what
We will). And We cause whom We will to remain in the wombs for
an appointed term, then We bring you out as infants, then (give
you growth) that you may reach your age of full strength. And
among you there is he who dies (young), and among you there is
he who is brought back to the miserable old age, so that he knows
nothing after having known. And you see the earth barren, but
when We send down water (rain) on it, it is stirred (to life), it
swells and puts forth every lovely kind (of growth).*

Quran 22:7-9

*And surely, the Hour is coming, there is no doubt about it, and
certainly, Allâh will resurrect those who are in the graves. (7) And
among men is he who disputes about Allâh, without knowledge or
guidance, or a Book giving light (from Allâh), (8) Bending his neck
in pride (far astray from the Path of Allâh), and leading (others)
too (far) astray from the Path of Allâh. For him there is disgrace in
this worldly life, and on the Day of Resurrection We shall make
him taste the torment of burning (Fire).*

Quran 22:17

*Verily, those who believe (in Allâh and in His Messenger
Muhammad), and those who are Jews, and the Sabians, and the
Christians, and the Majus, and those who worship others besides
Allâh, truly, Allâh will judge between them on the Day of
Resurrection. Verily! Allâh is Witness over all things a witness.*

Quran 22:47

And they ask you to hasten on the torment! And Allâh fails not His Promise. And verily, a day with your Lord is as a thousand years of what you reckon.

Quran 22:55-57

And those who disbelieved will not cease to be in doubt about it (this Qur'ân) until the Hour comes suddenly upon them, or there comes to them the torment of the Day after which there will be no night (i.e. the Day of Resurrection). (55) The sovereignty on that Day will be that of Allâh (the one Who has no partners). He will judge between them. So those who believed (in the Oneness of Allâh Islâmic Monotheism) and did righteous good deeds will be in Gardens of delight (Paradise). (56) And those who disbelieved and belied Our Verses (of this Qur'ân), for them will be a humiliating torment (in Hell).

Quran 22:69

"Allâh will judge between you on the Day of Resurrection about that wherein you used to differ."

Quran 23:16

Then (again), surely, you will be resurrected on the Day of Resurrection.

Quran 23:101

Then, when the Trumpet is blown, there will be no kinship among them that Day, nor will they ask of one another.

Quran 24:24-25

On the Day when their tongues, their hands, and their legs (or feet) will bear witness against them as to what they used to do. (24) On that Day Allâh will pay them the recompense of their deeds in full, and they will know that Allâh, He is the Manifest Truth.

Quran 24:64

Certainly, to Allâh belongs all that is in the heavens and the earth. Surely, He knows your condition and (He knows) the Day when they will be brought back to Him, then He will inform them of what they did. And Allâh is All-Knower of everything.

Quran 25:17-19

And on the Day when He will gather them together and that which they worship besides Allâh [idols, angels, pious men, saints, 'Îsā (Jesus) son of Maryam (Mary), etc.]. He will say: "Was it you who misled these My slaves or did they (themselves) stray from the (Right) Path?" (17) They will say: "Glorified are You! It was not for us to take any Auliyâ' (Protectors, Helpers) besides You, but You gave them and their fathers comfort till they forgot the warning, and became a lost people (doomed to total loss). (18) Thus they (false gods – all deities other than Allâh) will belie you (polytheists) regarding what you say (that they are gods besides Allâh), then you can neither avert (the punishment), nor get help. And whoever among you does wrong (i.e. sets up rivals to Allâh), We shall make him taste a great torment.

Quran 25:22-30

On the Day they will see the angels, – no glad tidings will there be for the Mujrimûn (criminals, disbelievers, polytheists, sinners) that day. And they (angels) will say: "All kinds of glad tidings are forbidden to you," [none will be allowed to enter Paradise except the one who said: Lâ ilâha ill-allâh, "(none has the right to be worshipped but Allâh) and acted practically on its legal orders and obligations.] (22) And We shall turn to whatever deeds they (disbelievers, polytheists, sinners) did, and We shall make such deeds as scattered floating particles of dust. (23) The dwellers of Paradise (i.e. those who deserved it through their Islamic Monotheistic Faith and their deed of righteousness) will, on that Day, have the best abode, and have the fairest of places for repose. (24) And (remember) the Day when the heaven shall be rent asunder with clouds, and the angels will be sent down, with a grand descending. (25) The sovereignty on that Day will be the true (sovereignty), belonging to the Most Gracious (Allâh), and it will be a hard Day for the disbelievers (those who disbelieve in the Oneness of Allâh Islâmic Monotheism). (26) And (remember) the Day when the Zâlim (wrong-doer, oppressor, polytheist) will bite at his hands, he will say: "Oh! Would that I had taken a path with the Messenger (Muhammad). (27) "Ah! Woe to me! Would that I had never taken so-and-so as a Khalil (an intimate friend)! (28) "He indeed led me astray from the Reminder (this Qur'ân) after it had come to me. And Shaitân (Satan) is to man ever a deserter in the hour of need." (29) And the Messenger (Muhammad) will say: "O my Lord! Verily, my people deserted this Qur'ân (neither listened to it, nor acted on its laws and teachings).

Quran 26:87-102

And disgrace me not on the Day when (all the creatures) will be resurrected; (87) The Day whereon neither wealth nor sons will avail, (88) Except him who brings to Allâh a clean heart [clean from Shirk (polytheism) and Nifâq (hypocrisy)]. (89) And Paradise will be brought near to the Muttaqûn (pious and righteous persons). (90) And the (Hell) Fire will be placed in full view of the erring. (91) And it will be said to them: "Where are those (the false gods whom you used to set up as rivals with Allâh) that you used to worship. (92) "Instead of Allâh? Can they help you or (even) help themselves?" (93) Then they will be thrown on their faces into the (Fire), They and the Ghâwûn (devils, and those who were in error). (94) And the whole hosts of Iblîs (Satan) together. (95) They will say while contending therein, (96) By Allâh, we were truly in a manifest error, (97) When We held you (false gods) as equals (in worship) with the Lord of the 'Alamîn (mankind, jinn and all that exists); (98) And none has brought us into error except the Mujrimûn [Iblîs (Satan) and those of human beings who commit crimes, murderers, polytheists, oppressors], (99) Now we have no intercessors, (100) Nor a close friend (to help us). (101) (Alas!) If we only had a chance to return (to the world), we shall truly be among the believers!

Quran 27:83-85

And (remember) the Day when We shall gather out of every nation a troop of those who denied Our Ayât (proofs, evidences, verses, lessons, signs, revelations, etc.), and (then) they (all) shall be set in array (gathered and driven to the place of reckoning), (83) Till, when they come (before their Lord at the place of reckoning), He will say: "Did you deny My Ayât (proofs, evidences, verses, lessons, signs, revelations, etc.) where as you comprehended them not by knowledge (of their truth or falsehood), or what (else) was it that you used to do?" (84) And the Word (of torment) will be fulfilled against them, because they have done wrong, and they will be unable to speak (in order to defend themselves).

Quran 27:87-90

And (remember) the Day on which the Trumpet will be blown — and all who are in the heavens and all who are on the earth, will be terrified except him whom Allâh will (exempt). And all shall come to Him humbled. (87) And you will see the mountains and think them solid, but they shall pass away as the passing away of the clouds. The Work of Allâh, Who perfected all things, verily! He is Well-Acquainted with what you do. (88) Whoever brings a good deed (i.e. Belief in the Oneness of Allâh along with every deed of righteousness), will have better than its worth, and they will be safe from the terror on that Day. (89) And whoever brings an evil deed (i.e. Shirk — polytheism, disbelief in the Oneness of Allâh and every evil sinful deed), they will be cast down (prone) on their faces in the Fire. (And it will be said to them) "Are you being recompensed anything except what you used to do?"

Quran 28:62-67

And (remember) the Day when He will call to them, and say: "Where are My (so-called) partners whom you used to assert?" (62) Those about whom the Word will have come true (to be punished) will say: "Our Lord! These are they whom we led astray. We led them astray, as we were astray ourselves. We declare our innocence (from them) before You. It was not us they worshipped." (63) And it will be said (to them): "Call upon your (so-called) partners (of Allâh), and they will call upon them, but they will give no answer to them, and they will see the torment. (They will then wish) if only they had been guided! (64) And (remember) the Day (Allâh) will call to them, and say: "What answer gave you to the Messengers?" (65) Then the news of a good answer will be obscured to them on that day, and they will not be able to ask one another. (66) But as for him who repented (from polytheism and sins), believed (in the Oneness of Allâh, and in His Messenger Muhammad), and did righteous deeds (in the life of this world), then he will be among those who are successful.

Quran 28:74-75

And (remember) the Day when He (your Lord — Allâh) will call to them (those who worshipped others along with Allâh), and will say: "Where are My (so-called) partners, whom you used to assert?" (74) And We shall take out from every nation a witness, and We shall say: "Bring your proof." Then they shall know that the truth is with Allâh (Alone), and the lies (false gods) which they invented will disappear from them.

Quran 29:13

And verily, they shall bear their own loads, and other loads besides their own, and verily, they shall be questioned on the Day of Resurrection about that which they used to fabricate.

Quran 30:12-16

And on the Day when the Hour will be established, the Mujrimûn (disbelievers, sinners, criminals, polytheists) will be plunged into destruction with (deep regrets, sorrows, and) despair. (12) No intercessors will they have from those whom they made equal with

Allâh (partners i.e. their so¬called associate gods), and they will (themselves) reject and deny their partners. (13) And on the Day when the Hour will be established, that Day shall (all men) be separated (i.e the believers will be separated from the disbelievers). (14) Then as for those who believed (in the Oneness of Allâh - Islâmic Monotheism) and did righteous good deeds, such shall be honored and made to enjoy luxurious life (forever) in a Garden of Delight (Paradise). (15) And as for those who disbelieved and belied Our Ayât (proofs, evidences, verses, lessons, signs, revelations, Allâh's Messengers, Resurrection, etc.), and the Meeting of the Hereafter, such shall be brought forth to the torment (in the Hell-fire).

Quran 30:55-57

And on the Day that the Hour will be established, the Mujrimûn (criminals, disbelievers, polytheists, sinners) will swear that they stayed not but an hour, thus were they ever deluded [away from the truth (i.e they used to tell lies and take false oaths, and turn away from the truth) in this life of the world]. (55) And those who have been bestowed with knowledge and faith will say: "Indeed you have stayed according to the Decree of Allâh, until the Day of Resurrection, so this is the Day of Resurrection, but you knew not." (56) So on that Day no excuse of theirs will avail those who did wrong (by associating partners in worship with Allâh, and by denying the Day of Resurrection), nor will they be allowed (then) to return to seek Allâh's Pleasure (by having Islâmic Faith with righteous deeds and by giving up polytheism, sins and crimes with repentance).

Quran 32:25

Verily, your Lord will judge between them on the Day of Resurrection, concerning that wherein they used to differ

Quran 32:28-29

They say: "When will this Fath (Decision) be (between us and you, i.e. the Day of Resurrection), if you are telling the truth?" (28) Say: "On the Day of Al¬Fath (Decision), no profit will it be to those who disbelieve if they (then) believe! Nor will they be granted a respite."

Quran 34:3-5

Those who disbelieve say: "The Hour will not come to us." Say: "Yes, by my Lord, the All¬Knower of the unseen, it will come to you." not even the weight of an atom or less than that or greater, escapes His Knowledge in the heavens or in the earth, but it is in a Clear Book (Al¬Lauh Al¬Mahfûz). (3) That He may recompense those who believe (in the Oneness of Allâh Islâmic Monotheism) and do righteous good deeds. Those, theirs is forgiveness and Rizq Karîm (generous provision, i.e. Paradise). (4) But those who strive against Our Ayât (proofs, evidences, verses, lessons, signs, revelations, etc.) to frustrate them, those, for them will be a severe painful torment.

Quran 34:25-26

Say "You will not be asked about our sins, nor shall we be asked of what you do." (25) Say: "Our Lord will assemble us all together (on the Day of Resurrection), then He will judge between us with truth. And He is the Just judge, the All-Knower of the true state of affairs."

Quran 34:29-33

And they say: "When is this promise (i.e. the Day of Resurrection) if you are truthful?" (29) Say: "The appointment to you is for a Day, which you cannot put back for an hour (or a moment) nor put forward." (30) And those who disbelieve say: "We believe not in this Qur'ân nor in that which was before it," but if you could see when the Zâlimûn (polytheists and wrong¬doers) will be made to stand before their Lord, how they will cast the (blaming) word one to another! Those who were deemed weak will say to those who were arrogant: "Had it not been for you, we should certainly have been believers!" (31) And those who were arrogant will say to those who were deemed weak: "Did we keep you back from guidance after it had come to you? Nay, but you were Mujrimûn (polytheists, sinners, disbeliveres, criminals). (32) Those who were deemed weak will say to those who were arrogant: "Nay, but it was your plotting by night and day, when you ordered us to disbelieve in Allâh and set up rivals to Him!" And each of them (parties) will conceal their own regrets (for disobeying Allâh during this worldly life), when they behold the torment. And We shall put iron collars round the necks of those who disbelieved. Are they requited aught except what they used to do?

Quran 34:40-42

And (remember) the Day when He will gather them all together, then He will say to the angels: "Was it you that these people used to worship?" (40) They (the angels) will say: "Glorified are You! You are our Walî (Lord) instead of them. Nay, but they used to worship the jinn; most of them were believers in them." (41) So Today (i.e. the Day of Resurrection), none of you can profit or harm one another. And We shall say to those who did wrong [i.e. worshipped others (like angels, jinn, prophets, saints, righteous persons) along with Allâh]: "Taste the torment of the Fire which you used to belie.

Quran 36:48-65

And they say: "When will this promise (i.e. Resurrection) be fulfilled, if you are truthful?" (48) They await only but a single Saihah (shout), which will seize them while they are disputing! (49) Then they will not be able to make bequest, nor they will return to their family. (50) And the Trumpet will be blown (i.e. the second blowing) and behold from the graves they will come out quickly to their Lord. (51) They will say: "Woe to us! Who has raised us up from our place of sleep." (It will be said to them): "This is what the Most Gracious (Allâh) had promised, and the Messengers spoke truth!" (52) It will be but a single Saihah (shout), so behold! They will all be brought up before Us! (53) This Day (Day of Resurrection), none will be wronged in anything, nor will you be requited anything except that which you used to do. (54) Verily, the dwellers of the Paradise, that Day, will be busy with joyful things. (55) They and their wives will be in pleasant shade, reclining on thrones. (56) They will have therein fruits (of all kinds) and all that they ask for. (57) (It will be said to them): Salâm (peace be on you), — a Word from the Lord (Allâh), Most Merciful. (58) (It will be said): "And O you Mujrimûn (criminals, polytheists, sinners, disbelievers in the Islâmic Monotheism, wicked evil ones)! Get you apart this Day (from the believers). (59) Did I not command for you, O Children of Adam, that you should not worship Shaitân (Satan). Verily, he is a plain enemy to you. (60) And that you should worship Me [Alone, and set up not

rivals, associate-gods with Me]. That is the Straight Path. (61)
And indeed he (Satan) did lead astray a great multitude of you.
Did you not, then, understand? (62) This is Hell which you were
promised! (63) Burn therein this Day, for that you used to
disbelieve. (64) This Day, We shall seal up their mouths, and their
hands will speak to Us, and their legs will bear witness to what
they used to earn.

Quran 36:74-75

And they have taken besides Allâh âlihah (gods), hoping that they
might be helped (by those so – called gods). (74) They cannot help
them, but they will be brought forward as a troop against those
who worshipped them (at the time of Reckoning).

Quran 37:15-33

And they say: "This is nothing but evident magic! (15) "When we
are dead and have become dust and bones, shall we (then) verily be
resurrected? (16) "And also our fathers of old?" (17) Say: "Yes,
and you shall then be humiliated." (18) It will be a single Zajrah
[shout (i.e. the second blowing of the Trumpet)], and behold, they
will be staring! (19) They will say: "Woe to us! This is the Day of
Recompense!" (20) (It will be said): "This is the Day of Judgement
which you used to deny." (21) It will be said to the angels):
"Assemble those who did wrong, together with their companions
(from the devils) and what they used to worship (22) "Instead of
Allâh, and lead them on to the way of flaming Fire (Hell); (23)
"But stop them, verily they are to be questioned. (24) "What is the
matter with you? Why do you not help one another (as you used to
do in the world)?" (25) Nay, but that Day they shall surrender,
(26) And they will turn to one another and question one another.

(27) They will say: "It was you who used to come to us from the right side [i.e. from the right side of one of us and beautify for us every evil, enjoin on us polytheism, and stop us from the truth i.e. Islâmic Monotheism and from every good deed]." (28) They will reply: "Nay, you yourselves were not believers. (29) "And we had no authority over you. Nay! But you were Taghun (transgressing) people (polytheists, and disbelievers). (30) "So now the Word of our Lord has been justified against us, that we shall certainly (have to) taste (the torment). (31) "So we led you astray because we were ourselves astray." (32) Then verily, that Day, they will (all) share in the torment.

Quran 39:7

If you disbelieve, then verily, Allâh is not in need of you, He likes not disbelief for His slaves. And if you are grateful (by being believers), He is pleased therewith for you. No bearer of burdens shall bear the burden of another. Then to your Lord is your return, and He will inform you what you used to do. Verily, He is the All-Knower of that which is in (men's) breasts.

Quran 39:24

Is he then, who will confront with his face the awful torment on the Day of Resurrection (as he who enters peacefully in Paradise)? And it will be said to the Zâlimûn (polytheists and wrong-doers): "Taste what you used to earn!"

Quran 39:30-35

Verily, you (O Muhammad) will die and verily, they (too) will die. (30) Then, on the Day of Resurrection, you will be disputing before your Lord. (31) Then, who does more wrong than one who utters a lie against Allâh, and denies the truth [this Qur'ân, the Prophet (Muhammad), and the Islâmic Monotheism] when it comes to him! Is there not in Hell an abode for the disbelievers? (32) And he (Muhammad) who has brought the truth (this Qur'ân and Islâmic Monotheism) and (those who) believed therein (i.e. the true believers of Islâmic Monotheism), those are Al- Muttaqûn (the pious and righteous persons) (33) They shall have all that they will desire with their Lord. That is the reward of Muhsinûn (good-doers) (34) So that Allâh may expiate from them the evil of what they did and give them the reward, according to the best of what they used to do

Quran 39:44

Say: "To Allâh belongs all intercession. His is the Sovereignty of the heavens and the earth, Then to Him you shall be brought back."

Quran 39:46-48

Say: "O Allâh! Creator of the heavens and the earth! All-Knower of the Ghaib (unseen) and the seen. You will judge between your slaves about that wherein they used to differ." (46) And those who did wrong (the polytheists and disbelievers in Allâh), if they had all that is in earth and therewith as much again, they verily, would offer it to ransom themselves therewith on the Day of Resurrection from the evil torment, and there will become apparent to them from Allâh, what they had not been reckoning (47) And the evils of that which they earned will become apparent to them, and they will be encircled by that which they used to mock at!

Quran 39:60-61

And on the Day of Resurrection you will see those who lied against Allâh (i.e. attributed to Him sons, partners) — their faces will be black. Is there not in Hell an abode for the arrogant? (60) And Allâh will deliver those who are the Muttaqûn (pious) to their places of success (Paradise). Evil shall touch them not, nor shall they grieve.

Quran 39:67-75

They made not a just estimate of Allâh such as is due to Him. And on the Day of Resurrection the whole of the earth will be grasped by His Hand and the heavens will be rolled up in His Right Hand. Glorified is He, and High is He above all that they associate as partners with Him! (67) And the Trumpet will be blown, and all who are in the heavens and all who are on the earth will swoon away, except him whom Allâh wills. Then it will blown a second time and behold, they will be standing, looking on (waiting). (68) And the earth will shine with the light of its Lord (Allâh, when He will come to judge among men) and the Book will be placed (open) and the Prophets and the witnesses will be brought forward, and it will be judged between them with truth, and they will not be wronged. (69) And each person will be paid in full of what he did; and He is Best Aware of what they do. (70) And those who disbelieved will be driven to Hell in groups, till, when they reach it, the gates thereof will be opened (suddenly like a prison at the arrival of the prisoners). And its keepers will say, "Did not the Messengers come to you from yourselves, reciting to you the Verses of your Lord, and warning you of the Meeting of this Day of yours?" They will say: "Yes, but the Word of torment has been justified against the disbelievers!" (71) It will be said (to them): "Enter you the gates of Hell, to abide therein. And (indeed) what an evil abode of the arrogant!" (72) And those who kept their duty to their Lord will be led to Paradise in groups, till, when they reach it, and its gates will be opened (before their arrival for their reception) and its keepers will say: Salâmun 'Alaikum (peace be upon you)! You have done well, so enter here to abide therein." (73) And they will say: "All the praises and thanks are to Allâh Who has fulfilled His Promise to us and has made us inherit (this) land. We can dwell in Paradise where we will; how excellent a reward for the (pious good) workers!" (74) And you will see the angels surrounding the Throne (of Allâh) from all round, glorifying the praises of their Lord (Allâh). And they (all the creatures) will be judged with truth, and it will be said. All the praises and thanks are to Allâh, the Lord of the 'Alamîn (mankind, jinn and all that exists)."

Quran 40:15-18

(He is Allâh) Owner of High Ranks and Degrees, the Owner of the Throne. He sends the revelation by His Command to any of His slaves He wills, that he (the person who receives revelation) may warn (men) of the Day of Mutual Meeting (i.e. The Day of Resurrection). (15) The Day when they will (all) come out, nothing of them will be hidden from Allâh. Whose is the kingdom this Day? (Allâh Himself will reply to His Question): It is Allâh's the One, the Irresistible! (16) This Day shall every person be recompensed for what he earned. This day no injustice (shall be done to anybody). Truly, Allâh is Swift in reckoning. (17) And warn them (O Muhammad) of the Day that is drawing near (i.e. the Day of Resurrection), when the hearts will be choking the

throats, and they can neither return them (hearts) to their chests nor can they throw them out. There will be no friend, nor an intercessor for the Zâlimûn (polytheists and wrong-doers), who could be given heed to.

Quran 41:47-48

To Him (Alone) is referred the knowledge of the Hour. No fruit comes out of its sheath, nor does a female conceive, nor brings forth (young), except by His Knowledge. And on the Day when He will call unto them (polytheists) (saying): "Where are My (so-called) partners (whom you did invent)?" They will say: "We inform You that none of us bears witness to it (that they are Your partners)!" (47) And those whom they used to invoke before before (in this world) shall disappear from them, and they will perceive that they have no place of refuge (from Allâh's punishment)

Quran 42:47

Answer the Call of your Lord (i.e. accept the Islâmic Monotheism, O mankind, and jinn) before there comes from Allâh a Day which cannot be averted. (i.e. the Day of Resurrection) You will have no refuge on that Day nor there will be for you any denying (of your crimes as they are all recorded in the Book of your deeds)

Quran 43:36-39

And whosoever turns away blindly from the remembrance of the Most Gracious (Allâh) (i.e. this Qur'ân and worship of Allâh), We appoint for him Shaitân (Satan devil) to be a Qarîn (a intimate companion) to him. (36) And verily, they (Satans / devils) hinder them from the Path (of Allâh), but they think that they are guided

*aright! (37) Till, when (such a one) comes to Us, he says [to his
Qarîn (Satan / devil companion)] "Would that between me and
you were the distance of the two easts (or the east and west)" a
worst (type of) companion (indeed)! (38) It will profit you not this
Day (O you who turn away from Allâh's remembrance and His
worship) as you did wrong, (and) that you will be sharers (you and
your Qarîn) in the punishment.*

Quran 43:66-70

*Do they only wait for the Hour that it shall come upon them
suddenly, while they perceive not? (66) Friends on that Day will
be foes one to another except Al-Muttaqûn (pious) (67) (It will be
said to the true believers of Islâmic Monotheism): My worshippers!
No fear shall be on you this Day, nor shall you grieve, (68) (You)
who believed in Our Ayât (proofs, verses, lessons, signs,
revelations, etc.) and were Muslims (i.e. who submit totally to
Allâh's Will, and believe in the Oneness of Allâh - Islâmic
Monotheism) (69) Enter Paradise, you and your wives, in
happiness.*

Quran 44:40-42

*Verily, the Day of Judgement (when Allâh will judge between the
creatures) is the time appointed for all of them, − (40) The Day
when Maula (a near relative) cannot avail Maula (a near relative)
in aught, and no help can they receive, (41) Except him on whom
Allâh has Mercy. Verily, He is the All-Mighty, the Most Merciful.*

Quran 45:27-35

And to Allâh belongs the kingdom of the heavens and the earth. And on the Day that the Hour will be established − on that Day the followers of falsehood (polytheists, disbelievers, worshippers of false deities) shall lose (everything). (27) And you will see each nation humbled to their knees (kneeling), each nation will be called to its Record (of deeds). This Day you shall be recompensed for what you used to do. (28) This Our Record speaks about you with truth. Verily, We were recording what you used to do (i.e. Our angels used to record your deeds). (29) Then, as for those who believed (in the Oneness of Allâh − Islâmic Monotheism) and did righteous good deeds, their Lord will admit them to His Mercy. That will be the evident success. (30) But as for those who disbelieved (it will be said to them): "Were not Our Verses recited to you? But you were proud, and you were a people who were Mujrimûn (polytheists, disbelievers, sinners, criminals)." (31) And when it was said: "Verily! Allâh's Promise is the truth, and there is no doubt about the coming of the Hour," you said; "We know not what is the Hour, we do not think it but as a conjecture, and we have no firm convincing belief (therein)." (32) And the evil of what they did will appear to them, and that which they used to mock at will completely encircle them. (33) And it will be said: "This Day We will forget you as you forgot the Meeting of this Day of yours. And your abode is the Fire, and there is none to help you." (34) This, because you took the revelations of Allâh (this Qur'ân) in mockery, and the life of the world deceived you. So this Day, they shall not be taken out from there (Hell), nor shall they be returned to the worldly life, (so that they repent to Allâh, and beg His Pardon for their sins).

Quran 46:6

And when mankind are gathered (on the Day of Resurrection), they (false deities) will become their enemies and will deny their worshipping.

Quran 46:19-20

And for all, there will be degrees according to that which they did, that He (Allâh) may recompense them in full for their deeds. And they will not be wronged. (19) On the Day when those who disbelieve (in the Oneness of Allâh Islâmic Monotheism) will be exposed to the Fire (it will be said): "You received your good things in the life of the world, and you took your pleasure therein. Now this Day you shall be recompensed with a torment of humiliation, because you were arrogant in the land without a right, and because you used to rebel against Allah's Command (disobey Allâh).

Quran 46:34-35

And on the Day when those who disbelieve will be exposed to the Fire (it will be said to them): "Is this not the truth?" They will say: "Yes, By our Lord!" He will say: "Then taste the torment, because you used to disbelieve!" (34) Therefore be patient (O Muhammad) as did the Messengers of strong will and be in no haste about them (disbelievers). On the Day when they will see that (torment) with which they are promised (i.e. threatened, it will be) as if they had not stayed more than an hour in a single day. (O mankind, this Qur'ân is sufficient as) a clear Message (or proclamation to save yourself from destruction). But shall any be destroyed except the people who are Al-Fâsiqûn (the rebellious against Allâh's Command, the disobedient to Allâh)?

Quran 50:20-35

*And the Trumpet will be blown − that will be the Day whereof
warning (had been given) (i.e. the Day of Resurrection). (20) And
every person will come forth along with an (angel) to drive (him),
and an (angel) to bear witness. (21) (It will be said to the sinners):
"Indeed you were heedless of this, now We have removed your
covering, and sharp is your sight this Day!" (22) And his
companion (angel) will say: "Here is (this Record) ready with
me!" (23) (Allah will say to the angels): "Both of you throw into
Hell, every stubborn disbeliever (in the Oneness of Allâh, in His
Messengers) − (24) "Hinderer of good, transgressor, doubter, (25)
"Who set up another ilâh (god) with Allâh, Then both of you cast
him in the severe torment." (26) His companion (Satan − devil)]
will say: "Our Lord! I did not push him to transgression, (in
disbelief, oppression, and evil deeds) but he was himself in error far
astray." (27) Allâh will say: "Dispute not in front of Me, I had
already, in advance, sent you the threat. (28) The Sentence that
comes from Me cannot be changed, and I am not unjust to the
slaves." (29) On the Day when We will say to Hell: "Are you
filled?" It will say: "Are there any more (to come)?" (30) And
Paradise will be brought near to the Muttaqûn (pious) not far off.
(31) (It will be said): "This is what you were promised, - (it is) for
those oft-returning (to Allâh) in sincere repentance, and those who
preserve their covenant with Allâh (by obeying Him in all what He
has ordered, and worshipping none but Allâh Alone, i.e. follow
Allâh's religion, Islâmic Monotheism). (32) "Who feared the Most
Gracious (Allâh) in the Ghaib (unseen) and brought a heart turned
in repentance (to Him - and absolutely free from each and every
kind of polytheism). (33) "Enter you therein in peace and security*

— *this is a Day of eternal life!" (34) There they will have all that they desire — and We have more (for them, i.e. a glance at the All-Mighty, All-Majestic)*

Quran 50:41-44

And listen on the Day when the caller will call from a near place, (41) The Day when they will hear As-Saihah (shout) in truth, that will be the Day of coming out (from the graves i.e. the Day of Resurrection). (42) Verily, We it is Who give life and cause death; and to Us is the final return, (43) On the Day when the earth shall be cleft, from off them, (they will come out) hastening forth. That will be a gathering, quite easy for Us.

Quran 51:12-19

They ask; "When will be the Day of Recompense?" (12) (It will be) a Day when they will be tried (punished i.e. burnt) over the Fire! (13) "Taste you your trial (punishment i.e. burning)! This is what you used to ask to be hastened!" (14) Verily, the Muttaqûn (pious) will be in the midst of Gardens and Springs (in the Paradise), (15) Taking joy in the things which their Lord has given them. Verily, they were before this Muhsinûn (good-doers) (16) They used to sleep but little by night [invoking their Lord (Allâh) and praying, with fear and hope]. (17) And in the hours before dawn, they were (found) asking (Allâh) for forgiveness, (18) And in their properties there was the right of the Sa'il (the beggar who asks), and the Mahrûm (the poor who does not ask the others)

Quran 52:7-28

Verily, the Torment of your Lord will surely come to pass, (7) There is none that can avert it; (8) On the Day when the heaven will shake with a dreadful shaking, (9) And the mountains will move away with a (horrible) movement. (10) Then woe that Day to the beliers; (11) Who are playing in falsehood. (12) The Day when they will be pushed down by force to the Fire of Hell, with a horrible, forceful pushing. (13) This is the Fire which you used to belie. (14) Is this magic, or do you not see? (15) Taste you therein its heat, and whether you are patient of it or impatient of it, it is all the same. You are only being requited for what you used to do. (16) Verily, the Muttaqûn (pious) will be in Gardens (Paradise), and Delight. (17) Enjoying in that which their Lord has bestowed on them, and (the fact that) their Lord saved them from the torment of the blazing Fire. (18) "Eat and drink with happiness because of what you used to do." (19) They will recline (with ease) on thrones arranged in ranks. And We shall marry them to Hûr (female, fair ones) with wide lovely eyes. (20) And those who believe and whose offspring follow them in Faith, to them shall We join their offspring, and We shall not decrease the reward of their deeds in anything. Every person is a pledge for that which he has earned. (21) And We shall provide them with fruit and meat, such as they desire. (22) There they shall pass from hand to hand a (wine) cup, free from any Laghw (dirty, false, evil vain talk between them), and free from sin (because it will be lawful for them to drink). (23) And there will go round boy-servants of theirs, to serve them as if they were preserved pearls. (24) And some of them draw near to others, questioning. (25) Saying: "Aforetime, we were afraid (of the punishment of Allâh) in the midst of our families. (26) "So Allâh has been gracious to us, and has saved us from the torment of the Fire. (27) "Verily, We used to invoke Him (Alone and none else) before. Verily, He is Al¬Barr (the Most Subtle, Kind, Courteous, and Generous), the Most Merciful."

Quran 52:45-46

So leave them alone till they meet their Day, in which they will sink into a fainting (with horror). (45) The Day when their plotting shall not avail them at all nor will they be helped (i.e. they will receive their torment in Hell).

Quran 53:57-58

The Day of Resurrection draws near, (57) None besides Allâh can avert it, (or advance it, or delay it).

Quran 54:6-8

So (O Muhammad) withdraw from them. The Day that the caller will call (them) to a terrible thing. (6) They will come forth, with humbled eyes from (their) graves as if they were locusts spread abroad, (7) Hastening towards The caller, the disbelievers will say: "This is a hard Day."

Quran 54:46-55

Nay, but the Hour is their appointed time (for their full recompense), and the Hour will be more grievous and more bitter. (46) Verily, the Mujrimûn (polytheists, disbelievers, sinners, criminals) are in error (in this world) and will burn (in the Hell-fire in the Hereafter). (47) The Day they will be dragged on their faces into the Fire (it will be said to them): "Taste you the touch of Hell!" (48) Verily, We have created all things with Qadar (Divine Preordainments of all things before their creation, as written in the

Book of Decrees Al-Lauh Al-Mahfûz). (49) And Our Commandment is but one, as the twinkling of an eye. (50) And indeed, We have destroyed your likes, then is there any that will remember (or receive admonition)? (51) And everything they have done is noted in (their) Records (of deeds). (52) And everything, small and big, is written down (in Al-Lauh Al-Mahfûz already beforehand i.e. before it befalls, or is done by its doer) (53) Verily, The Muttaqûn (the pious), will be in the midst of Gardens and Rivers (Paradise). (54) In a seat of truth (i.e. Paradise), near the Omnipotent King (Allâh the one, the All-Blessed, the Most High, the Owner of Majesty and Honour).

Quran 55:37-44

Then when the heaven is rent asunder, and it becomes rosy or red like red-oil, or red hide (37) Then which of the Blessings of your Lord will you both (jinn and men) deny? (38) So on that Day no question will be asked of man or jinni as to his sin, [because they have already been known from their faces either white (dwellers of Paradise - true believers of Islamic Monotheism) or black (dwellers of Hell - polytheists; disbelievers, criminals)]. (39) Then which of the Blessings of your Lord will you both (jinn and men) deny? (40) The Mujrimûn (polytheists, criminals, sinners) will be known by their marks (black faces), and they will be seized by their forelocks and their feet. (41) Then which of the Blessings of your Lord will you both (jinn and men) deny? (42) This is Hell which the Mujrimûn (polytheists, criminals, sinners) denied. (43) They will go between it (Hell) and the fierce boiling water!

Quran 56:1-56

When the Event (i.e. the Day of Resurrection) befalls. (1) And there can be no denial of its befalling. (2) Bringing low (some — those who will enter Hell) Exalting (others- those who will enter Paradise). (3) When the earth will be shaken with a terrible shake. (4) And the mountains will be powdered to dust. (5) So that they will become floating dust particles. (6) And you (all) will be in three groups. (7) So those on the Right Hand (i.e. those who will be given their Records in their right hands) — how (fortunate) will be those on the Right Hand! (As a respect for them, because they will enter Paradise). (8) And those on the Left Hand (i.e. those who will be given their Record in their left hands) — how (unfortunate) will be those on the Left Hand? (As a disgrace for them, because they will enter Hell). (9) And those foremost [(in Islâmic Faith of Monotheism and in performing righteous deeds) in the life of this world on the very first call for to embrace Islâm,] will be foremost (in Paradise). (10) These will be those nearest (to Allâh). (11) In the Gardens of Delight (Paradise). (12) A multitude of those (foremost) will be from the first generations (who embraced Islâm). (13) And a few of those (foremost) will be from the later generations. (14) (They will be) on thrones woven with gold and precious stones, (15) Reclining thereon, face to face. (16) Immortal boys will go around them (serving). (17) With cups, and jugs, and a glass of the flowing wine, (18) Wherefrom they will get neither any aching of the head, nor any intoxication. (19) And with fruit, that they may choose. (20) And with the flesh of fowls that they desire. (21) And (there will be) Hur (fair females) with wide, lovely eyes (as wives for the pious), (22) Like unto preserved pearls. (23) A reward for what they used to do. (24) No Laghw (dirty, false, evil vain talk) will they hear therein, nor any sinful speech (like backbiting). (25) But only the saying of: Salâm!, Salâm! (greetings

with peace) ! (26) And those on the Right Hand- how (fortunate)
will be those on the Right Hand? (27) (They will be) among
thornless lote-trees, (28) And Among Talh (banana-trees) with
fruits piled one above another, (29) In shade long-extended, (30)
And by water flowing constantly, (31) And fruit in plenty, (32)
Whose supply is not cut off (by change of season) nor are they out
of reach. (33) And on couches or thrones, raised high. (34) Verily,
We have created them (maidens) of special creation. (35) And made
them virgins. (36) Loving (their husbands only), (and) of equal
age. (37) For those on the Right Hand. (38) A multitude of those
(on the Right Hand) will be from the first generation (who
embraced Islâm). (39) And a multitude of those (on the Right
Hand) will be from the later generations. (40) And those on the
Left Hand how (unfortunate) will be those on the Left Hand? (41)
In fierce hot wind and boiling water. (42) And shadow of black
smoke. (43) (That shadow) neither cool, nor (even) pleasant, (44)
Verily, before that, they indulged in luxury, (45) And were
persisting in great sin (joining partners in worship along with
Allâh, committing murder and other crimes). (46) And they used
to say: "When we die and become dust and bones, shall we then
indeed be resurrected? (47) "And also our forefathers?" (48) Say
(O Muhammad): "(Yes) verily, those of old, and those of later
times. (49) "All will surely be gathered together for appointed
Meeting of a known Day. (50) "Then moreover, verily, you the
erring-ones, the deniers (of Resurrection)! (51) "You verily will
eat of the trees of Zaqqûm. (52) "Then you will fill your bellies
therewith, (53) "And drink boiling water on top of it. (54) "And
you will drink (that) like thirsty camels!" (55) That will be their
entertainment on the Day of Recompense!

Quran 57:19

And those who believe in (the Oneness of) Allâh and His Messengers, they are the Siddiqûn (i.e. those followers of the Prophets who were first and foremost to believe in them), and the martyrs with their Lord, they shall have their reward and their light. But those who disbelieve (in the Oneness of Allâh - Islâmic Monotheism) and deny Our Ayât (proofs, evidences, verses, lessons, signs, revelations, etc.), they shall be the dwellers of the blazing Fire.

Quran 58:5-7

Verily, those who oppose Allâh and His Messenger (Muhammad) will be disgraced, as those before them (among the past nation), were disgraced. And We have sent down clear Ayât (proofs, evidences, verses, lessons, signs, revelations, etc.). And for the disbelievers is a disgracing torment. (5) On the Day when Allâh will resurrect them all together (i.e. on the Day of Resurrection) and inform them of what they did. Allâh has kept account of it, while they have forgotten it. And Allâh is Witness over all things. (6) Have you not seen that Allâh knows whatsoever is in the heavens and whatsoever is on the earth? There is no Najwa (secret counsel) of three, but He is their fourth (with His Knowledge, while He Himself is over the Throne, over the seventh heaven), nor of five but He is their sixth (with His Knowledge), not of less than that or more, but He is with them (with His Knowledge) wheresoever they may be; And afterwards on the Day of Resurrection, He will inform them of what they did. Verily, Allâh is the All-Knower of everything.

Quran 64:9-10

(And remember) the Day when He will gather you (all) on the Day of Gathering, that will be the Day of mutual loss and gain (i.e. loss for the disbelievers as they will enter the Hell-fire and gain for the believers as they will enter Paradise). And whosoever believes in Allâh and performs righteous good deeds, He will expiate from him his sins, and will admit him to Gardens under which rivers flow (Paradise) to dwell therein forever, that will be the great success. (9) But those who disbelieved (in the Oneness of Allâh - Islâmic Monotheism) and denied Our Ayât (proofs, evidences, verses, lessons, signs, revelations, etc.), they will be the dwellers of the Fire, to dwell therein forever. And worst indeed is that destination

Quran 67:24-27

Say: "It is He Who has created you from the earth, and to Him shall you be gathered (in the Hereafter)." (24) They say: "When will this promise (i.e. the Day of Resurrection) come to pass if you are telling the truth?" (25) Say (O Muhammad): "The knowledge (of its exact time) is with Allâh only, and I am only a plain warner." (26) But when they will see it (the torment on the Day of Resurrection) approaching, the faces of those who disbelieve will change and turn black with sadness and in grief and it will be said (to them): "This is (the promise) which you were calling for!"

Quran 68:42-43

(Remember) the Day when the Shin shall be laid bare (i.e. the Day of Resurrection) and they shall be called to prostrate themselves (to Allâh), but they (hypocrites) shall not be able to do so. (42) Their eyes will be cast down and ignominy will cover them; they used to

be called to prostrate themselves (offer prayers), while they were healthy and good (in the life of the world, but they did not).

Quran 69:13-37

Then when the Trumpet will be blown with one blowing (the first one), (13) And the earth and the mountains shall be removed from their places, and crushed with a single crushing. (14) Then on that Day shall the (Great) Event befall. (15) And the heaven will be wrent asunder, for that Day it (the heaven) will be frail, and torn up. (16) And the angels will be on its sides, and eight angels will, that Day, bear the Throne of your Lord above them. (17) That Day shall you be brought to Judgement, not a secret of you will be hidden. (18) Then as for him who will be given his Record in his right hand will say: "Here! read my Record! (19) "Surely, I did believe that I shall meet my Account!" (20) So he shall be in a life, well-pleasing. (21) In a lofty Paradise, (22) The fruits in bunches whereof will be low and near at hand. (23) Eat and drink at ease for that which you have sent on before you in days past! (24) But as for him who will be given his Record in his left hand, will say: "I wish that I had not been given my Record! (25) "And that I had never known, how my Account is! (26) "Would that it had been my end (death)! (27) "My wealth has not availed me; (28) "My power (and arguments to defend myself) have gone from me!" (29) (It will be said): "Seize him and fetter him; (30) Then throw him in the blazing Fire. (31) "Then fasten him with a chain whereof the length is seventy cubits!" (32) Verily, He used not to believe in Allâh, the Most Great, (33) And urged not on the feeding of Al¬Miskîn (the poor), (34) So no friend has he here this Day, (35) Nor any food except filth from the washing of wounds, (36) None will eat it except the Khâti'ûn (sinners, disbelievers, polytheists).

Quran 69:50

And indeed it (this Qur'ân) will be an anguish for the disbelievers (on the Day of Resurrection).

Quran 70:1-17

A questioner asked concerning a torment about to befall (1) Upon the disbelievers, which none can avert, (2) From Allâh, the Lord of the ways of ascent. (3) The angels and the Rûh [Jibril (Gabriel)] ascend to Him in a Day the measure whereof is fifty thousand years. (4) So be patient, with a good patience. (5) Verily! they see it (the torment) afar off. (6) But We see it (quite) near. (7) The Day that the sky will be like the boiling filth of oil, (or molten copper or silver or lead). (8) And the mountains will be like flakes of wool. (9) And no friend will ask a friend (about his condition), (10) Though they shall be made to see one another [(i.e. on the Day of Resurrection), there will be none but see his father, children and relatives, but he will neither speak to them nor will ask them for any help]. The Mujrim, (criminal, sinner, disbeliever) would desire to ransom himself from the punishment of that Day by his children. (11) And his wife and his brother, (12) And his kindred who sheltered him, (13) And all that are in the earth, so that it might save him. (14) By no means! Verily, it will be the Fire of Hell! (15) Taking away (burning completely) the head skin! (16) Calling (all) such as turn their backs and turn away their faces (from Faith) [picking and swallowing them up from that great gathering of mankind on the Day of Resurrection just as a bird picks up a grain from the earth with its beak and swallows it up].

Quran 70:43-44

The Day when they will come out of the graves quickly as racing to a goal, (43) With their eyes lowered in fear and humility, ignominy covering them (all over)! That is the Day which they were promised!

Quran 73:14-18

On the Day when the earth and the mountains will be in violent shake, and the mountains will be a heap of sand poured out. (14) Verily, We have sent to you (O men) a Messenger (Muhammad) to be a witness over you, as We did send a Messenger [Mûsa (Moses)] to Fir'aun (Pharaoh) (15) But Fir'aun (Pharaoh) disobeyed the Messenger [Mûsa (Moses)], so We seized him with a severe punishment. (16) Then how can you avoid the punishment, if you disbelieve, on a Day (i.e. the Day of Resurrection) that will make the children grey-headed? (17) Whereon the heaven will be cleft asunder? His Promise is certainly to be accomplished

Quran 74:8-11

Then, when the Trumpet is sounded (i.e. the second blowing of horn); (8) Truly, that Day will be a Hard Day (9) Far from easy for the disbelievers. (10) Leave Me Alone (to deal) with whom I created Alone!

Quran 75:1-15

I swear by the Day of Resurrection; (1) And I swear by the self-reproaching person (a believer). (2) Does man (a disbeliever) think that We shall not assemble his bones? (3) Yes, We are Able to put together in perfect order the tips of his fingers. (4) Nay! (Man denies Resurrection and Reckoning.) So he desires to continue committing sins. (5) He asks: "When will be this Day of Resurrection?" (6) So, when the sight shall be dazed, (7) And the moon will be eclipsed, (8) And the sun and moon will be joined together (by going one into the other or folded up or deprived of their light). (9) On that Day man will say: "Where (is the refuge) to flee?" (10) No! There is no refuge! (11) Unto your Lord (Alone) will be the place of rest that Day. (12) On that Day man will be informed of what he sent forward (of his evil or good deeds), and what he left behind (of his good or evil traditions). (13) Nay! Man will be a witness against himself [as his body parts (skin, hands, legs, etc.) will speak about his deeds]. (14) Though he may put forth his excuses (to cover his evil deeds).

Quran 75:22-25

Some faces that Day shall be Nâdirah (shining and radiant). (22) Looking at their Lord (Allâh); (23) And some faces, that Day, will be Bâsirah (dark, gloomy, frowning, and sad), (24) Thinking that some calamity is about to fall on them

Quran 77:7-15

Surely, what you are promised must come to pass. (7) Then when the stars lose their lights; (8) And when the heaven is cleft asunder; (9) And when the mountains are blown away; (10) And when the Messengers are gathered to their time appointed; (11) For what Day are these signs postponed? (12) For the Day of sorting out (the men of Paradise from the men destined for Hell). (13) And what will explain to you what is the Day of sorting out? (14) Woe that Day to the deniers (of the Day of Resurrection)!

Quran 77:28-49

Woe that Day to the deniers (of the Day of Resurrection)! (28) (It will be said to the disbelievers): "Depart you to that which you used to deny! (29) "Depart you to a shadow (of Hell-fire smoke ascending) in three columns, (30) "Neither shady, nor of any use against the fierce flame of the Fire." (31) Verily, It (Hell) throws sparks (huge) as Al-Qasr [a fort or a (huge log of wood)], (32) As if they were yellow camels or bundles of ropes. (33) Woe that Day to the deniers (of the Day of Resurrection)! (34) That will be a Day when they shall not speak (during some part of it), (35) And they will not be permitted to put forth any excuse. (36) Woe that Day to the deniers (of the Day of Resurrection)! (37) That will be a Day of Decision! We have brought you and the men of old together! (38) So if you have a plot, use it against Me (Allâh)! (39) Woe that Day to the deniers (of the Day of Resurrection)! (40) Verily, the Muttaqûn (pious) shall be amidst shades and springs. (41) And fruits, such as they desire. (42) "Eat and drink comfortably for that which you used to do. (43) Verily, thus We reward the Muhsinûn (good-doers) (44) Woe that Day to the deniers (of the Day of Resurrection)! (45) (O you disbelievers)! Eat and enjoy yourselves (in this worldly life) for a little while. Verily, you are the Mujrimûn (polytheists, disbelievers, sinners, criminals). (46) Woe that Day to the deniers (of the Day of Resurrection)! (47) And when it is said to them: "Bow down yourself (in prayer)!" They bow not down (offer not their prayers). (48) Woe that Day to the deniers (of the Day of Resurrection)!

Quran 78:17-40

Verily, the Day of Decision is a fixed time, (17) The Day when the Trumpet will be blown, and you shall come forth in crowds (groups after groups). (18) And the heaven shall be opened, and it

*will become as gates, (19) And the mountains shall be moved away
from their places and they will be as if they were a mirage. (20)
Truly, Hell is a place of ambush — (21) A dwelling place for the
Tâghûn (those who transgress the boundry limits set by Allâh like
polytheists, disbelievers in the Oneness of Allâh, hyprocrites,
sinners, criminals), (22) They will abide therein for ages, (23)
Nothing cool shall they taste therein, nor any drink. (24) Except
boiling water, and dirty wound discharges — (25) An exact
recompense (according to their evil crimes) (26) For verily, they
used not to look for a reckoning. (27) But they belied Our Ayât
(proofs, evidences, verses, lessons, signs, revelations, and that
which Our Prophet brought) completely. (28) And all things We
have recorded in a Book. (29) So taste you (the results of your evil
actions); No increase shall We give you, except in torment. (30)
Verily, for the Muttaqûn, there will be a success (Paradise); (31)
Gardens and vineyards, (32) And young full-breasted (mature)
maidens of equal age, (33) And a full cup (of wine). (34) No Laghw
(dirty, false, evil talk) shall they hear therein, nor lying; (35) A
reward from your Lord, an ample calculated gift (according to the
best of their good deeds). (36) (From) the Lord of the heavens and
the earth, and whatsoever is in between them, the Most Gracious
with whom they dare to speak (on the Day of Resurrection except
by His Leave). (37) The Day that Ar-Rûh [Jibril (Gabriel) or
another angel] and the angels will stand forth in rows, none they
will not speak except him whom the Most Gracious (Allâh) allows,
and he will speak what is right. (38) That is (without doubt) the
True Day, so, whosoever wills, let him seek a place with (or a way
to) His Lord (by obeying Him in this worldly life)! (39) Verily, We
have warned you of a near torment — the Day when man will see*

that (the deeds) which his hands have sent forth, and the disbeliever will say: "Woe to me! Would that I were dust!"

Quran 79:6-14

On the Day (when the first blowing of the Trumpet is blown), the earth and the mountains will shake violently (and everybody will die), (6) The second blowing of the Trumpet follows it (and everybody will be resurrected), (7) (Some) hearts that Day will shake with fear and anxiety. (8) Their eyes will be downcast. (9) They say: "Shall we indeed be returned to (our) former state of life? (10) "Even after we are crumbled bones?" (11) They say: "It would in that case, be a return with loss!" (12) But, it will be only a single Zajrah [shout (i.e., the second blowing of the Trumpet)]. (13) When, behold, they find themselves on the surface of the earth alive after their death

Quran 79:34-46

But when there comes the greatest catastrophe (i.e. the Day of Recompense), (34) The Day when man shall remember what he strove for, (35) And Hell-fire shall be made apparent in full view for (every) one who sees, (36) Then, for him who transgressed all bounds (in disbelief, oppression and evil deeds of disobedience to Allâh). (37) And preferred the life of this world (by following his evil desires and lusts), (38) Verily, his abode will be Hell-fire; (39) But as for him who feared standing before his Lord, and restrained himself from impure evil desires, and lusts. (40) Verily, Paradise will be his abode. (41) They ask you (O Muhammad) about the Hour, - when will be its appointed time? (42) You have no knowledge to say anything about it, (43) To your Lord belongs (the knowledge of) the term thereof? (44) You (O Muhammad) are only

*a warner for those who fear it, (45) The Day they see it, (it will be)
as if they had not tarried (in this world) except an afternoon or a
morning.*

Quran 80:33-42

*Then, when there comes As-Sâkhkhah (the second blowing of the
Trumpet on the Day of Resurrection) — (33) That Day shall a
man flee from his brother, (34) And from his mother and his father,
(35) And from his wife and his children. (36) Everyman, that Day,
will have enough to make him careless of others. (37) Some faces
that Day, will be bright (true believers of Islâmic Monotheism).
(38) Laughing, rejoicing at good news (of Paradise). (39) And
other faces, that Day, will be dust-stained; (40) Darkness will
cover them, (41) Such will be the Kafarah (disbelievers in Allâh, in
His Oneness, and in His Messenger Muhammad, etc.), the Fajarah
(wicked evil doers).*

Quran 81:1-14

*When the sun is wound round and lost its light (is lost and is
overthrown). (1)And when the stars fall; (2) And when the
mountains are made to pass away; (3) And when the pregnant she-
camels are neglected; (4) And when the wild beasts are gathered
together; (5) And when the seas become as blazing Fire or
overflow; (6) And when the souls are joined with their bodies (the
good with the good and bad with the bad). (7) And when the female
(infant) buried alive (as the pagan Arabs used to do) is questioned.
(8) For what sin was she killed? (9) And when the (written) pages
[of deeds (good and bad) of every person] are laid open; (10) And
when the heaven is stripped off and taken away from its place; (11)
And when Hell-fire is set ablaze. (12) And when Paradise is*

brought near, (13) (Then) every person will know what he has brought (of good and evil).

Quran 82:1-5

When the heaven is cleft asunder. (1) And when the stars have fallen and scattered; (2) And when the seas are burst forth; (3) And when the graves are turned upside down (and bring out their contents). (4) (Then) a person will know what he has sent forward and (what he has) left behind (of good or bad deeds).

Quran 82:13-19

Verily, the Abrâr (pious and righteous) will be in Delight (Paradise); (13) And verily, the Fujjâr (the wicked, disbelievers, polytheists sinners and evil-doers) will be in the blazing Fire (Hell), (14) Therein they will enter, and taste its burning flame on the Day of Recompense, (15) And they (Al-Fujjâr) will not be absent therefrom. (16) And what will make you know what the Day of Recompense is? (17) Again, what will make you know what the Day of Recompense is? (18) (It will be) the Day when no person shall have power (to do) anything for another, and the Decision, that Day, will be (wholly) with Allâh.

Quran 83:4-12

Do they not think that they will be resurrected (for reckoning), (4) On a Great Day, (5) The Day when (all) mankind will stand before the Lord of the 'Alamîn (mankind, jinn and all that exists)? (6) Nay! Truly, the Record (writing of the deeds) of the Fujjâr (disbelievers, polytheists sinners, evil-doers and wicked) is (preserved) in Sijjîn. (7) And what will make you know what

Sijjîn is? (8) A Register inscribed. (9) Woe, that Day, to those who deny. (10) Those who deny the Day of Recompense. (11) And none can deny it except every transgressor beyond bounds, (in disbelief, oppression and disobedience to Allâh), the sinner!

Quran 83:15-28

Nay! Surely, they (evil-doers) will be veiled from seeing their Lord that Day. (15) Then, verily they will indeed enter (and taste) the burning flame of Hell. (16) Then, it will be said to them: "This is what you used to deny!" (17) Nay! Verily, the Record (writing of the deeds) of Al-Abrâr (the pious and righteous), is (preserved) in 'Illiyyûn. (18) And what will make you know what 'Illiyyûn is? (19) A Register inscribed. (20) To which bear witness those nearest (to Allâh, i.e. the angels). (21) Verily, Al-Abrâr (the pious who fear Allâh and avoid evil) will be in Delight (Paradise). (22) On thrones, looking (at all things). (23) You will recognize in their faces the brightness of delight. (24) They will be given to drink of pure sealed wine. (25) The last thereof (that wine) will be the smell of Musk, and for this let (all) those strive who want to strive (i.e. hasten earnestly to the obedience of Allâh). (26) It (that wine) will be mixed with Tasnîm. (27) A spring whereof drink those nearest to Allâh.

Quran 83:34-36

But this Day (the Day of Resurrection) those who believe will laugh at the disbelievers (34) On (high) thrones, looking (at all things). (35) Are not the disbelievers paid (fully) for what they used to do?

Quran 84:1-12

When the heaven is split asunder, (1) And listens to and obeys its Lord — and it must do so; (2) And when the earth is stretched forth, (3) And has cast out all that was in it and become empty, (4) And listens to and obeys its Lord, and it must do so; (5) O man! Verily, you are returning towards your Lord with your deeds and actions (good or bad), a sure returning, and you will meet (i.e. the results of your deeds which you did). (6) Then, as for him who will be given his Record in his right hand, (7) He surely will receive an easy reckoning, (8) And will return to his family in joy! (9) But whosoever is given his Record behind his back, (10) He will invoke (for his) destruction, (11) And he shall enter a blazing Fire, and be made to taste its burning.

Quran 86:9-10

Verily, (Allâh) is Able to bring him back (to life)! (8) The Day when all the secrets (deeds, prayers, fasting, etc.) will be examined (as to their truth) (9) Then he will have no power, nor any helper.

Quran 88:1-16

Has there come to you the narration of the overwhelming (i.e. the Day of Resurrection)? (1) Some faces, that Day, will be humiliated (in the Hell-fire, i.e. the faces of all disbelievers, Jews and Christians). (2) Labouring (hard in the worldly life by worshipping others besides Allâh), weary (in the Hereafter with humility and disgrace). (3) They will enter in the hot blazing Fire, (4) They will be given to drink from a boiling spring, (5) No food will there be for them but a poisonous thorny plant, (6) Which will neither nourish nor avail against hunger (7) (Other) faces, that Day, will be joyful, (8) Glad with their endeavour (for their good deeds which they did in this world, along with the true Faith of Islâmic

Monotheism). (9 In a lofty Paradise (10) Where they shall neither hear harmful speech nor falsehood, (11) Therein will be a running spring, (12)Therein will be thrones raised high, (13) And cups set at hand (14) And cushions set in rows, (15) And rich carpets (all) spread out

Quran 89:21-30

Nay! When the earth is ground to powder, (21) And your Lord comes with the angels in rows, (22) And Hell will be brought near that Day. On that Day will man remember, but how will that remembrance (then) avail him? (23) He will say: "Alas! Would that I had sent forth (good deeds) for (this) my life!" (24) So on that Day, none will punish as He will punish (25) And none will bind (the wicked, disbelivers and polytheists) as He will bind. (26) (It will be said to the pious − believers of Islamic Monothesim): "O (you) the one in (complete) rest and satisfaction! (27) "Come back to your Lord, Well-pleased (yourself) and well-pleasing (unto Him)! (28) "Enter you, then, among My (honoured) slaves, (29) "And enter you My Paradise!"

Quran 99:1-8

When the earth is shaken with its (final) earthquake. (1) And when the earth throws out its burdens, (2) And man will say: "What is the matter with it?" (3) That Day it will declare its information (about all that happened over it of good or evil). (4) Because your Lord will inspire it. (5) That Day mankind will proceed in scattered groups that they may be shown their deeds. (6) So whosoever does good equal to the weight of an atom shall see it. (7) And whosoever does evil equal to the weight of an atom shall see it.

Quran 100:9-11

Knows he not that when the contents of the graves are poured forth (all mankind is resurrected)? (9) And that which is in the breasts (of men) is made known? (10) Verily, that Day (i.e. the Day of Resurrection) their Lord will be Well-Acquainted with them (as to their deeds and will reward them for their deeds).

Quran 101:1-11

Al-Qâri'ah (the striking Hour i.e. the Day of Resurrection), (1) What is the striking (Hour)? (2) And what will make you know what the striking (Hour) is? (3) It is a Day whereon mankind will be like moths scattered about, (4) And the mountains will be like carded wool, (5) Then as for him whose balance (of good deeds) will be heavy, (6) He will live a pleasant life (in Paradise). (7) But as for him whose balance (of good deeds) will be light, (8) He will have his home in Hawiyah (pit, i.e. Hell) (9) And what will make you know what it is? (10) (It is) a fierce blazing Fire!

Quran 102:3-8

Nay! You shall come to know! (3) Again, Nay! You shall come to know! (4) Nay! If you knew with a sure knowledge (5) Verily, You shall see the blazing Fire (Hell)! (6) And again, you shall see it with certainty of sight! (7) Then, on that Day, you shall be asked about the delights (you indulged in, in this world)!

Narrated Al--A`mash:

Abu Huraira said, "Allah's Messenger said, 'Between the two sounds of the trumpet, there will be forty." Somebody asked Abu Huraira, "Forty days?" But he refused to reply. Then he asked,

"Forty months?" He refused to reply. Then he asked, "Forty years?" Again, he refused to reply. Abu Huraira added. "Then (after this period) Allah will send water from the sky and then the dead bodies will grow like vegetation grows, There is nothing of the human body that does not decay except one bone; that is the little bone at the end of the coccyx of which the human body will be recreated on the Day of Resurrection."

Source: Sahih Bukhari USC-MSA web (English) reference : Vol. 6, Book 60, Hadith 457

'A'isha reported:

Umm Habiba and Umm Salama made a mention before the Messenger of Allah of a church which they had seen in Abyssinia and which had pictures in it. The Messenger of Allah said: When a pious person amongst them (among the religious groups) dies they build a place of worship on his grave, and then decorate it with such pictures. They would be the worst of creatures on the Day of judgment in the sight of Allah.

Source: Sahih Muslim 528 a

Narrated Ibn `Umar:

The Prophet said, "Oppression will be a darkness on the Day of Resurrection."

Source: Sahih al-Bukhari 2447

Narrated Anas:

The Prophet said, ''Every betrayer will have a flag on the Day of Resurrection'' One of the two sub-narrators said that the flag would be fixed, and the other said that it would be shown on the Day of Resurrection, so that the betrayer might be recognized by it.

Source: Sahih al-Bukhari 3186

Narrated Abu Huraira:

Allah's Messenger said, "We (Muslims) are the last (people to come in the world) but (will be) the foremost (on the Day of Resurrection)."

Source: Sahih al-Bukhari 238

Narrated Abu Huraira:

The Prophet said, "The sun and the moon will be folded up (deprived of their light) on the Day of Resurrection."

Source: Sahih al-Bukhari 3200

Narrated `Abdullah:

The Prophet said, "The cases which will be decided first (on the Day of Resurrection) will be the cases of blood-shedding. "

Source: Sahih al-Bukhari 6533

Abdullah bin Busr narrated that :

the Prophet said: "On the day of Resurrection, my nation will be radiant from prostrating and shining from Wudu."

Source: Jami` at-Tirmidhi 607 Graded Sahih by Darussalam

Narrated Abu Hurayrah:

The Prophet said: If anyone rescinds a sale with a Muslim, Allah will cancel his slip, on the Day of Resurrection.

Source: Sunan Abi Dawud 3460 Graded Sahih by Albani

Narrated Ammar:

The Prophet said: He who is two-faced in this world will have two tongues of fire on the Day of Resurrection.

Source: Sunan Abi Dawud 4873 Graded Sahih by Albani

It was narrated from Jabir that the Messenger of Allah (ﷺ) said:

"People will be gathered (on the Day of Resurrection) according to their intentions."

Source: Sunan ibn Majah

English reference : Vol. 5, Book 37, Hadith 4230

Graded Sahih by Darussalam

Narrated Abu Huraira:

Allah's Messenger said, "On the Day of Resurrection, a huge fat man will come who will not weigh, the weight of the wing of a mosquito in Allah's Sight." and then the Prophet added, 'We shall not give them any weight on the Day of Resurrection ' (18.105)

Source: Sahih Bukhari USC-MSA web (English) reference : Vol. 6, Book 60, Hadith 253

Narrated Abu Huraira:

The Prophet said, "On the Day of Resurrection Abraham will meet his father Azar whose face will be dark and covered with dust.(The Prophet Abraham will say to him): 'Didn't I tell you not to disobey me?' His father will reply: 'Today I will not disobey you.' 'Abraham will say: 'O Lord! You promised me not to disgrace me on the Day of Resurrection; and what will be more disgraceful to me than cursing and dishonoring my father?' Then Allah will say (to him):' 'I have forbidden Paradise for the disbelievers." Then he will be addressed, 'O Abraham! Look! What is underneath your feet?' He will look and there he will see a Dhabh (an animal,) blood-stained, which will be caught by the legs and thrown in the (Hell) Fire."

Source: Sahih al-Bukhari 3350

Narrated Abu Hurayrah:

The Prophet said: If anyone lies on his side where he does not remember Allah, deprivation will descend on him on the Day of Resurrection; and if anyone sits in a place where he does not remember Allah, deprivation will descend on him on the Day of Resurrection.

Source: Sunan Abi Dawud 5059 Graded Hasan by Albani

It was narrated from Ibn 'Abbas that the Messenger of Allah (ﷺ) said:

"Wailing over the dead is one of the affairs of the Days of Ignorance and if the woman who wails does not repent before she dies, she will be resurrected on the Day of Resurrection wearing a

~ 118 ~

shirt of pitch (tar), over which she will wear a shirt of flaming fire."

Source: Sunan ibn Majah

English reference : Vol. 1, Book 6, Hadith 1582

Graded Hasan by Darussalam

Narrated Salim's father (i.e. `Abdullah):

The Prophet said, "Whoever takes a piece of the land of others unjustly, he will sink down the seven earths on the Day of Resurrection."

Source: Sahih al-Bukhari 2454

Narrated `Abdullah bin `Umar:

Allah's Messenger said, "Whoever drags his clothes (on the ground) out of pride and arrogance, Allah will not look at him on the Day of Resurrection."

Source: Sahih al-Bukhari 5791

Narrated Aisha:

Allah's Messenger said, "The painter of these pictures will be punished on the Day of Resurrection, and it will be said to them, Make alive what you have created.' "

Source: Sahih al-Bukhari 7557

Buraidah Al-Aslami narrated that :

the Prophet said: "*Give glad tiding to those who walk to the Masajid in the dark; of a complete light on the Day of Resurrection.*"

Source: Jami` at-Tirmidhi 223 Graded Sahih by Darussalam

Abu Ad-Darda narrated that the Messenger of Allah said:

"*Whoever protects his brother's honor, Allah protects his face from the Fire on the Day of Resurrection.*"

Source: Jami` at-Tirmidhi 1931

Graded Hasan by Darussalam

Narrated Abu Hurayrah:

The Prophet said: He who is asked something he knows and conceals it will have a bridle of fire put on him on the Day of Resurrection.

Source: Sunan Abi Dawud 3658

Graded Hasan Sahih by Albani

Narrated Abdullah ibn Umar:

The Prophet as saying: If anyone wears a garment for gaining fame, Allah will clothe him in a similar garment on the Day of Resurrection.

Source: Sunan Abi Dawud 4029 Graded Hasan by Albani

It was narrated that Ibn 'Umar said:

"The Messenger of Allah said: 'Whoever wears a garment of pride and vanity, Allah will clothe him, on the Day of Resurrection, in a garment of humiliation.'"

Source: Sunan ibn Majah

English reference : Vol. 4, Book 32, Hadith 3606

Graded Hasan by Darussalam

Abu Hurairah reported the prophet (ﷺ) as saying:

If anyone removes his brother's anxiety of this world, Allah will remove for him one of the anxieties of the Day of resurrection; if anyone makes easy for an impoverished man, Allah will make easy for him in this world and on the day of resurrection; if anyone conceals a Muslim's secrets, Allah will conceal his secrets in this world and on the Day of resurrection; Allah will remain in the aid of a servant so long as the servant remains in the aid of his brother.

Abu Dawud said: 'Uthman did not transmit the following words from Abu Mu'awiyah: "if anyone makes easy for an impoverished man".

Source: Sunan Abi Dawud 4946 Graded Sahih by Albani

Abu Huraira reported Allah's Apostle (ﷺ) as saying:

The servant (who conceals) the faults of others in this world, Allah would conceal his faults on the Day of Resurrection.

Source: Sahih Muslim 2590 b

Umm Darda' reported on the authority of Abu Darda' as saying:

I heard Allah's Messenger as saying: The invoker of curse would neither be witness nor intercessor on the Day of Resurrection.

Source: Sahih Muslim 2598 c

Abu Musa' reported that Allah's Messenger (ﷺ) said:

When it will be the Day of Resurrection Allah would deliver to every Muslim a Jew or a Christian and say: That is your rescue from Hell-Fire.

Source: Sahih Muslim 2767 a

Narrated Abu Huraira:

The Prophet said, "A wound which a Muslim receives in Allah's cause will appear on the Day of Resurrection as it was at the time of infliction; blood will be flowing from the wound and its color will be that of the blood but will smell like musk."

Source: Sahih al-Bukhari 237

Narrated Abu Huraira:

The Prophet said, "By Him in Whose Hands my soul is, I will drive some people out from my (sacred) Fount on the Day of Resurrection as strange camels are expelled from a private trough."

Source: Sahih al-Bukhari 2367

Narrated Khaula Al-Ansariya:

I heard Allah's Messenger saying, "Some people spend Allah's Wealth (i.e. Muslim's wealth) in an unjust manner; such people will be put in the (Hell) Fire on the Day of Resurrection."

Source: Sahih al-Bukhari 3118

Narrated Abu Huraira:

Allah's Messenger said, "The Kanz (money, the Zakat of which is not paid) of anyone of you will appear in the form of bald-headed poisonous male snake on the Day of Resurrection."

Source: Sahih Bukhari USC-MSA web (English) reference : Vol. 6, Book 60, Hadith 182

Narrated Abu Huraira:

The Prophet said, "The worst people in the Sight of Allah on the Day of Resurrection will be the double faced people who appear to some people with one face and to other people with another face."

Source: Sahih al-Bukhari 6058

Narrated Ibn `Umar:

The Prophet said, "For every betrayer (perfidious person), a flag will be raised on the Day of Resurrection, and it will be announced (publicly) 'This is the betrayal (perfidy) of so-and-so, the son of so-and-so.' "

Source: Sahih al-Bukhari 6177

Narrated Abu Huraira:

Allah's Messenger said, "The most awful name in Allah's sight on the Day of Resurrection, will be (that of) a man calling himself Malik Al-Amlak (the king of kings).

Source: Sahih al-Bukhari 6205

Narrated Abu Huraira:

Allah's Messenger said, "The people will sweat so profusely on the Day of Resurrection that their sweat will sink seventy cubits deep into the earth, and it will rise up till it reaches the people's mouths and ears."

Source: Sahih al-Bukhari 6532

Narrated Abu Huraira:

The Prophet said, "On the Day of Resurrection Allah will hold the whole earth and fold the heaven with His right hand and say, 'I am the King: where are the kings of the earth?"

Source: Sahih al-Bukhari 7382

Narrated Jarir:

Allah's Messenger came out to us on the night of the full moon and said, "You will see your Lord on the Day of Resurrection as you see this (full moon) and you will have no difficulty in seeing Him."

Source: Sahih al-Bukhari 7436

Narrated Abu Huraira:

Allah's Messenger said, "For every Prophet there is one invocation which is definitely fulfilled by Allah, and I wish, if Allah will, to keep my that (special) invocation as to be the intercession for my followers on the Day of Resurrection."

Source: Sahih al-Bukhari 7474

Abdullah bin Mas'ud narrated that the Messenger of Allah said:

"Hell will be brought forth on that Day (of Resurrection) having seventy thousand bridles, and with every handle will be seventy thousand angels dragging it'".

Source: Jami at-Tirmidhi

English reference: Vol. 4, Book 13, Hadith 2573

Graded Sahih by Darussalam

It was narrated that Samurah bin Jundab said:

"The Messenger of Allah said: 'Begging will be but lacerations on a man's face (on the Day of Resurrection). Unless he asks a man in authority or when he has no alternative."'

Source: Sunan an-Nasa'i 2600 Graded Sahih by Darussalam

Abdullah bin 'Amr said:

"The Messenger of Allah said: ' A man will keep on asking until on the Day of Resurrection he will come without even a shred of skin on his face. "'

Source: Sunan an-Nasa'i 2585 Graded Sahih by Darussalam

It was narrated from 'Aishah that the Prophet said:

"You will be gathered (one the Day of Resurrection) barefoot and naked." I said: "Men and women looking at one another?" he said: "The matter will be too difficult for people to pay attention to that."

Source: Sunan an-Nasa'i 2084 Graded Sahih by Darussalam

It was narrated from Ibn 'Abbas that the Prophet said:

"The people will be gathered on the Day of Resurrection naked and uncircumcised. The first one to be clothed will be Ibrahim." Then he recited: As We began the first creation, We shall repeat it

Source: Sunan an-Nasa'i 2082 Graded Sahih by Darussalam

Narrated Abu Hurayrah:

The Prophet said: When a man has two wives and he is inclined to one of them, he will come on the Day of resurrection with a side hanging down.

Source: Sunan Abi Dawud 2133 Graded Sahih by Albani

It was narrated that 'Esa bin Talhah said:

"I heard Mu'awiyah bin Abu Sufyan say that Messenger of Allah said: "The Mu'adh-dhin will have the longest necks of all people on the Day of Resurrection."

Source: Sunan Ibn Majah 725 Graded Sahih by Darussalam

It was narrated from Anas bin Malik that the Messenger of Allah (ﷺ) said:

"Whoever goes out in the cause of Allah will have the equivalent of the dust that got on him, in musk, on the Day of Resurrection."

Source: Sunan ibn Majah

English reference : Vol. 4, Book 24, Hadith 2775

Graded Hasan by Darussalam

It was narrated from Ibn 'Abbas that the Messenger of Allah (ﷺ) said:

"Whoever tells of a false dream, will be ordered (on the Day of Resurrection) to tie two grains of barley together, and he will be punished for that."

Source: Sunan Ibn Majah 3916 Graded Sahih by Darussalam

It was narrated from Abu Dharr that the Messenger of Allah (ﷺ) said:

"The wealthiest will be the lowest on the Day of Resurrection, except those who do such and such with their money, and earn it from good sources."

Source: Sunan ibn Majah

English reference : Vol. 5, Book 37, Hadith 4130

Graded Hasan by Darussalam

It was narrated from Abu Hurairah that the Messenger of Allah (ﷺ) said:

"There is no part of man that will not disintegrate, apart from a single bone at the base of the coccyx, from which he will be recreated on the Day of Resurrection."

Source: Sunan ibn Majah

English reference : Vol. 5, Book 37, Hadith 4266

Graded Sahih by Darussalam

It was narrated from Bahz bin Hakim, from his father, that his grandfather said:

"The Messenger of Allah said: 'On the Day of Resurrection, we will complete seventy nations, of whom we are the last and the best.'"

Source: Sunan ibn Majah

English reference : Vol. 5, Book 37, Hadith 4287

Graded: Hasan by Darussalam

It was narrated that Jabir said:

"I heard the Messenger of Allah say: 'My intercession on the Day of Resurrection will be for those among my nation who committed major sins.'"

Source: Sunan ibn Majah

English reference : Vol. 5, Book 37, Hadith 4310

Graded Hasan by Darussalam

It is narrated by Abu Huraira and Huraira that the Messenger of Allah (ﷺ) said:

It was Friday from which Allah diverted those who were before us. For the Jews (the day set aside for prayer) was Sabt (Saturday), and for the Christians it was Sunday. And Allah turned towards us and guided us to Friday (as the day of prayer) for us. In fact, He (Allah) made Friday, Saturday and Sunday (as days of prayer). In this order would they (Jews and Christians) come after us on the Day of Resurrection. We are the last of (the Ummahs) among the people in this world and the first among the created to be judged on the Day of Resurrection. In one narration it is: ', to be judged among them".

Source: Sahih Muslim 856 a

Abu Huraira reported Allah's Messenger (ﷺ) as saying:

A bulky person would be brought on the Day of judgment and he would not carry the weight to the eye of Allah equal even to that of a gnat. Nor shall We set up a balance for them on the Day of Resurrection"

Source: Sahih Muslim 2785

It was narrated from Ibn Buraidah that his father told that the Messenger of Allah(ﷺ) said:

"The Quran will come on the Day of Resurrection, like a pale man, and will say: 'I am the one that kept you awake at night and made you thirsty during the day."

Source: Sunan Ibn Majah 3781 Graded Hasan by Darussalam

Narrated Anas bin Malik:

A man said, "O Allah's Prophet! Will Allah gather the non-believers on their faces on the Day of Resurrection?" He said, "Will not the One Who made him walk on his feet in this world, be able to make him walk on his face on the Day of Resurrection?" (Qatada, a subnarrator, said: Yes, By the Power of Our Lord!)

Source: Sahih Bukhari USC-MSA web (English) reference : Vol. 6, Book 60, Hadith 283

Narrated `Abdullah bin `Umar:

Allah's Messenger said, "A Muslim is a brother of another Muslim, so he should not oppress him, nor should he hand him over to an oppressor. Whoever fulfilled the needs of his brother, Allah will fulfill his needs; whoever brought his (Muslim) brother out of a discomfort, Allah will bring him out of the discomforts of the Day of Resurrection, and whoever screened a Muslim, Allah will screen him on the Day of Resurrection . "

Source: Sahih al-Bukhari 2442

Narrated `Aisha:

Allah's Messenger, said, "None will be called to account on the Day of Resurrection, but will be ruined." I said "O Allah's Messenger! Hasn't Allah said: 'Then as for him who will be given his record in his right hand, he surely will receive an easy reckoning? (84.7-8) -- Allah's Messenger said, "That (Verse) means only the presentation of the accounts, but anybody whose account (record) is questioned on the Day of Resurrection, will surely be punished."

Source: Sahih al-Bukhari 6537

Narrated `Abdullah bin `Umar:

Allah's Messenger said, "When anyone of you dies, he is shown his place both in the morning and in the evening. If he is one of the people of Paradise; he is shown his place in it, and if he is from the people of the Hell-Fire; he is shown his place there-in. Then it is said to him, 'This is your place till Allah resurrect you on the Day of Resurrection."

Source: Sahih al-Bukhari 1379

In the hadith narrated by Shu'ba the words are:

Verily the Messenger of Allah said: He who took an oath on a religion other than Islam as a liar would become so as he said, and he who slaughtered himself with a thing would be slaughtered with that on the Day of Resurrection.

Sahih Muslim 110 d

Ibn 'Umar reported Allah's Messenger (ﷺ) as saying:

He who patiently endures the hardships of it (of this city of Medina), I would be an intercessor or a witness on his behalf on the Day of Resurrection.

Source: Sahih Muslim 1377 a

Abu Huraira reported that Abu'l-Qasim (one of the names of Allah's Messenger [may peace be upon him]) said:

He who accused his slave of adultery, punishment would be imposed upon him on the Day of Resurrection, except in case the accusation was as he had said.

Source: Sahih Muslim 1660 a

Abu Huraira reported Allah's Messenger (ﷺ) as saying:

Verily. Allah would say on the Day of Resurrection: Where are those who have mutual love for My Glory's sake? Today I shall shelter them in My shadow when there is no other shadow but the shadow of Mine.

Source: Sahih Muslim 2566

Abu Huraira reported Allah's Messenger (ﷺ) as saying:

The claimants would get their claims on the Day of Resurrection so much so that the hornless sheep would get its claim from the horned sheep.

Source: Sahih Muslim 2582

Malik reported Allah's Messenger (ﷺ) as saying:

He, who brought up two girls properly till they grew up, he and I would come (together) (very closely) on the Day of Resurrection, and he interlaced his fingers (for explaining the point of nearness between him and that person).

Source: Sahih Muslim 2631

Sahl bin Sa'd reported that Allah's Messenger (ﷺ) said:

The people will be assembled on the Day of Resurrection on a white plain with a reddish tinge like the loaf of white bread with no marks set up for anyone.

Source: Sahih Muslim 2790

Narrated Abu Huraira:

I heard Abu-l-Qasim (the Prophet) saying, "If somebody slanders his slave and the slave is free from what he says, he will be flogged on the Day of Resurrection unless the slave is really as he has described him."

Source: Sahih al-Bukhari 6858

Abu Huraira narrated that the Prophet (ﷺ) said:

"On the Day of Resurrection a group of companions will come to me, but will be driven away from the Lake-Fount, and I will say, 'O Lord (those are) my companions!' It will be said, 'You have no knowledge as to what they innovated after you left; they turned apostate as renegades (reverted from Islam).

Source: Sahih al-Bukhari 6585

It was narrated that Abu Hurairah said:

"The Messenger of Allah said: "There are three to whom Allah, the Mighty and Sublime, will not speak on the Day of Resurrection: An old man who commits adultery, a poor man who is arrogant, and an Imam who tells lies."'

Source: Sunan an-Nasa'i 2575 Graded Hasan by Darussalam

Bahz bin Hakim narrated from his father that his grandfather said:

"No man comes to his Mawla and asks him for something from the surplus of what he has, and he withholds it from him, but on the Day of Resurrection a bald-headed Shuja'a will be called to him and will be licking the surplus that he withheld."

Source: Sunan an-Nasa'i 2566 Graded Hasan by Darussalam

Abu Hurairah said:

"The Messenger of Allah said: '(On the Day of Resurrection) camels will come to their owner in the best state of health that they ever had (in this world) and if he did not pay what was due on them, they will trample him with their hooves. Sheep will come to their owner in the best state of health that they ever had (in this world) and if he did not pay what was due on them, they will trample him with their cloven hooves and gore him with their horns. And among their rights are that they should be milked with water in the front of them. I do not want any one of you to come on the Day of Resurrection with a groaning camel on his neck, saying O Muhammad, and I will say: I cannot do anything for you, I conveyed the message. I do not want any one of you to come on the Day of Resurrection with a bleating sheep on his neck, saying, "O Muhammad," and I will say: "I cannot do anything for you, I conveyed the message." And on the Day of Resurrection the hoarded treasure of one of you will be a blad-headed Shujaa from which its owner will flee, but it will chase him (saying), I am your hoarded treasure, and it will keep (chasing him) until he gives it his finger to swallow."'

Source: Sunan an-Nasa'i 2448 Graded Sahih by Darussalam

It was narrated that 'Amr bin Sharid said:

"I heard Sharid say: 'I heard the Messenger of Allah say: Whoever kills a small bird for no reason, it will beseech Allah on the Day of Resurrection saying: O Lord, so and so killed me for no reason. And he did not kill me for any beneficial purpose." '

Source: Sunan an-Nasa'i 4446 Graded Hasan by Darussalam

Uqbah bin Amir said, I heard the Messenger of Allah(ﷺ) say:

"Whoever has three daughters and is patient towards them, and feeds them, gives them to drink, and clothes them from his wealth; they will be a shield for him from the Fire on the Day of Resurrection.' "

Source: Sunan Ibn Majah 3669 Graded Sahih by Darussalam

It was narrated that 'Atiyyah bin 'Amir Al-Juhani said:

"I heard Salman, when he was forced to eat food, say: 'It is sufficient for me that I heard the Messenger of Allah say: The people who most eat their fill in this world will be the most hungry on the Day of Resurrection.'"

Source: Sunan ibn Majah

English reference: Vol. 4, Book 29, Hadith 3351

Graded Hasan by Darussalam

It was narrated from Sahl bin Mu'adh bin Anas, from his father, that the Messenger of Allah (ﷺ) said:

"Whoever restrains his anger when he is able to implement it, Allah will call him before all of creation on the Day of Resurrection, and will give him his choice of any houri that he wants."

Source: Sunan ibn Majah

English reference : Vol. 5, Book 37, Hadith 4186

Graded Hasan by Darussalam

It was narrated from Abu Sa'eed Al-Khudri that the Prophet (ﷺ) said:

"I have a Cistern, (as large as the distance) between the Ka'bah and Baitul-Maqdis (Jerusalem). (It is) whiter than milk, and its vessels are the number of the stars. I will be the Prophet with the most followers on the Day of Resurrection."

Source: Sunan ibn Majah

English reference: Vol. 5, Book 37, Hadith 4301

Graded Sahih by Darussalam

Abu Umama said he heard Allah's Messenger (ﷺ) say:

Recite the Qur'an, for on the Day of Resurrection it will come as an intercessor for those who recite It. Recite the two bright ones, al-Baqara and Surah Al 'Imran, for on the Day of Resurrection they will come as two clouds or two shades, or two flocks of birds in ranks, pleading for those who recite them. Recite Surah al-Baqara, for to take recourse to it is a blessing and to give it up is a cause of grief, and the magicians cannot confront it. (Mu'awiya said: It has been conveyed to me that here Batala means magicians.)

Source: Sahih Muslim 804 a

Narrated `Ali:

I heard the Prophet saying, "In the last days (of the world) there will appear young people with foolish thoughts and ideas. They will give good talks, but they will go out of Islam as an arrow goes out of its game, their faith will not exceed their throats. So, wherever you find them, kill them, for there will be a reward for their killers on the Day of Resurrection."

Source: Sahih al-Bukhari 5057

It was narrated that 'Ubadah bin Samit said:

"The Messenger of Allah led us in prayer on the Day of Hunain, beside a camel that was part of the spoils of war. Then he took something from the camel, and extracted from it a hair, which he placed between two of his fingers. Then he said: 'O people, this is part of your spoils of war. Hand over a needle and thread and anything greater than that or less than that. For stealing from the spoils of war will be a source of shame for those who do it, and ignominy and Fire, on the Day of Resurrection.'"

Source: Sunan ibn Majah

English reference: Vol. 4, Book 24, Hadith 2850

Graded Hasan by Darussalam

It was narrated from Abu Sa'd bin Abu Fadalah Al-Ansari, who was one of the Companions, that the Messenger of Allah (ﷺ) said:

"When Allah assembles the first and the last on the Day of Resurrection, a day concerning which there is no doubt, a caller will cry out: 'Whoever used to associate anyone else in an action that he did for Allah, let him seek his reward from someone other than Allah, for Allah is so self-sufficient that He has no need of any associate.'"

Source: Sunan ibn Majah

English reference : Vol. 5, Book 37, Hadith 4203

Graded Hasan by Darussalam

Narrated Jabir bin `Abdullah:

Allah's Messenger said, "Whoever after listening to the Adhan says, 'Allahumma Rabba hadhihi-dda`watit-tammah, was-salatil qa'imah, ati Muhammadan al-wasilata wal-fadilah, wa b`ath-hu maqaman mahmudan-il-ladhi wa`adtahu' [O Allah! Lord of this perfect call (perfect by not ascribing partners to You) and of the regular prayer which is going to be established, give Muhammad the right of intercession and illustriousness, and resurrect him to the best and the highest place in Paradise that You promised him (of)], then my intercession for him will be allowed on the Day of Resurrection".

Source: Sahih al-Bukhari 614

~ 138 ~

Narrated Abu Huraira:

The Prophet said, "(There are) three (types of persons to whom) Allah will neither speak to them on the Day of Resurrections, nor look at them (They are):--(1) a man who takes a false oath that he has been offered for a commodity a price greater than what he has actually been offered; (2) and a man who takes a false oath after the `Asr (prayer) in order to grab the property of a Muslim through it; (3) and a man who forbids others to use the remaining superfluous water. To such a man Allah will say on the Day of Resurrection, 'Today I withhold My Blessings from you as you withheld the superfluous part of that (water) which your hands did not create.'"

Source: Sahih al-Bukhari 7446

Narrated Tarif Abi Tamima:

I saw Safwan and Jundab and Safwan's companions when Jundab was advising. They said, "Did you hear something from Allah's Messenger?" Jundab said, "I heard him saying, 'Whoever does a good deed in order to show off, Allah will expose his intentions on the Day of Resurrection (before the people), and whoever puts the people into difficulties, Allah will put him into difficulties on the Day of Resurrection.'" The people said (to Jundab), "Advise us." He said, "The first thing of the human body to purify is the `Abdomen, so he who can eat nothing but good food (Halal and earned lawfully) should do so, and he who does as much as he can that nothing intervene between him and Paradise by not shedding even a handful of blood, (i.e. murdering) should do so."

Source: Sahih al-Bukhari 7152

Abu Huraira reported Allah's Messenger (ﷺ) as saying:

*He who recites in the morning and in the evening (these words):"
Hallowed be Allah and all praise is due to Him" one hundred
times, he would not bring on the Day of Resurrection anything
excellent than this except one who utters these words or utters
more than these words.*

Source: Sahih Muslim 2692

Abu Huraira reported Allah's Messenger (ﷺ) as saying:

*There are one hundred (parts of) mercy for Allah and He has sent
down out of these one part of mercy upon the jinn and human
beings and animals and the insects, and it is because of this (one
part) that they love one another, show kindness to one another and
even the beast treats its young one with affection, and Allah has
reserved ninety nine parts of mercy with which He would treat His
servants on the Day of Resurrection.*

Source: Sahih Muslim 2752 c

Narrated Anas bin Malik:

*Allah's Prophet used to say, "A disbeliever will be brought on the
Day of Resurrection and will be asked. "Suppose you had as much
gold as to fill the earth, would you offer it to ransom yourself?" He
will reply, "Yes." Then it will be said to him, "You were asked for
something easier than that (to join none in worship with Allah i.e.
to accept Islam,) but you refused.*

Source: Sahih al-Bukhari 6538

Narrated Nu`am Al-Mujmir:

Once I went up the roof of the mosque, along with Abu Huraira. He perform ablution and said, "I heard the Prophet saying, "On the Day of Resurrection, my followers will be called "Al-Ghurr-ul-Muhajjalun" from the trace of ablution and whoever can increase the area of his radiance should do so (i.e. by performing ablution regularly).' "

Source: Sahih al-Bukhari 136

Narrated `Abdur-Rahman:

Abu Sa`id Al-Khudri told my father, "I see you liking sheep and the wilderness. So whenever you are with your sheep or in the wilderness and you want to pronounce Adhan for the prayer raise your voice in doing so, for whoever hears the Adhan, whether a human being, a jinn or any other creature, will be a witness for you on the Day of Resurrection." Abu Sa`id added, "I heard it (this narration) from Allah's Messenger."

Source: Sahih al-Bukhari 609

Narrated Abu Huraira:

The Prophet said, "Allah says, 'I will be against three persons on the Day of Resurrection: -1. One who makes a covenant in My Name, but he proves treacherous. -2. One who sells a free person (as a slave) and eats the price, -3. And one who employs a laborer and gets the full work done by him but does not pay him his wages.' "

Source: Sahih al-Bukhari 2227

Narrated Abu Huraira:

Allah's Messenger said, "Whoever has oppressed another person concerning his reputation or anything else, he should beg him to forgive him before the Day of Resurrection when there will be no money (to compensate for wrong deeds), but if he has good deeds, those good deeds will be taken from him according to his oppression which he has done, and if he has no good deeds, the sins of the oppressed person will be loaded on him."

Source: Sahih al-Bukhari 2449

Narrated Abu Sa`id:

The Prophet said, 'People will be struck unconscious on the Day of Resurrection and I will be the first to regain consciousness, and behold! There I will see Moses holding one of the pillars of Allah's Throne. I will wonder whether he has become conscious before me of he has been exempted, because of his unconsciousness at the Tur (mountain) which he received (on the earth).

Source: Sahih al-Bukhari 3398

Narrated Jundub:

The Prophet said, "He who lets the people hear of his good deeds intentionally, to win their praise, Allah will let the people know his real intention (on the Day of Resurrection), and he who does good things in public to show off and win the praise of the people, Allah will disclose his real intention (and humiliate him).

Source: Sahih al-Bukhari 6499

Narrated `Adi bin Hatim:

The Prophet said, "There will be none among you but will be talked to by Allah on the Day of Resurrection, without there being an interpreter between him and Him (Allah) . He will look and see nothing ahead of him, and then he will look (again for the second time) in front of him, and the (Hell) Fire will confront him. So, whoever among you can save himself from the Fire, should do so even with one half of a date (to give in charity).

Source: Sahih al-Bukhari 6539

Narrated Anas bin Malik:

The Prophet said, "Allah will say to the person who will have the minimum punishment in the Fire on the Day of Resurrection, 'If you had things equal to whatever is on the earth, would you ransom yourself (from the punishment) with it?' He will reply, Yes. Allah will say, 'I asked you a much easier thing than this while you were in the backbone of Adam, that is, not to worship others besides Me, but you refused and insisted to worship others besides Me."'

Source: Sahih al-Bukhari 6557

Narrated An-Nu`man bin Bashir:

I heard the Prophet saying, "The least punished person of the (Hell) Fire people on the Day of Resurrection will be a man under whose arch of the feet two smoldering embers will be placed, because of which his brain will boil just like Al-Mirjal (copper vessel) or a Qum-qum (narrow-necked vessel) is boiling with water."

Source: Sahih al-Bukhari 6562

Narrated `Itban bin Malik:

Once Allah's Messenger came to me in the morning, and a man among us said, "Where is Malik bin Ad- Dukhshun?" Another man from us replied, "He is a hypocrite who does not love Allah and His Apostle." The Prophet said, "Don't you think that he says: None has the right to be worshipped but Allah, only for Allah's sake?" They replied, "Yes" The Prophet said, "Nobody will meet Allah with that saying on the Day of Resurrection, but Allah will save him from the Fire."

Source: Sahih al-Bukhari 6938

Narrated Mu'adh bin Jabal :

That the Prophet said: "Whoever fought in the cause of Allah - a Muslim man - for the time it takes for two milkings of a camel, then Paradise is obligatory for him. And whoever suffered a wound in the cause of Allah, or he suffers from an injury, then he will come on the Day of Resurrection while (his blood will be) more copius that it ever was, its color the color of saffron, and its scent like that of musk."

Source: Jami` at-Tirmidhi 1657 Graded Sahih by Darussalam

It was narrated from Salim bin 'Abdullah that his father said:

"The Messenger of Allah said: "There are three at whom Allah will not look on the Day of Resurrection: The one who disobeys his parents, the woman who imitates men in her outward appearance,

and the cuckold. And there are three who will not enter Paradise:
The one who disobeys his parents, the drunkard, and the one who
reminds people of what he has given them." '

Source: Sunan an-Nasa'i 2562 Graded Hasan by Darussalam

It was narrated that 'Awf bin Malik said:

"The Messenger of Allah came out with a stick in his hand, and a
man had hung up a bunch of dry and bad dates. He started hitting
that bunch of dates and said: 'I wish that the one who gave this
Sadaqah had given something better than this, for the one who
gave these dry, bad dates will eat dry, bad dates on the Day of
Resurrection." '

Source: Sunan an-Nasa'i 2493 Graded Hasan by Darussalam

It was narrated from 'Amr bin Shu 'aib, from his father,
from his grandfather, that:

a woman from among the people of Yemen came to the Messenger
of Allah with a daughter of hers, and on the daughter's hand were
two thick bangles of gold. He said: "Do you pay Zakah on these?
She said: "No." He said: "Would it please you if Allah were to put
two bangles of fire on you on the Day of Resurrection? " So she
took them off and gave them to the Messenger of Allah and said:
"They are for Allah and His Messenger."

Source: Sunan an-Nasa'i 2479 Graded Hasan by Darussalam

It was narrated from Abu Hurairah that he heard the
Messenger of Allah say when the Verse of Mula'anah
(Li'an) was revealed:

"Any woman who falsely attributes a man to people to whom he does not belong, has no share from Allah, and Allah will not admit her to His Paradise. Any man who denies his son while looking at him (knowing that he is indeed his son), Allah, the Mighty and Sublime, will cast him away, and disgrace him before the first and the last on the Day of Resurrection."

Source: Sunan an-Nasa'i 3481 Graded Hasan by Darussalam

It was narrated that Abu 'Imran Al-Jawni said:

"Jundab said: 'So and so told me that the Messenger of Allah said: The slain will bring his killer on the Day of Resurrection and will say: Ask him why he killed me. He will say: I killed him defending the kingdom of so and so.'" Jundab said: "So be careful.'"

Source: Sunan an-Nasa'i 3998 Graded Sahih by Darussalam

It was narrated from 'Abdullah bin Murrah, from Al-Harith, from 'Abdullah, who said:

"The one who consumes Riba(usury/interest), the one who pays it, and the one who writes it down, if they know that it is Riba(usury/interest); the woman who does tattoos and the woman who has that done for the purpose of beautification; the one who withholds Sadaqah (Zakah); and the one who reverts to the life of a Bedouin after having emigrated- they will (all) be cursed upon the tongue of Muhammad on the Day of Resurrection."

Source: Sunan an-Nasa'i 5102 Graded Hasan by Darussalam

It was narrated from Abu Hurairah that the Prophet (ﷺ) said:

"The first thing for which a person will be brought to account on the Day of Resurrection will be his Salah. If it is found to be complete then it will be recorded as complete, and if anything is lacking He will say: 'Look and see if you can find any voluntary prayers with which to complete what he neglected of his obligatory prayers.' Then the rest of his deeds will be reckoned in like manner."

Source: Sunan an-Nasa'i 466 Graded Sahih by Darussalam

It was narrated from Sulaiman bin Buraidah that his father said:

"The Messenger of Allah said: 'The sanctity of the wives of the Mujahidin to those who stay behind is like the sanctity of their mothers. There is no man who takes on the responsibility of looking after the wife of one of the Mujahidin and betrays him with her but he (the betrayer) will be made to stand before him on the Day of Resurrection and he will take whatever he wants of his (good) deeds. So what do you think?'"

Source: Sunan an-Nasa'i 3189 Graded Sahih by Darussalam

Narrated Hudhayfah ibn al-Yaman:

Zirr ibn Hubaysh said: Hudhayfah traced, I think, to the Messenger of Allah the saying: He who spits in the direction of the qiblah will come on the Day of Resurrection in the state that his saliva will be between his eyes; and he who eats from this noxious vegetable should not come near our mosque, saying it three times.

Source: Sunan Abi Dawud 3824 Graded Sahih by Albani

Narrated Abdur Rahman:

I asked Abu Sa'id al-Khudri about wearing lower garment. He said: You have come to the man who knows it very well. The Messenger of Allah said: The way for a believer to wear a lower garment is to have it halfway down his legs and he is guilty of no sin if it comes halfway between that and the ankles, but what comes lower than the ankles is in Hell. On the day of Resurrection. Allah will not look at him who trails his lower garment conceitedly.

Source: Sunan Abi Dawud 4093 Graded Sahih by Albani

'Amr b. Shu'aib, on his father's authority, told that his grandfather reported the Messenger of Allah (ﷺ) said:

Do not pluck out grey hair. If any believer grows a grey hair in Islam, he will have light on the Day of Resurrection. (This is Sufyan's version). Yahya's version says: Allah will record on his behalf a good deed for it, and will blot out a sin for it.

Source: Sunan Abi Dawud 4202

Graded Hasan Sahih by Albani

Narrated Mu'adh ibn Anas:

The Prophet said: If anyone guards a believer from a hypocrite, Allah will send an angel who will guard his flesh on the Day of Resurrection from the fire of Jahannam; but if anyone attacks a Muslim saying something by which he wishes to disgrace him, he will be restrained by Allah on the bridge over Jahannam till he is acquitted of what he said.

Source: Sunan Abi Dawud 4883 Graded Hasan by Albani

It was narrated from Abu Salam, the servant of the Prophet, that :

the Prophet said: "There is no Muslim - or no person, or slave (of Allah) - who says, in the morning and evening: 'Radaytu billahi Rabban wa bil-Islami dinan wa bi Muhammadin nabiyyan (I am content with Allah as my Lord, Islam as my religion and Muhammad as my Prophet),' but he will have a promise from Allah to make him pleased on the Day of Resurrection."

Source: Sunan Ibn Majah 3870 Graded Hasan by Darussalam

It was narrated from Isma'il bin 'Ubaid bin Rifa'ah, from his father, that his grandfather Rifa'ah said:

"We went out with the Messenger of Allah and the people were trading early in the morning. He called them: 'O merchants!' and when they looked up and craned their necks, he said : 'The merchants will be raised on the Day of Resurrection as immoral people, apart from those who fear Allah and act righteously and speak the truth (i.e. those who are honest)."'

Source: Sunan ibn Majah

English reference : Vol. 3, Book 12, Hadith 2146

Graded Hasan by Darussalam

It was narrated that Rifa'ah bin Shaddad Al-Qitbani said:

"Were it not for a word that I heard from 'Amr bin Hamiq Khuza'i, I would have separated the head of Al-Mukhtar from his

~ 149 ~

body. I heard him saying: "The Messenger of Allah said: 'If a man trusts someone with his life then he kills him, he will carry a banner of treachery on the day of Resurrection.'"

Source: Sunan ibn Majah

English reference : Vol. 3, Book 21, Hadith 2688

Graded Sahih by Darussalam

It was narrated from Abu Hurairah that the Messenger of Allah (ﷺ) said:

There are three whose supplications are not turned back: A just ruler, and a fasting person until he breaks his fast. And, the supplication of one who has been wronged is raised by Allah up to the clouds on the Day of Resurrection, and the gates of heaven are opened for it, and Allah says, 'By My Might I will help you (against the wrongdoer) even if it is after a while.'"

Source: Sunan ibn Majah

English reference : Vol. 1, Book 7, Hadith 1752

Graded Hasan by Darussalam

It was narrated from Abu Hurairah that the Messenger of Allah (ﷺ) said:

"Whoever dies being prepared in the cause of Allah, will be given continuously the reward for the good deeds that he used to do, and he will be rewarded with provision, and he will be kept safe from Fattan, and Allah will raise him on the Day of Resurrection free of fright."

Source: Sunan ibn Majah

English reference : Vol. 4, Book 24, Hadith 2767

Graded Sahih by Darussalam

It was narrated that 'Ubadah bin Samit said:

"I heard the Messenger of Allah say: 'Five prayers that Allah has enjoined upon His slaves, so whoever does them, and does not omit anything out of negligence, on the Day of Resurrection Allah will make a covenant with him that He will admit him to Paradise. But whoever does them but omits something from them out of negligence, will not have such a covenant with Allah; if He wills He will punish him, and if He wills, He will forgive him.'"

Source: Sunan ibn Majah

English reference : Vol. 1, Book 5, Hadith 1401

Graded Hasan by Darussalam

It was narrated from Thawban that the Prophet (ﷺ) said:

"I certainly know people of my nation who will come on the Day of Resurrection with good deeds like the mountains of Tihamah, but Allah will make them like scattered dust." Thawban said: "O Messenger of Allah, describe them to us and tell us more, so that we will not become of them unknowingly." He said: "They are your brothers and from your race, worshipping at night as you do, but they will be people who, when they are alone, transgress the sacred limits of Allah."

Source: Sunan ibn Majah

English reference : Vol. 5, Book 37, Hadith 4245

Graded Hasan by Darussalam

Al-Aswad ibn Sari' reported:

The Prophet, peace and blessings be upon him, said, "There are four kinds of people on the Day of Resurrection: a deaf man who cannot hear anything, a mad man, a senile man, and a man who died in the period before Islam. The deaf man will say: O Lord, Islam came and I could not hear anything. The mad man will say: O Lord, Islam came and the children threw filth at me. The senile man will say: O Lord, Islam came and I could not understand anything. The man who died before Islam will say: O Lord, there was no messenger from you who came to me. Allah will make them promise to obey Him. Then, he will command them to enter the fire. By the one in whose hand is the soul of Muhammad, if they enter the fire, it will become cool and peaceful."

Source: Musnad Ah☐mad 15866

Graded Sahih by Albani

Abu Dharr reported that Allah's Messenger (ﷺ) said:

I know the last of the inhabitants of Paradise to enter it and the last of the inhabitants of Hell to come out of it. He is a man who would be brought on the Day of Resurrection and it will be said: Present his minor sins to him, and withhold from him his serious sins. Then the minor sins would be placed before him, and it would be said: On such and such a day you did so and so and on such and such a day you did so and so. He would say: Yes. It will not be possible for him to deny, while he would be afraid lest serious sins should be presented before him. It would be said to him: In place of every evil deed you will have a good deed. He will say: My Lord! I have done things I do not see here. I indeed saw the Messenger of Allah laugh till his front teeth were exposed.

Source: Sahih Muslim 190 a

Abu al-Sa'id Khudri reported Allah's Messenger (ﷺ) as saying that the earth would turn to be one single bread on the Day of Resurrection and the Almighty would turn it in His hand as one of you turns a loaf while on a journey. It would be a feast arranged in the honor of the people of Paradise. He (the narrator) further narrated that a person from among the Jews came and he said:

Abu al-Qasim, may the Compassionate Lord be pleased with you! May I inform you about the feast arranged in honour of the people of Paradise on the Day of Resurrection? He said: Do it, of course. He said: The earth would become one single bread. Then Allah's Messenger looked towards us and laughed until his molar teeth became visible. He then again said: May I inform you about that with which they would season it? He said: Do it, of course. He said: Their seasoning would be balim and fish. The Companions of the Prophet said: What is this balam? He said: Ox and fish from whose excessive livers seventy thousand people would be able to eat.

Source: Sahih Muslim 2792

Abu Burda reported Allah's Messenger (ﷺ) as saying:

There would come people amongst the Muslims on the Day of Resurrection with as heavy sins as a mountain, and Allah would forgive them and He would place in their stead the Jews and the Christians. (As far as I think), Abu Raub said: I do not know as to who is in doubt. Abu Burda said: I narrated it to 'Umar b. 'Abd al-'Aziz, whereupon he said: Was it your father who narrated it to you from Allah's Apostle? I said: Yes.

Source: Sahih Muslim 2767 d

A'isha reported that a person sought permission from Allah's Apostle (ﷺ) to see him. He said:

Grant him permission. (and also added:) He is a bad son of his tribe or he is a bad person of his tribe. When he came in he used kind words for him. 'A'isha reported that she said: Allah's Messenger, you said about him what you had to say and then you treated him with kindness. He said: A'isha, verily in the eye of Allah, worst amongst the person in rank on the Day of Resurrection is one whom the people abandon or desert out of the fear of indecency.

Source: Sahih Muslim 2591 a

It was narrated that Anas said:

"The Messenger of Allah passed by a dome-shaped structure at the door of a man among the Ansar and said: 'What is this? 'They said: 'A dome that was built by so-and-so.' The Messenger of Allah said: 'All wealth that is like this (extravagant) will bring evil consequences to its owner on the Day of Resurrection.' News of that reached the Ansari, so he demolished it. Then the Prophet

passed by (that place) later on and did not see it. He asked about it and was told that its owner had demolished it because of what he had heard from him. He said: 'May Allah have mercy on him, may Allah have mercy on him.'"

Source: Sunan ibn Majah

English reference : Vol. 5, Book 37, Hadith 4161

Graded Hasan by Darussalam

It was narrated from Anas bin Malik that the Messenger of Allah (ﷺ) said:

"On the Day of Resurrection the disbeliever who lived the most luxurious will be brought, and it will be said: 'Dip him once in Hell.' So he will be dipped in it, then it will be said to him: 'O so-and-so, have you every enjoyed any pleasure?' He will say: 'No, I have never enjoyed any pleasure.' Then the believer who suffered the most hardship and trouble will be brought and it will be said: 'Dip him once in Paradise.' So he will be dipped in it and it will be said to him: 'O so-and-so, have you ever suffered any hardship or trouble?' He will say: 'I have never suffered any hardship or trouble.'"

Source: Sunan ibn Majah

English reference: Vol. 5, Book 37, Hadith 4321

Graded Sahih by Darussalam

Abu Huraira reported Allah's Messenger (ﷺ) as saying:

*Do you know who is poor? They (the Companions of the Prophet)
said: A poor man amongst us is one who has neither dirham with
him nor wealth. He (the Prophet) said: The poor of my Umma
would be he who would come on the Day of Resurrection with
prayers and fasts and Zakat but (he would find himself bankrupt
on that day as he would have exhausted his funds of virtues) since
he hurled abuses upon others, brought calumny against others and
unlawfully consumed the wealth of others and shed the blood of
others and beat others, and his virtues would be credited to the
account of one (who suffered at his hand). And if his good deeds
fall short to clear the account, then his sins would be entered in
(his account) and he would be thrown in the Hell-Fire.*

Source: Sahih Muslim 2581

It was narrated from Abu Hurairah that :

*The Messenger of Allah said: "There are seven whom Allah, the
Mighty and Sublime, will shade with His shade on the Day of
Resurrection, the Day when there will be no shade but His: A just
ruler, a young man who grows up worshipping Allah, the Mighty
and Sublime; a man who remembers Allah when he is alone and
his eyes flow (with tears); a man whose heart is attached to the
Masjid; two men who love each other for the sake of Allah, the
Mighty and Sublime; a man who is called (to commit sin) by a
woman of high status and beauty, but he says: 'I fear Allah'; and a
man who gives charity and conceals it, so that his left hand does
not know what his right hand is doing."*

Source: Sunan an-Nasa'i 5380 Graded Sahih by Darussalam

Narrated Umar ibn al-Khattab:

reported the Prophet as saying: *There are people from the servants of Allah who are neither prophets nor martyrs; the prophets and martyrs will envy them on the Day of Resurrection for their rank from Allah, the Most High.*

They (the people) asked: Tell us, Messenger of Allah, who are they? He replied: They are people who love one another for the spirit of Allah (i.e. the Qur'an), without having any mutual kinship and giving property to one. I swear by Allah, their faces will glow and they will be (sitting) in (pulpits of) light. They will have no fear (on the Day) when the people will have fear, and they will not grieve when the people will grieve.

He then recited the following Qur'anic verse: "Behold! Verily for the friends of Allah there is no fear, nor shall they grieve."

Source: Sunan Abi Dawud 3527 Graded Sahih by Albani

Abu Huraira reported Allah's Messenger as saying:

If any owner of gold or silver does not pay what is due on him, when the Day of Resurrection would come, plates of fire would be beaten out for him; these would then be heated in the fire of Hell and his sides, his forehead and his back would be cauterized with them. Whenever these cool down, (the process is) repeated during a day the extent of which would be fifty thousand years, until judgment is pronounced among servants, and he sees whether his path is to take him to Paradise or to Hell. It was said: Messenger of Allah, what about the camel? He (the Prophet) said: If any owner of the camel does not pay what is due on him, and of his due in that (camel) is (also) to milk it on the day when it comes down to water. When the Day of Resurrection comes a soft sandy plain would be set for him, as extensive as possible, (he will find) that not a single young one is missing, and they will trample him with their hoofs and bite him with their mouths. As often as the first of them passes him, the last of them would be made to return during a day the extent of which would be fifty thousand years, until judgment is pronounced among servants and he sees whether his path is to take him to Paradise or to Hell. It was (again) said: Messenger of Allah, what about cows (cattle) and sheep? He said: If any owner of the cattle and sheep does not pay what is due on them, when the Day of Resurrection comes a soft sandy plain would be spread for them, he will find none of them missing, with twisted horns, without horns or with a broken horn, and they will gore him with their horns and trample him with their hoofs. As often as the first of them passes him the last of them would be made to return to him during a day the extent of which would be fifty thousand years, until judgment would be pronounced among the servants. And he would be shown his path-path leading him to Paradise or to Hell. It was said: Messenger of Allah, what about the horse? Upon this he said: The horses are of three types. To one than (these are) a burden, and to another man (these are) a covering, and still to another man (these are) a source of reward. The one for whom these are a burden is the person who rears them in order to show off, for vainglory and for opposing the Muslims; so they are a burden for him. The one for whom these are a covering is the person who rears them for the sake of Allah but does not forget the right of Allah concerning their backs and their necks, and so they are a covering for him. As for those which bring reward (these refer to) the person who rears them for the sake of Allah to be used for Muslims and he puts them in meadow and field. And whatever thing do these eat from that meadow and field would be recorded on his behalf as good *deeds, as would also the amount of their dung and urine. And these would not break their halter and prance a course or two without having got recorded the amount of their hoof marks and their dung as a good deed on his behalf (on behalf of their owner). And their master does not bring them past a river from which they drink, though he did not intend to quench their thirst, but Allah would record for him the amount of what they drink on his behalf as deeds. It was said: Messenger of Allah, what about the asses?, Upon this he said: Nothing has been revealed to me in regard to the asses (in particular) except this one verse of a comprehensive nature:" He who does an atom's weight of good will see it, and he who does an atom's weight of evil will see it" (xcix. 7)*

Source: Sahih Muslim 987 a

Narrated Abu Sa`id Al-Khudri:

During the lifetime of the Prophet some people said, : O Allah's Messenger! Shall we see our Lord on the Day of Resurrection?" The Prophet said, "Yes; do you have any difficulty in seeing the sun at midday when it is bright and there is no cloud in the sky?" They replied, "No." He said, "Do you have any difficulty in seeing the moon on a full moon night when it is bright and there is no cloud in the sky?" They replied, "No." The Prophet said, "(Similarly) you will have no difficulty in seeing Allah on the Day of Resurrection as you have no difficulty in seeing either of them. On the Day of Resurrection, a call-maker will announce, "Let every nation follow that which they used to worship." Then none of those who used to worship anything other than Allah like idols and other deities but will fall in Hell (Fire), till there will remain none but those who used to worship Allah, both those who were obedient (i.e. good) and those who were disobedient (i.e. bad) and the remaining party of the people of the Scripture. Then the Jews will be called upon and it will be said to them, 'Who do you use to worship?' They will say, 'We used to worship Ezra, the son of Allah.' It will be said to them, 'You are liars, for Allah has never taken anyone as a wife or a son. What do you want now?' They will say, 'O our Lord! We are thirsty, so give us something to drink.' They will be directed and addressed thus, 'Will you drink,' whereupon they will be gathered unto Hell (Fire) which will look like a mirage whose different sides will be destroying each other. Then they will fall into the Fire. Afterwards the Christians will be called upon and it will be said to them, 'Who do you use to worship?' They will say, 'We used to worship Jesus, the son of Allah.' It will be said to them, 'You are liars, for Allah has never taken anyone as a wife or a son,' Then it will be said to them, 'What do you want?' They will say what the former people have said. Then, when there remain (in the gathering) none but those who used to worship Allah (Alone, the real Lord of the Worlds) whether they were obedient or disobedient. Then (Allah) the Lord of the worlds will come to them in a shape nearest to the picture they had in their minds about Him. It will be said, 'What are you waiting for?' Every nation have followed what they used to worship.' They will reply, 'We left the people in the world when we were in great need of them and we did not take them as friends. Now we are waiting for our Lord Whom we used to worship.' Allah will say, 'I am your Lord.' They will say twice or thrice, 'We do not worship any besides Allah.' "

Source: Sahih Bukhari USC-MSA web (English) reference : Vol. 6, Book 60, Hadith 105

Abu Huraira narrated on the authority of Abu Bakr that the Messenger of Allah (ﷺ) said:

Three are the persons with whom Allah would neither speak on the Day of Resurrection, nor would He look towards them, nor would purify them (from sins), and there would be a tormenting chastisement for them: a person who in the waterless desert has more water (than his need) and he refuses to give it to the traveller and a person who sold a commodity to another person in the afternoon and took an oath of Allah that he had bought it at such and such price and he (the buyer) accepted it to be true though it was not a fact, and a person who pledged allegiance to the Imam but for the sake of the world (material gains). And if the Imam bestowed on him (something) out of that (worldly riches) he stood by his allegiance and if he did not give him, he did not fulfil the allegiance.

Source: Sahih Muslim 108 a

Thauban reported Allah's Apostle (ﷺ) as saying:

I would be pushing back from my Cistern the crowd of people. I would strike away from it (the Cistern) with my staff the people of Yemen until the water (of the Haud) would spout forth upon them. He was asked about its breadth. He said: From this place of mine to 'Amman, and he was asked about the drink and he said: It is whiter than milk and sweeter than honey. There would spout into it two streamlets having their sources in Paradise. the one is from gold and the other is from silver. This hadith has been narrated on the authority of Hisham with the same chain of transmitters and the words are:" I would be on the Day of Resurrection near the bank of the Cistern."

Source: Sahih Muslim 2301 a, b

Miqdad b. Aswad reported:

I heard Allah's Messenger as saying: On the Day of Resurrection, the sun would draw so close to the people that there would be left only a distance of one mile. Sulaim b. Amir said: By Allah, I do not know whether he meant by" mile" the mile of the (material) earth or an instrument used for applying collyrium to the eye. (The Prophet is, however, reported to have said): The people would be submerged in perspiration according to their deeds, some up to their knees, some up to the waist and some would have the bridle of perspiration and, while saying this, Allah's Apostle pointed his hand towards his mouth.

Source: Sahih Muslim 2864

Narrated Abu Huraira:

The Prophet said, "The first man to be called on the Day of Resurrection will be Adam who will be shown his offspring, and it will be said to them, 'This is your father, Adam.' Adam will say (responding to the call), 'Labbaik and Sa`daik' Then Allah will say (to Adam), 'Take out of your offspring, the people of Hell.' Adam will say, 'O Lord, how many should I take out?' Allah will say, 'Take out ninety-nine out of every hundred." They (the Prophet's companions) said, "O Allah's Apostle! If ninety-nine out of every one hundred of us are taken away, what will remain out of us?"

He said, "My followers in comparison to the other nations are like a white hair on a black ox."

Source: Sahih al-Bukhari 6529

Narrated Adi ibn Umayrah al-Kindi:

The Prophet said: O people, if any of you is put in an administrative post on our behalf and conceals from us a needle or more, he is acting unfaithfully, and will bring it on the Day of Resurrection. A black man from the Ansar, as if I am seeing him, stood and said: Messenger of Allah, take back from me my post. He asked: What is that? He replied: I heard you say such and such. He said: And I say that. If we appoint anyone to an office, he must bring what is connected with it, both little and much. What he is given, he may take, and he must refrain from what is kept away from him.

Source: Sunan Abi Dawud 3581 Graded Sahih by Albani

Anas b. Malik said:

The Messenger of Allah dozed for a short while and raised his head smiling. He either said to them(people) or they said to him: Messenger of Allah! Why did you laugh? He said: A surah has been revealed to me just now, and then he recited: "In the name of Allah, Most Gracious. Most Merciful. To thee We have granted the fount (of abundance)" up to the end. When he recited, he asked: Do you know what al-kauthar is? They replied: Allah and his Apostle know best. He said: It is a river which my Lord, the Exalted, has promised me(to grant) in Paradise: there is abundance of good and upon it there is a pond which my people will approach on the Day of Resurrection. There are vessels as numerous as stars(in the sky).

Source: Sunan Abi Dawud 4747 Graded Hasan by Albani

It was narrated that 'Alqamah bin Waqqas said that a man passed by him, who held a prominent position, and 'Alqamah said to him:

"You have kinship and rights, and I see you entering upon these rulers and speaking to them as Allah wills you should speak. But I heard Bilal bin Harith Al-Muzani, the Companion of the Messenger of Allah, say that the Messenger of Allah said: 'One of you may speak a word that pleases Allah, and not know how far it reaches, but Allah will record for him as pleasure, until the Day of Resurrection due to that word. And one of you may speak a word that angers Allah, and not know how far it reaches, but Allah will record against him his anger, until the Day he meets Him due to that word." 'Alqamah said: "So look, woe to you, at what you say and what you speak about, for there is something that I wanted to say but I refrained because of what I heard from Bilal bin Harith."

Source: Sunan Ibn Majah 3969 Graded Hasan by Darussalam

Abdullah bin 'Amr narrated that the Messenger of Allah (ﷺ) said:

"A man from my nation will be called before all of creation on the Day of Resurrection, and ninety-nine scrolls will be spread out for him, each one extending as far as the eye can see. Then Allah will say: "Do you deny anything of this?" He will say: "No, O Lord." He will say: "Have My recording scribes been unfair to you?"

Then He will say: "Apart from that, do you have any good deeds?"
The man will be terrified and will say: "No." (Allah) will say:
"Indeed, you have good deeds with Us, and you will not be treated
unjustly this Day." Then a card will be brought out on which is
written Ash-hadu an la ilaha illallah wa anna Muhammadan
'abduhu wa rasuluhu (I bear witness that none has the right to be
worshipped but Allah, and that Muhammad is His slave and
Messenger). He will say: "O Lord, what is this card compared with
these scrolls?" He will say: "You will not be treated unjustly."
Then the scrolls will be placed in one side of the Balance and the
card in the other. The scrolls will go up (i.e., be light) and the card
will go down (i.e., will weigh heavily)."

Source: Sunan ibn Majah

English reference : Vol. 5, Book 37, Hadith 4300

Graded Sahih by Darussalam

Safwan b. Muhriz reported that a person said to Ibn 'Umar:

How did you hear Allah's Messenger as saying something about
intimate conversation? He said: I heard him say: A believer will be
brought to his Lord, the Exalted and Glorious, on the Day of
Resurrection and He would place upon him His veil (of Light) and
make him confess his faults and say: Do you recognize (your
faults)? He would say: My Lord, I do recognize (them). He (the
Lord) would say: I concealed them for you in the world. And today
I forgive them. And he would then be given the Book containing
(the account of his) good deeds. And so far as the non-believers and
hypocrites are concerned, there would be general announcement

about them before all creation telling them that these (people, i. e. non-believers and hypocrites) told a lie about Allah.

Source: Sahih Muslim 2768

Shaqiq reported that it was said to Usama b. Zaid:

Why don't you visit 'Uthman and talk to him? Thereupon he said: Do you think that I have not talked to him but that I have made you hear? By Allah. I have talked to him (about things) concerning me and him and I did not like to divulge those things about which I had to take the initiative and I do not say to my ruler: "You are the best among people," after I heard Allah's Messenger as saying: A man will be brought on the Day of Resurrection and thrown in Hell-Fire and his intestines will pour forth in Hell and he will go round along with them, as an ass goes round the mill stone. The denizens of Hell would gather round him and say: O, so and so, what has happened to you? Were you not enjoining us to do what was reputable and forbid us to do what was disreputable? He will say: Of course, it is so; I used to enjoin (upon people) to do what was reputable but did not practice that myself. I had been forbidding people to do what was disreputable, but practiced it myself.

Source: Sahih Muslim 2989 a

Narrated Abu Sa`id Al-Khudri:

Once the Prophet sat on a pulpit and we sat around him. Then he said, "The things I am afraid of most for your sake (concerning what will befall you after me) is the pleasures and splendors of the world and its beauties which will be disclosed to you." Somebody said, "O Allah's Messenger! Can the good bring forth evil?" The Prophet remained silent for a while. It was said to that person, "What is wrong with you? You are talking to the Prophet (p.b.u.h) while he is not talking to you." Then we noticed that he was being inspired divinely. Then the Prophet wiped off his sweat and said, "Where is the questioner?" It seemed as if the Prophet liked his question. Then he said, "Good never brings forth evil. Indeed it is like what grows on the banks of a water-stream which either kill or make the animals sick, except if an animal eats its fill the Khadira (a kind of vegetable) and then faces the sun, and then defecates and urinates and grazes again. No doubt this wealth is sweet and green. Blessed is the wealth of a Muslim from which he gives to the poor, the orphans and to needy travelers. (Or the Prophet said something similar to it) No doubt, whoever takes it illegally will be like the one who eats but is never satisfied, and his wealth will be a witness against him on the Day of Resurrection."

Source: Sahih al-Bukhari 1465

Narrated Abu Sa`id Al-Khudri:

The Prophet said, "Allah will say (on the Day of Resurrection), 'O Adam.' Adam will reply, 'Labbaik wa Sa`daik', and all the good is in Your Hand.' Allah will say: 'Bring out the people of the fire.' Adam will say: 'O Allah! How many are the people of the Fire?' Allah will reply: 'From every one thousand, take out nine-hundred-and ninety-nine.' At that time children will become hoary headed, every pregnant female will have a miscarriage, and one will see mankind as drunken, yet they will not be drunken, but dreadful will be the Wrath of Allah." The companions of the Prophet asked, "O Allah's Apostle! Who is that (excepted) one?"

He said, "Rejoice with glad tidings; one person will be from you and one-thousand will be from Gog and Magog." The Prophet further said, "By Him in Whose Hands my life is, hope that you will be one-fourth of the people of Paradise." We shouted, "Allahu Akbar!" He added, "I hope that you will be one-third of the people of Paradise." We shouted, "Allahu Akbar!" He said, "I hope that you will be half of the people of Paradise." We shouted, "Allahu Akbar!" He further said, "You (Muslims) (compared with non-Muslims) are like a black hair in the skin of a white ox or like a white hair in the skin of a black ox (i.e. your number is very small as compared with theirs)."

Source: Sahih al-Bukhari 3348

Narrated `Abdullah:

Allah's Messenger said, "If somebody is ordered (by the ruler or the judge) to take an oath, and he takes a false oath in order to grab the property of a Muslim, then he will incur Allah's Wrath when he will meet Him." And Allah revealed in its confirmation: 'Verily! Those who purchase a small gain at the cost of Allah's covenants and their own oaths.' (3.77) (The sub-narrator added:) Al-Ash'ath bin Qais entered, saying, "What did Abu `Abdur-Rahman narrate to you?" They said, "So-and-so," Al-Ash'ath said, "This verse was revealed in my connection. I had a well on the land of my cousin (and we had a dispute about it). I reported him to Allah 's Apostle who said (to me). "You should give evidence (i.e. witness) otherwise the oath of your opponent will render your claim invalid." I said, "Then he (my opponent) will take the oath, O Allah's Messenger." Allah's Messenger said, "Whoever is ordered (by the ruler or the judge) to give an oath, and he takes a false oath in order to grab the property of a Muslim, then he will incur Allah's Wrath when he meets Him on the Day of Resurrection."

Source: Sahih al-Bukhari 6676, 6677

Abu Huraira reported Allah's Messenger (ﷺ) as saying:

Verily, Allah, the Exalted and Glorious, would say on the Day of Resurrection: O son of Adam, I was sick but you did not visit Me. He would say: O my Lord; how could I visit Thee whereas Thou art the Lord of the worlds? Thereupon He would say: Didn't you know that such and such servant of Mine was sick but you did not visit him and were you not aware of this that if you had visited him, you would have found Me by him? O son of Adam, I asked food from you but you did not feed Me. He would say: My Lord, how could I feed Thee whereas Thou art the Lord of the worlds? He said: Didn't you know that such and such servant of Mine asked food from you but you did not feed him, and were you not aware that if you had fed him you would have found him by My side? (The Lord would again say:) O son of Adam, I asked drink from you but you did not provide Me. He would say: My Lord, how could I provide Thee whereas Thou art the Lord of the worlds? Thereupon He would say: Such and such of servant of Mine asked you for a drink but you did not provide him, and had you provided him drink you would have found him near Me.

Source: Sahih Muslim 2569

'Abd al-Rahman al-Hubuli reported:

I heard that a person asked 'Abdullah b. 'Amr b. 'As and heard him saying: Are we not amongst the destitute of the emigrants? Abdullah said to him: Have you a spouse with whom you live? He said: Yes. Abdullah asked: Do you not have a home in which you reside? The man replied "Yes." Abdullah said: Then you are amongst the rich. He said: I have a servant also. Thereupon he (Abdullah b. 'Amr b. 'As) said: Then you are amongst the kings. Abu 'Abd al-Rahman reported that three persons came to 'Abdullah b. Amr b. 'As while I was sitting with him and they said: By Allah, we have nothing with us either in the form of provision, riding animals or wealth. Thereupon he said to them: I am prepared to do whatever you like. If you come to us, we would give you what Allah would make available for you. and if you like I would make a mention of your case to the ruler, and if you like you can show patience also. for I have heard Allah's Messenger as saying: The destitute amongst the emigrants would precede the rich emigrants by forty years in getting into Paradise on the Day of Resurrection. Thereupon they said: We then, show patience and do not ask for anything.

Source: Sahih Muslim 2979 a, b

Abu Hurairah narrated that the Messenger of Allah said:

"Allah will gather mankind on the Day of Resurrection on a single plane, then the Lord of the Worlds will come to them and say: 'Let every person follow what they used to worship.' So to the worshipper of the cross, his cross shall be symbolized to him, and to the worshipper of images his images, and to the worshipper of fire his fire. They will follow what they used to worship, and the Muslims will remain. Then the Lord of the Worlds will come to

~ 170 ~

them and say: 'Do you not follow the people?' So they will say: 'We seek refuge in Allah from you, we seek refuge in Allah from you, Allah is our Lord, and we shall remain here until we see our Lord.' And He orders them and makes them firm.' "They said: "And you will see Him, O Messenger of Allah?" He said: "Are you harmed in seeing the moon on the night of a full moon?" They said: "No, O Messenger of Allah." He said: "So you will not be harmed in seeing Him at that hour. Then He will conceal Himself, then He will come, and He will make them recognize Him, then He will say: "I am your Lord, so follow Me." So the Muslims will arise and the Sirat shall be placed, and they shall be placed, and they shall pass by it the like of excellent horses and camels and their statement upon it shall be, "Grant them safety, grant them safety." And the people of Fire shall remain, then a party of them shall be cast down into it, and it shall be said (to the Fire): 'Have you become full?' So it shall say: Is there more? Then a party of them shall be cast down into it, and it shall be said: 'Have you become full?' So it shall say: Is there more? Until when they are all included into it, Ar-Rahman (the Most-Merciful) shall place His foot in it and its sides shall be all brought together, then He will say: 'Enough.' It will say 'Enough, enough.' So when Allah, the Exalted, has admitted the people of Paradise into Paradise and the people of Fire into Fire"- [He said:]- "Death shall be brought in by the collar and stood on the wall that is between the people of Paradise and the people of the Fire, then it will be said: 'O people of Paradise!' They will come near, afraid. Then it will be said: 'O people of the Fire!' They will come rejoicing, hoping for intercession. Then it will be said to the people of Paradise and the people of the Fire: 'Do you recognize this?' So they will-both of them-say: 'We recognize it. It is Death which was given charge of us,' so it will be laid down and slaughtered upon the wall [the one that is between Paradise and the Fire], then it will be said: 'O people of Paradise! Everlasting life without death!' And 'O people of the Fire! Everlasting life without death!'"

Source: Jami at-Tirmidhi

English reference : Vol. 4, Book 12, Hadith 2557

Graded Sahih by Darussalam

It was narrated from Abu Hurairah, that one of the people of Ash-Sham said to him:

"O Shaikh, tell me of a Hadith that you heard from the Messenger of Allah." He said: "Yes; I heard the Messenger of Allah say: 'The first of people for whom judgment will be passed on the Day of Resurrection are three. A man who was martyred. He will be brought and Allah will remind him of His blessings and he will acknowledge them. He will say: What did you do with them? He will say: I fought for Your sake until I was martyred. He will say: You are lying. You fought so that it would be said that so-and-so is brave, and it was said. Then He will order that he be dragged on his face and thrown into the Fire. And (the second will be) a man who acquired knowledge and taught others, and read Qur'an. He will be brought, and Allah will remind him of His blessings, and he will acknowledge them. He will say: What did you do with them? He will say: I acquired knowledge and taught others, and read the Qur'an for Your sake. He will say: You are lying. You acquired knowledge so that it would be said that you were a scholar; and you read Qur'an so that it would be said that you were a reciter, and it was said. Then He will order that he be

~ 172 ~

dragged on his face and thrown into the Fire. And (the third will be) a man whom Allah made rich and gave him all kinds of wealth. He will be brought and Allah will remind him of His blessings, and he will acknowledge them. he will say: What did you do with them? He will say: I did not leave any way that You like wealth to be spent - Abu 'Abdur-Rahman (An-Nasa'i) said: I did not understand "what You like" as I wanted to - "but I spent it." He will say: "You are lying. You spent it so that it would be said that he was generous, and it was said." Then he will order that he be dragged on his face and thrown into the Fire.'"

Source: Sunan an-Nasa'i 3137 Graded Sahih by Darussalam

Abu Haraira reported:

The people said to the Messenger of Allah: Messenger of Allah, shall we see our Lord on the Day of Resurrection? The Messenger of Allah said: Do you feel any trouble in seeing the moon on the night when it is full? They said: Messenger of Allah, no. He (the Messenger) further said: Do you feel any trouble in seeing the sun, when there is no cloud over it? They said: Messenger of Allah. no. He (the Prophet) said: Verily you would see Him like this (as you see the sun and the moon). God will gather people on the Day of Resurrection and say: Let every people follow what they worshipped. Those who worshipped the sun would follow the sun, and those who worshipped the moon would follow the moon, and those who worshipped the devils would follow the devils. This Ummah (of Islam) alone would be left behind and there would be hypocrites too amongst it. Allah would then come to them in a form other than His own Form, recognizable to them, and would say: I am your Lord. They would say: We take refuge with Allah from thee. We will stay here till our Lord comes to us. and when our Lord would come we would recognise Him. Subsequently Allah would come to them in His own Form, recognizable to them, and say: I am your Lord. They would say: Thou art our Lord. And they would follow Him, and a bridge would be set over the Hell; and I (the Prophet) and my Ummah would be the first to pass over it; and none but the messengers would speak on that day, and the prayer of the messengers on that day would be: O Allah! grant safety, grant safety. In Hell, there would be long spits like the thorns of Sa'dan He (the Prophet) said: Have you seen Sa'dan? They replied: Yes, Messenger of Allah. He said: Verily those (hooks) would be like the thorns of Sa'dan, but no one knows their size except Allah. These would seize people for their misdeeds. Some of them would escape for their (good) deeds, and some would be rewarded for their deeds till they get salvation. When Allah would finish judging His bondsmen and because of His mercy decide to take out of Hell such people as He pleases. He would command the angels to bring out those who had not associated anything with Allah; to whom Allah decided to show mercy. those who would say: There is no god but Allah. They (the angels) would recognize them in the Fire by the marks of prostration, for Hell-fire will devour everything (limb) of the sons of Adam except the marks of prostration. Allah has forbidden the fire to consume the marks of prostration. They will be taken out of the Fire having been burnt, and the water of life would be poured over them, and they will sprout as seed does In the silt carried by flood. Then Allah would finish judging amongst His bondsmen; but a man who will be the last to enter Paradise will remain facing Hell and will say: O my Lord I turn my face away from Hell, for its air has poisoned me and its blaze has burnt me. He will then call to Allah as long as

Allah would wish that he should call to Him. Then Allah, Blessed and Exalted, would say: If I did that, perhaps you would ask for more than that. He would say: I would not ask You more than this, and he would give his Lord covenants and agreements as Allah wished, and so He would turn his face away from the Fire When he turns towards the Paradise and sees it, he will remain silent as long as Allah wishes him to remain so. He will then say: O my Lord I bring me forward to the gate of the Paradise. Allah would say to him: Did you not give covenants and agreements that you would not ask for anything besides what I had given you. Woe to thee! O son of Adam, how treacherous you are! He would say: O my Lord! and would continue calling to Allah till He would say to him: If I grant you that, perhaps you will ask for more. He will reply: No, by Thy greatness, and he will give His Lord promises and covenants as Allah had wished. He would then bring him to the gate of the Paradise, and when he would stand at the gate of the Paradise, it would lay open before him. and he would see the bounty and the joy that there is in it. He would remain quiet as long as Allah would desire him to remain silent. He would then say: O my Lord, admit me to Paradise. Allah. Blessed and Exalted, would say: Did you not give covenants and agreements that you would not ask for anything more than what I had granted you? Woe to you! son of Adam, how treacherous you are! And he would say: O my Lord, I do not wish to be the most miserable of Thy creatures. He would continue calling upon Allah till Allah, Blessed and Exalted, would laugh. When Allah would laugh at him, He would say: Enter the Paradise. When he would enter, Allah would say: State your wish. He would express his wishes till Allah would remind him (the desire of) such and such (things). When his desires would be exhausted Allah would say: That is for thee and, besides it, the like of it also. 'Ata' b. Yazid said: Abu Sa'id al-Khudri was with Abu Huraira and he did not reject anything from the hadith narrated by him, but when Abu Huraira narrated:" Allah said to that man; and its like along with it," Abu Sa'id said:" Ten like it along with it," O Abu Huraira. Abu Huraira said: I do not remember except the words:" That is for you and a similar one along with it." Abu Sa'id said: I bear witness to the fact that I remembered from the Messenger of Allah his words:" That is for thee and ten like it." Abu Huraira said: That man was the last of those deserving of Paradise to enter Paradise.

Source: Sahih Muslim 182 a

Abdullah bin Mas'ud narrated that :

Allah's Messenger said: "The person closest to me on the Day of Judgement is the one who sent the most Salat upon me."

Source: Jami` at-Tirmidhi 484 Graded Hasan by Darussalam

Abu Hurairah reported the Messenger of Allah (ﷺ) as saying:

If anyone drinks poison, the poison will be in his hand (on the Day of Judgement) and he will drink it in Hell-fire and he will live in it eternally.

Source: Sunan Abi Dawud 3872 Graded Sahih by Albani

Narrated Abu Ayyub:

"I heard the Messenger of Allah saying: 'Whoever separates a mother from her child, Allah separates him and his most beloved on the Day of Judgement.'"

Source: Jami` at-Tirmidhi 1283

Graded Hasan by Darussalam

Jabir narrated that the Messenger of Allah said:

"Indeed the most beloved among you to me, and the nearest to sit with me on the Day of Judgment is the best of you in character. And indeed, the most disliked among you to me, and the one sitting furthest from me on the Day of Judgement are the Thartharun, and the Mutashaddiqun and the Muthafaihiqun."
They said: "O Messenger of Allah! We know about the Thartharun, and the Mutashaddiqun, but what about the Muthafaihiqun?"' He said: "The arrogant."

Source: Jami` at-Tirmidhi 2018

Graded Hasan by Darussalam

Sahl bin Mu'adh bin Anas Al-Juhani narrated from his father, that the Messenger of Allah said:

"Whoever leaves(valuable) dress out of humility to Allah while he is able to (afford it), Allah will call him before the heads of creation on the Day of Judgement so that he can chose whichever Hulal of faith he wishes to wear."

Source: Jami at-Tirmidhi

English reference : Vol. 4, Book 11, Hadith 2481

Graded Hasan by Darussalam

'Amr bin Shu'aib narrated from his father, from his grandfather from the Prophet who said:

"The proud will be gathered on the Day of Judgement resembling tiny particles in the image of men. They will be covered with humiliation everywhere, they will be dragged into a prison in Hell called Bulas, submerged in the Fire of Fires, drinking the drippings of the people of the Fire, filled with derangement."

Source: Jami at-Tirmidhi

English reference : Vol. 4, Book 11, Hadith 2492

Graded Hasan by Darussalam

Narrated Abu Hurairah:

that the Prophet said: "The one who memorized the Qur'an shall come on the Day of Judgement and (the reward for reciting the Qur'an) says: 'O Lord! Decorate him." So he is donned with a crown of nobility. Then it says: "O Lord! Give him more!' So he is donned with a suit of nobility. Then it says: "O Lord! Be pleased with him.' So He is pleased with him and says: "Recite and rise up, and be increased in reward with every Ayah.'"

Source: Jami at-Tirmidhi

English reference : Vol. 5, Book 42, Hadith 2915

Graded Hasan by Darussalam

Abu Salih reported from Aabil Huraurah and Abu Sa'eed that the Messenger of allah said:

"The servant will be brought on the Day of Judgement, and He will say to him: 'Did I not give you hearing. Sight, wealth, children, and did I not make the cattle and tillage subservient to you, and did I not leave you as the head of people taking from their wealth? Did you not think that you would have to meet with Me on this Day of yours?' So he will say: 'No.' So it will be said to him: 'Today you shall be forgotten just as you have forgotten Me.'"

Source: Jami at-Tirmidhi

English reference : Vol. 4, Book 11, Hadith 2428

Graded Sahih by Darussalam

Narrated 'Abdul-Hamid bin Ja'far:

"My father informed me, from Ibn Mina, from Abu Sa'eed bin Abi Fadalah Al-Ansari - and he was one of the Companions - who said: 'I heard the Messenger of Allah said: "When Allah gathers the people on the Day of Judgement - a Day in which there is no doubt in - a caller will call out: 'Whoever committed Shirk in any of his deeds he did for Allah - then let him seek his reward from other than Allah. For indeed Allah is the most free of the partners from any need of Shirk."

Source: Jami at-Tirmidhi

English reference: Vol. 5, Book 44, Hadith 3154

Graded Hasan by Darussalam

Al-Walid bin Abi Al-Wald abu 'Utthman Al-Mada'ini narrated that 'Uqbah bin Muslim narrated to him, that shufaiy Al-Asbahi narrated he entered Al-Madinah and saw a man around whom people had gathered. He asked:

" Who is this?" They said: "Abu Hurairah." (He said): So I got close to him until I was sitting in front of him as he was narrating to the people. When he was silent and alone, I said to him: " I ask you absolute truth if you would narrate to me a Hadith which you heard from the Messenger of Allah, That you understand and know." So Abu Hurairah said: "You want me to narrate a Hadith to you which the Messenger of Allah narrated to me that I understand and know." Then Abu Hurairah began sobbing profusely. We sat for a while, then he recovered and said: "I shall narrate to you a Hadith which the Messenger of Allah narrated in this House, while there was no one with us other than he and I." Then, again, Abu Hurairah began sobbing severely. Then he recovered, and wiped his face, and said: "you want me to narrate to you a Hadith which the Messenger of Allah narrated while he and I were sitting in this House, and no one was with us but he and I." Then Abu Hurairah began sobbing severely. Then he bent, falling on his face, so I supported him for a long time. Then he recovered and said: "The Messenger of Allah narrated to me that on the Day of Judgement, Allah, Most High, will descend to His slaves to judge between them. Every nation shall be kneeling. The first of those who will be called before him will be a man who memorized the Qur'an, and a man who was killed in Allah's cause, and a wealthy man. Allah will say to the reciter: 'Did I not teach you what I revealed to My Messenger?" He says: 'Of course O Lord!'

He says: 'Then what did you do with what you learned?' He said: 'I would stand (in prayer reciting) with it during all hours of the night and all hours of the day.' Then Allah would say to him: 'You have lied.' And the angels will say: 'You have lied.' Allah will say to him: 'Rather, you wanted it to be said that so-and-so is a reciter. And that was said.' The person with the wealth will be brought, and Allah will say to him: 'Was I not so generous with you, such that I did not leave you having any need from anyone?' He will say: 'Of course O Lord!' He says: 'Then what did you do with what I gave to you?' He says: 'I would nurture the ties of kinship and give charity.' Then Allah will say to him: 'You have lied.' And the angels will say to him: 'You have lied.' Allah, Most High, will say: 'Rather, you wanted it to be said that so-and-so is so generous, and that was said.' Then the one who was killed in Allah's cause shall be brought, and Allah will say to him : 'For what were you killed?' So he says: 'I was commanded to fight in Your cause ,so I fought until I was killed.' Allah [Most High] will say to him: 'You have lied.' And the angels will say to him: 'You have lied.' Allah [Most High] will say: 'Rather, you wanted it be said that so-and-so is brave, and that was said.' "Then the Messenger of Allah hit me on my knees and said: 'O Abu Hurairah! These first three are the creatures of Allah with whom the fire will be enflamed on the Day of Judgement.'" Al-Walid Abu 'Uthman Al-Mada'ini said: "So 'Uqbah bin Muslim informed me that Shaufaiy, is the one who entered upon Mu'awiyah to inform him about this." Abu Uthman said: 'This has been done with these people, then how about with those who remain among the people?" Then Mu'awiyah begin weeping so intensely, that we thought that he will kill himself with excessive weeping. We said: "This man came to us to cause evil." Then Mu'awiyah recovered, wiped off his face and said: "Allah and

His Messenger told the truth: Whosoever desires the life of the world and its glitter, then we shall pay in full (the wages of) their deeds therein, and they shall have no diminution therein. They are those for whom there is nothing in the Hereafter Fire, and vain are the deeds they did therein. And of no effect is that which they used to do."

Source: Jami` at-Tirmidhi 2382 Graded Sahih by Darussalam

An-Nadr bin Anas bin Malik narrated from his father who said:

"I asked the Prophet to intercede for me on the Day of Judgement. He said: 'I am the one to do so.'" [He said:] "I said: 'O Messenger of Allah! Then where shall I seek you?' He said: 'Seek me, the first time you should seek me is on the Sirat.'" [He said:] "I said: 'If I do not meet you upon the Sirat?' He said: 'Then seek me at the Mizan.' I said:'And if I do not meet you at the Mizan?' He said: 'Then seek me at the Hawd, for indeed I will not me missed at these three locations.'"

Source: Jami at-Tirmidhi

English reference : Vol. 4, Book 11, Hadith 2433

Graded Hasan by Darussalam

Abu Hurairah narrated that:

the Prophet said: "The best day that the sun has risen upon is Friday. On it Adam was created, on it he entered Paradise, and on it, he was expelled from it. And the Hour will not be established except on Friday."

Source: Jami` at-Tirmidhi 488 Graded Sahih by Darussalam

Narrated Anas:

The Prophet said, "The believers will be kept (waiting) on the Day of Resurrection so long that they will become worried and say, "Let us ask somebody to intercede far us with our Lord so that He may relieve us from our place.

Then they will go to Adam and say, 'You are Adam, the father of the people. Allah created you with His Own Hand and made you reside in His Paradise and ordered His angels to prostrate before you, and taught you the names of all things will you intercede for us with your Lord so that He may relieve us from this place of ours? Adam will say, 'I am not fit for this undertaking.' He will mention his mistakes he had committed, i.e., his eating off the tree though he had been forbidden to do so. He will add, 'Go to Noah, the first prophet sent by Allah to the people of the Earth.' The people will go to Noah who will say, 'I am not fit for this undertaking' He will mention his mistake which he had done, i.e., his asking his Lord without knowledge.' He will say (to them), 'Go to Abraham, Khalil Ar-Rahman.' They will go to Abraham who will say, 'I am not fit for this undertaking. He would mention three words by which he told a lie, and say (to them). 'Go to Moses, a slave whom Allah gave the Torah and spoke to, directly and brought near Him, for conversation.'

They will go to Moses who will say, 'I am not fit for this undertaking. He will mention his mistake he made, i.e., killing a person, and will say (to them), 'Go to Jesus, Allah's slave and His Apostle, and a soul created by Him and His Word.' (Be: And it was.) They will go to Jesus who will say, 'I am not fit for this undertaking but you'd better go to Muhammad the slave whose past and future sins have been forgiven by Allah.' So they will come to me, and I will ask my Lord's permission to enter His House and then I will be permitted. When I see Him I will fall down in prostration before Him, and He will leave me (in prostration) as long as He will, and then He will say, 'O Muhammad, lift up your head and speak, for you will be listened to, and intercede, for your intercession will be accepted, and ask (for anything) for it will be granted:' Then I will raise my head and glorify my Lord with certain praises which He has taught me. Allah will put a limit for me (to intercede for a certain type of people) I will take them out and make them enter Paradise." (Qatada said: I heard Anas saying that), the Prophet said, "I will go out and take them out of Hell (Fire) and let them enter Paradise, and then I will return and ask my Lord for permission to enter His House and I will be permitted.

When I will see Him I will fall down in prostration before Him and He will leave me in prostration as long as He will let me (in that state), and then He will say, 'O Muhammad, raise your head and speak, for you will be listened to, and intercede, for your intercession will be accepted, and ask, your request will be granted.' " The Prophet added, "So I will raise my head and glorify and praise Him as He has taught me. Then I will intercede and He will put a limit for me (to intercede for a certain type of people). I will take them out and let them enter Paradise." (Qatada added: I heard Anas saying that) the Prophet said, 'I will go out and take them out of Hell (Fire) and let them enter Paradise, and I will return for the third time and will ask my Lord for permission to enter His house, and I will be allowed to enter.

When I see Him, I will fall down in prostration before Him, and will remain in prostration as long as He will, and then He will say, 'Raise your head, O Muhammad, and speak, for you will be listened to, and intercede, for your intercession will be accepted, and ask, for your request will be granted.' So I will raise my head and praise Allah as He has taught me and then I will intercede and He will put a limit for me (to intercede for a certain type of people). I will take them out and let them enter Paradise." (Qatada said: I heard Anas saying that) the Prophet said, "So I will go out and take them out of Hell (Fire) and let them enter Paradise, till none will remain in the Fire except those whom Quran will imprison (i.e., those who are destined for eternal life in the fire)." The narrator then recited the Verse:-- "It may be that your Lord will raise you to a Station of Praise and Glory.' (17.79) The narrator added: This is the Station of Praise and Glory which Allah has promised to your Prophet.

Source: Sahih al-Bukhari 7440

It was narrated from Abu Musa Al-Ash'ari that the Messenger of Allah (ﷺ) said:

"I was given the choice between being admitted to Paradise, and I chose intercession, because it is more general and more sufficient. Do you think it is for the pious? No, it is for the impure sinners."

Source: Sunan ibn Majah

English reference : Vol. 5, Book 37, Hadith 4311

Graded Hasan by Darussalam

It was narrated from 'Abdullah bin Abi Jad'a' that he heard the Prophet (ﷺ) say:

"More than (the members of the tribe of) Banu Tamim will enter Paradise through the intercession of a man from among my nation." They said: "O Messenger of Allah, besides you?" He said: "Besides me."

Source: Sunan ibn Majah

English reference : Vol. 5, Book 37, Hadith 4316

Graded Sahih by Darussalam

Abu Sa'id reported Allah's Messenger (ﷺ) as saying:

Death would be brought on the Day of Resurrection. in the form of a white-coloured ram. Abu Kuraib made this addition: Then it would be made to stand between the Paradise and the Hell. So far as the rest of the hadith is concerned there is perfect agreement (between the two narrators) and it would be said to the inmates of Paradise: Do you recognize this? They would raise up their necks and look towards it and say: Yes, ' it is death. Then it would be said to the inmates of Hell-Fire.. Do you recognize this? And they would raise up their necks and look and say: Yes, it is death. Then command would be given for slaughtering that and then it would be said: 0 inmates of Paradise, there is an everlasting life for you and no death. And then (addressing) to the inmates of the Hell-Fire, it would be said: 0 inmates of Hell-Fire, there is an everlasting living for you and no death. Allah's Messenger then recited this verse pointing with his hand to this (material) world:"

Warn them, this Day of dismay, and when their affairs would be decided and they would be un- mindful and they believe not" (xix. 39).

Source: Sahih Muslim 2849 a

It was narrated from Abu Sa'eed that the Messenger of Allah (ﷺ) said:

"I am the leader of the sons of Adam, and it is no boast. I will be the first one for whom the earth will be split open on the Day of Resurrection, and it is no boast. I will be the first to intercede and the first whose intercession will be accepted, and it is no boast. The banner of praise will be in my hand on the Day of Resurrection, and it is no boast."

Source: Sunan ibn Majah

English reference   : Vol. 5, Book 37, Hadith 4308

Graded Sahih by Darussalam

It was narrated from Sunabih Al-Ahmasi that the Messenger of Allah (ﷺ) said:

"I shall reach the Cistern (Haud) before you, and I will boast of your great numbers before the nations, so do not fight one another after I am gone.'"

Source: Sunan Ibn Majah 3944

Graded Sahih by Darussalam

It was narrated from Aishah that:

the Messenger of Allah said: "Marriage is part of my sunnah, and whoever does not follow my sunnah has nothing to do with me. Get married, for I will boast of your great numbers before the nations. Whoever has the means, let him get married, and whoever does not, then he should fast for it will diminish his desire."

Source: Sunan ibn Majah

English reference   : Vol. 3, Book 9, Hadith 1846

Graded Hasan by Darussalam

As a commentary, it is important to ensure one's lineage is boast-worthy <u>according to prophetic standards</u>. For if your descendants are disbelievers or don't follow the Sunnah according to the way of the prophet and salaf that is not boast-worthy and may be sinful for you to have procreated since you are a reason for the existence of a criminal. Hence it is vital to ensure the best parenting possible to ensure you have the best descendants possible. Whereas the most important factor in parenting, aside from the spouse you choose, is the country, state, city, neighborhood you choose to raise children. The environment is often as important if not more important than the parenting. Since most people stay and procreate where they were relatively raised Hijrah/Emigration to the believing lands of the pious is important for every parent. You don't want to come on the Day of Resurrection ashamed that your descendants include disbelievers or wicked people all because of the environment you birthed and raised them in. No matter where one lives now it is always possible to improve the environment and thereby the quality of your descendants via Hijrah.

Data about the Sirat and Mizan

Quran 4:175

So, as for those who believed in Allâh and held fast to Him, He will admit them to His Mercy and Grace (i.e. Paradise), and guide them to Himself by a Straight Path. (175)

Quran 7:8-9

And the weighing on that day (Day of Resurrection) will be the true (weighing). So as for those whose scale (of good deeds) will be heavy, they will be the successful (by entering Paradise). (8) And as for those whose scale will be light, they are those who will lose their ownselves (by entering Hell) because they denied and rejected Our Ayât (proofs, evidences, verses, lessons, signs, revelations).

Quran 7:46-49

And between them will be a (barrier) screen and on Al-A'râf (a wall with elevated places) will be men (whose good and evil deeds would be equal in scale), who would recognize all (of the Paradise and Hell people), by their marks (the dwellers of Paradise by their white faces and the dwellers of Hell by their black faces), they will call out to the dwellers of Paradise, "Salâmun 'Alaikûm" (peace be on you), and at that time they (men on Al-A'râf) will not yet have entered it (Paradise), but they will hope to enter (it) with certainty.

(46) And when their eyes will be turned towards the dwellers of the Fire, they will say: "Our Lord! Place us not with the people who are Zâlimûn (polytheists and wrong-doers)." (47) And the men on Al-A'râf (the wall) will call unto the men whom they would recognize by their marks, saying: "Of what benefit to you were your great numbers (and hoards of wealth), and your arrogance (against Faith)?" (48) Are they those, of whom you swore that Allâh would never show them mercy. (Behold! It has been said to them): "Enter Paradise, no fear shall be on you, nor shall you grieve."

Tafsir of the ayat by ibn Kathir

Mujahid said, "Al-A`raf is a barrier between Paradise and the Fire, a wall that has a gate." Ibn Jarir said, "Al-A`raf is plural for `Urf, where every elevated piece of land is known as `Urf to the Arabs." As-Suddi said, "Al-A`raf is so named because its residents recognize (Ya`rifun) the people. Al-A`raf's residents are those whose good and bad deeds are equal, as Hudhayfah, Ibn `Abbas, Ibn Mas`ud and several of the Salaf and later generations said." Ibn Jarir recorded that Hudhayfah was asked about the people of Al-A`raf and he said, "A people whose good and bad deeds are equal. Their evil deeds prevented them from qualifying to enter Paradise, and their good deeds qualified them to avoid the Fire. Therefore, they are stopped there on the wall until Allah judges them."

Quran 19:71-72

There is not one of you but will pass over it (Hell); this is with
your Lord; a Decree which must be accomplished (71) Then We
shall save those who use to fear Allâh and were dutiful to Him.
And We shall leave the Zâlimûn (polytheists and wrongdoers)
therein (humbled) to their knees (in Hell).

Tafsir of the ayat by Ibn Kathir

Ibn Jarir reported from `Abdullah that he said concerning
Allah's statement, (There is not one of you but will pass over
it.) "The bridge over Hell is like the sharp edge of a sword.
The first group to cross it will pass like a flash of lightning.
The second group will pass like the wind. The third group
will pass like the fastest horse. The fourth group will pass
like the fastest cow. Then, the rest will pass while the angels
will be saying, `O Allah save them, save them.' " This
narration has supporting narrations similar to it from the
Prophet in the Two Sahihs and other collections as well.
These narrations have been related by Anas, Abu Sa`id, Abu
Hurayrah, Jabir and other Companions, may Allah be
pleased with them all.

When all of the creatures passed over the Hellfire, and those
disbelievers and the disobedient people who are destined to
fall into it because of their disobedience, Allah will save the
believers and the righteous people from it because of their
deeds. Therefore, their passing over the bridge and their
speed will be based upon their deeds that they did in this
life. Then, the believers who performed major sins will be
allowed intercession. The angels, the Prophets and the

believers will all intercede. Thus, a large number of the sinners will be allowed to come out of Hell. The fire will have devoured much of their bodies, except the places of prostration on their faces. Their removal from the Hellfire will be due to the faith in their hearts. The first to come out will be he who has the weight of a Dinar of faith in his heart. Then, whoever has the next least amount after him. Then, whoever is next to that after him, and so forth. This will continue until the one who has the tiniest hint of faith in his heart, equal to the weight of an atom. Then, Allah will take out of the Fire whoever said "La ilaha illallah," even one day of his entire life, even if he never performed any good deed. After this, no one will remain in the Hellfire, except those it is obligatory upon to remain in the Hellfire forever.

Quran 21:47

And We shall set up balances of justice on the Day of Resurrection, then none will be dealt with unjustly in anything. And if there be the weight of a mustard seed, We will bring it. And Sufficient are We to take account.

Quran 23:102-103

Then, those whose scales (of good deeds) are heavy, - these, they are the successful. (102) And those whose scales (of good deeds) are light, they are those who lose their ownselves, in Hell will they abide.

Quran 57:12-15

On the Day you shall see the believing men and the believing women their light running forward before them and by their right hands. Glad tidings for you this Day! Gardens under which rivers flow (Paradise), to dwell therein forever! Truly, this is the great success! (12) On the Day when the hypocrites men and women will say to the believers: "Wait for us! Let us get something from your light!" It will be said: "Go back to your rear! Then seek a light!" So a wall will be put up between them, with a gate therein. Inside it will be mercy, and outside it will be torment." (13) (The hypocrites) will call the believers: "Were we not with you?" The believers will reply: "Yes! But you led yourselves into temptations, you looked forward for our destruction; you doubted (in Faith); and you were deceived by false desires, till the Command of Allâh came to pass. And the chief deceiver (Satan) deceived you in respect of Allâh." (14) So this Day no ransom shall be taken from you (hypocrites), nor of those who disbelieved, (in the Oneness of Allâh Islâmic Monotheism). Your abode is the Fire, That is your maula (friend), and worst indeed is that destination.

Tafsir of the ayat by ibn kathir

Allah the Exalted states that the believers who spend in charity will come on the Day of Resurrection with their light preceding them in the area of the Gathering, according to the level of their good deeds. As reported from `Abdullah bin Mas`ud: "They will pass over the Sirat according to their deeds. Some of them will have a light as large as a mountain, some as a date tree, some as big as a man in the standing position. The least among them has a light as big as his index finger, it is lit at times and extinguished at other times." Ibn

Abi Hatim and Ibn Jarir collected this Hadith. Ad-Dahhak commented on the Ayah, "Everyone will be given a light on the Day of Resurrection. When they arrive at the Sirat, the light of the hypocrites will be extinguished. When the believers see this, they will be concerned that their light also will be extinguished, just as the light of the hypocrites was. This is when the believers will invoke Allah, `O our Lord! Perfect our light for us.'"

Allah informs us in this Ayah of the terrible horrors, horrendous incidents and tremendous events that will take place on the Day of Resurrection in the Gathering Area. No one will be saved on that Day, except those who believed in Allah and His Messenger, obeyed Allah's commands and avoided His prohibitions. Al-`Awfi, Ad-Dahhak and others reported from Ibn `Abbas: "When the people are gathering in darkness, Allah will send light, and when the believers see the light they will march towards it. This light will be their guide from Allah to Paradise. When the hypocrites see the believers following the light, they will follow them. However, Allah will extinguish the light for the hypocrites. Al-Hasan and Qatadah said that the wall mentioned here is located between Paradise and Hellfire. Qatadah said, "They were deceived by Ash-Shaytan. By Allah! They remained deceived until Allah cast them into Hellfire." The meaning here is that the believers will answer the hypocrites by saying, "You were with us in bodies which were heartless and devoid of intentions. You were cast in doubt and suspicion. You were showing off for people and remembered Allah, little." Mujahid commented, "The hypocrites were with the believers in this life, marrying from among each other, yet betraying them even when they were associating with them. They were dead. They will both be given a light on the Day of Resurrection, but the light of the hypocrites will be extinguished when they reach the wall; this is when the two camps separate and part!"

Quran 57:28

O you who believe [in Mûsa (Moses) (i.e. Jews) and 'Īsā (Jesus) (i.e. Christians)]! Fear Allâh, and believe in His Messenger (Muhammad), He will give you a double portion of His Mercy, and He will give you a light by which you shall walk (straight), and He will forgive you. And Allâh is Oft-Forgiving, Most Merciful.

Quran 66:8

O you who believe! Turn to Allâh with sincere repentance! It may be that your Lord will expiate from you your sins, and admit you into Gardens under which rivers flow (Paradise) the Day that Allâh will not disgrace the Prophet (Muhammad) and those who believe with him, Their Light will run forward before them and (with their Records — Books of deeds) in their right hands They will say: "Our Lord! Keep perfect our Light for us [and do not put it off till we cross over the Sirât (a slippery bridge over the Hell) safely] and grant us forgiveness. Verily, You are Able to do all things

Narrated Abu Huraira:

Allah's Messenger said, "Whoever has wronged his brother, should ask for his pardon (before his death), as (in the Hereafter) there will be neither a Dinar nor a Dirham. (He should secure pardon in this life) before some of his good deeds are taken and paid to his brother, or, if he has done no good deeds, some of the bad deeds of his brother are taken to be loaded on him (in the Hereafter).

Source: Sahih Bukhari 6534

Narrated Masruq:

"'Aishah recited this Ayah: The Day when the earth will be changed to another earth (14:48). She said: 'O Messenger of Allah! Where will the people be?' He said: 'Upon the Sirat.'"

Source: Jami at-Tirmidhi

English reference : Vol. 5, Book 44, Hadith 3121

Graded Sahih by Darussalam

Abu Sa'eed narrated that the Messenger of Allah (ﷺ) said:

"The Sirat will be placed across Hell, on thorns like the thorns of Sa'dan plant. Then the people will cross it. Some will pass over safe and sound, some will be detained, and some will fall in headfirst."

Source: Sunan ibn Majah

English reference : Vol. 5, Book 37, Hadith 4280

Graded Hasan by Darussalam

It is narrated on the authority of Abu Sa'id al-Khudri:

We said: Messenger of Allah, shall we see our Lord? The Messenger of Allah said: Do you feel any trouble in seeing the sun on a cloudless day? We said: No. And the remaining part of the hadith has been narrated to the end like the hadith transmitted by Hafs b. Maisara with the addition of these words: Without the deed that they did or any good that they had sent before. It would be said to them: For you is whatever you see (in it) and with it the like of it. Abu Sa'id said: I have come to know that the bridge would be thinner even than the hair and sharper than the sword; and in the hadith narrated by Laith these words are not found: They would say, O our Lord! Thou hast bestowed upon us (favors) which thou didst not bestow on anyone else in the world.

Source: Sahih Muslim 183 b

Graded Hasan by Darussalam

It was narrated that 'Ata bin Yazid said:

"I was sitting with Abu Hurairah and Abu Sa'eed. One of them narrated the hadith about intercession and the other was listening. He said: 'Then the angels will come and intercede, and the messengers will intercede.' And he mentioned the Sirat, and said: "The Messenger of Allah said: 'I will be the first one to cross it, and when Allah has finished passing judgment among His creation, and has brought forth from the Fire those whom He wants to bring forth, Allah will command the angels and the messengers to intercede, and they will be recognized by their signs, for the Fire will consume all of the son of Adam apart from the

place of prostration. Then the water of life will be poured on them, and they will grow like seeds on the banks of a rainwater stream."

Source: Sunan an-Nasa'i 1140 Graded Sahih by Darussalam

Abu Hurairah narrated that the Messenger of Allah said:

"Allah will gather mankind on the Day of Resurrection on a single plane, then the Lord of the Worlds will come to them and say: 'Let every person follow what they used to worship.' So to the worshipper of the cross, his cross shall be symbolized to him, and to the worshipper of images his images, and to the worshipper of fire his fire. They will follow what they used to worship, and the Muslims will remain. Then the Lord of the Worlds will come to them and say: 'Do you not follow the people?' So they will say: 'We seek refuge in Allah from you, we seek refuge in Allah from you, Allah is our Lord, and we shall remain here until we see our Lord.' And He orders them and makes them firm.' "They said: "And you will see Him, O Messenger of Allah?" He said: "Are you harmed in seeing the moon on the night of a full moon?" They said: "No, O Messenger of Allah." He said: "So you will not be harmed in seeing Him at that hour. Then He will conceal Himself, then He will come, and He will make them recognize Him, then He will say: "I am your Lord, so follow Me." So the Muslims will arise and the Sirat shall be placed, and they shall be placed, and they shall pass by it the like of excellent horses and camels and their statement upon it shall be, "Grant them safety, grant them safety." And the people of Fire shall remain, then a party of them shall be cast down into it, and it shall be said (to the Fire): 'Have you become full?' So it shall say: Is there more? Then a party of them shall be cast down into it, and it shall be said: 'Have you

become full?' So it shall say: Is there more? Until when they are all included into it, Ar-Rahman (the Most-Merciful) shall place His foot in it and its sides shall be all brought together, then He will say: 'Enough.' It will say 'Enough, enough.' So when Allah, the Exalted, has admitted the people of Paradise into Paradise and the people of Fire into Fire"- [He said:]- "Death shall be brought in by the collar and stood on the wall that is between the people of Paradise and the people of the Fire, then it will be said: 'O people of Paradise!' They will come near, afraid. Then it will be said: 'O people of the Fire!' They will come rejoicing, hoping for intercession. Then it will be said to the people of Paradise and the people of the Fire: 'Do you recognize this?' So they will-both of them-say: 'We recognize it. It is Death which was given charge of us,' so it will be laid down and slaughtered upon the wall [the one that is between Paradise and the Fire], then it will be said: 'O people of Paradise! Everlasting life without death!' And 'O people of the Fire! Everlasting life without death!'"

Source: Jami at-Tirmidhi

English reference : Vol. 4, Book 12, Hadith 2557

Graded Sahih by Darussalam

Narrated Abu Huraira:

The people said, "O Allah's Messenger! Shall we see our Lord on the Day of Resurrection?" He replied, "Do you have any doubt in seeing the full moon on a clear (not cloudy) night?" They replied, "No, O Allah's Messenger!" He said, "Do you have any doubt in seeing the sun when there are no clouds?" They replied in the negative. He said, "You will see Allah (your Lord) in the same way. On the Day of Resurrection, people will be gathered and He will order the people to follow what they used to worship. So some of them will follow the sun, some will follow the moon, and some will follow other deities; and only this nation (Muslims) will be left with its hypocrites. Allah will come to them and say, 'I am Your Lord.' They will say, 'We shall stay in this place till our Lord comes to us and when our Lord will come, we will recognize Him. Then Allah will come to them again and say, 'I am your Lord.' They will say, 'You are our Lord.' Allah will call them, and As-Sirat (a bridge) will be laid across Hell and I (Muhammad) shall be the first amongst the Apostles to cross it with my followers. Nobody except the Apostles will then be able to speak and they will be saying then, 'O Allah! Save us. O Allah Save us.' There will be hooks like the thorns of Sa'dan in Hell. Have you seen the thorns of Sa'dan?" The people said, "Yes." He said, "These hooks will be like the thorns of Sa'dan but nobody except Allah knows their greatness in size and these will entangle the people according to their deeds; some of them will fall and stay in Hell forever; others will receive punishment (torn into small pieces) and will get out of Hell, till when Allah intends mercy on whomever He likes amongst the people of Hell, He will order the angels to take out of Hell those who worshipped none but Him alone. The angels will take them out by recognizing them from the traces of prostrations, for Allah has forbidden the (Hell) fire to eat away those traces. So they will come out of the Fire, it will eat away from the whole of the human body except the marks of the prostrations. At that time they will come out of the Fire as mere skeletons. The Water of Life will be poured on them and as a result they will grow like the seeds growing on the bank of flowing water. Then when Allah had finished from the Judgments amongst his creations, one man will *be left between Hell and Paradise and he will be the last man from the people of Hell to enter paradise. He will be facing Hell, and will say, 'O Allah! Turn my face from the fire as its wind has dried me and its steam has burnt me.' Allah will ask him, "Will you ask for anything more in case this favor is granted to you?' He will say, "No by Your (Honor) Power!" And he will give to his Lord (Allah) what he will of the pledges and the covenants. Allah will then turn his face from the Fire. When he will face Paradise and will see its charm, he will remain quiet as long as Allah will. He then will say, 'O my Lord! Let me go to the gate of Paradise.' Allah will ask him, 'Didn't you give pledges and make covenants (to the effect) that you would not ask for anything more than what you requested at first?' He will say, 'O my Lord! Do not make me the most wretched, amongst Your creatures.' Allah will say, 'If this request is granted, will you then ask for anything else?' He will say, 'No! By Your Power! I shall not ask for anything else.' Then he will give to his Lord what He will of the pledges and the covenants. Allah will then let him go to the gate of Paradise. On reaching then and seeing its life, charm, and pleasure, he will remain quiet as long as Allah wills and then will say, 'O my Lord ! Let me enter Paradise.' Allah will say, May Allah be merciful unto you, O son of Adam! How treacherous you are! Haven't you made covenants and given pledges that you will not ask for anything more than what you have been given?' He will say, 'O my Lord! Do not make me the most wretched amongst Your creatures.' So Allah will laugh and allow him to enter Paradise and will ask him to request as much as he likes. He will do so till all his desires have been fulfilled . Then Allah will say, 'Request more of such and such things.' Allah will remind him and when all his desires and wishes; have been fulfilled, Allah will say "All this is granted to* *you and a similar amount besides." Abu Sa`id Al-Khudri, said to Abu Huraira, 'Allah's Messenger said, "Allah said, 'That is for you and ten times more like it.' "Abu Huraira said, "I do not remember from Allah's Messenger except (his saying), 'All this is granted to you and a similar amount besides." Abu Sa`id said, "I heard him saying, 'That is for you and ten times more the like of it."*

Source: Sahih al-Bukhari 806

Abu Ad-Dardh narrated that the Messenger of Allah said:

"Nothing is heavier on the believer's Scale on the Day of Judgment than good character. For indeed Allah, Most High, is angered by the shameless obscene person."

Source: Jami` at-Tirmidhi 2002 Graded Sahih by Darussalam

Abu Ad-Dardh narrated that the Messenger of Allah said:

"Nothing is placed on the Scale that is heavier than good character. Indeed the person with good character will have attained the rank of the person of fasting and prayer."

Source: Jami` at-Tirmidhi 2003

Graded Hasan by Darussalam

Abu Hurairah narrated that:

The Messenger of Allah said: "There are two statements that are light on the tongue, heavy on the Scale, and beloved to Ar-Raḥmān: "Glory is to Allah and the praise; Glory is to Allah, the

Magnificent. (Subḥān Allāhi wa biḥamdih, Subḥān Allāhil-Aẓīm)"

Source: Jami` at-Tirmidhi 3467 Graded Sahih by Darussalam

Narrated Abu Sa`id Al-Khudri:

Allah's Messenger said, "When the believers pass safely over (the bridge across) Hell, they will be stopped at a bridge in between Hell and Paradise where they will retaliate upon each other for the injustices done among them in the world, and when they get purified of all their sins, they will be admitted into Paradise. By Him in Whose Hands the life of Muhammad is everybody will recognize his dwelling in Paradise better than he recognizes his dwelling in this world."

Source: Sahih al-Bukhari 2440

Narrated Mu'adh ibn Anas:

The Prophet said: If anyone guards a believer from a hypocrite, Allah will send an angel who will guard his flesh on the Day of Resurrection from the fire of Jahannam; but if anyone attacks a Muslim saying something by which he wishes to disgrace him, he will be restrained by Allah on the bridge over Jahannam till he is acquitted of what he said.

Source: Sunan Abi Dawud 4883 Graded Hasan by Albani

Jabir ibn 'Abdullah said:

"I purchased a camel and rode it hard for a month until I reached Syria. 'Abdullah ibn Unays was there, and I sent word to him, saying, 'Jabir is at the door.' The messenger returned and said, 'Jabir ibn 'Abdullah?' 'Yes,' I replied. So 'Abdullah came out and embraced me. I said, 'A hadith reached me which I had not heard before and I feared that one of us might die.'" He went on, "I heard the Prophet, may Allah bless him and grant him peace, say, 'Allah will gather His slaves or people naked, uncircumcised, without anything.' We asked, 'What is meant by "without anything"?' The Prophet said, 'They will have nothing with them.' (The Prophet went on,) 'They will be called by a voice that is heard from afar (and I think that he said, 'as if it was from close at hand'), saying, "I am the King. None of the people of the Garden will enter the Garden while any of the people of the Fire are seeking him for some injustice he did to him. None of the people of the Fire will enter the Fire while any of the people of the Garden are seeking him for an injustice he did to him."' I asked, 'How is this? We come to Allah naked and without any worldly goods?' He said, 'This applies to good actions and evil actions.'

Source: Al-Adab Al-Mufrad 970 Graded Hasan by Albani

Abu Huraira reported Allah's Messenger (ﷺ) as saying:

Do you know who is poor? They (the Companions of the Prophet) said: A poor man amongst us is one who has neither dirham with him nor wealth. He (the Prophet) said: The poor of my Umma would be he who would come on the Day of Resurrection with prayers and fasts and Zakat but (he would find himself bankrupt on that day as he would have exhausted his funds of virtues) since he hurled abuses upon others, brought calumny against others and unlawfully consumed the wealth of others and shed the blood of others and beat others, and his virtues would be credited to the account of one (who suffered at his hand). And if his good deeds fall short to clear the account, then his sins would be entered in (his account) and he would be thrown in the Hell-Fire.

Source: Sahih Muslim 2581

It is narrated on the authority of Abu Huraira and Hudhaifa that the Messenger of Allah (ﷺ) said:

Allah, the Blessed and Exalted, would gather people. The believers would stand till the Paradise would be brought near them. They would come to Adam and say: O our father, open for us the Paradise. He would say: What turned ye out from the Paradise was the sin of your father Adam. I am not in a position to do that; better go to my son Ibrahim, the Friend of Allah. He (the Prophet) said: He (Ibrahim) would say: I am not in a position to do that. Verily I had been the Friend (of Allah) from beyond, beyond; you better approach Moses (peace be upon him) with whom Allah conversed. They would come to Moses (peace be upon him), but he would say: I am not in a position to do that; you better go to Jesus, the Word of Allah and His Spirit. Jesus (peace be upon him) would say: I am not in a position to do that. So they would come to Muhammad. He would then be permitted (to open the door of Paradise). Trustworthiness and kinship would be dispatched, and these would stand on the right and left of the Path and the first of you would pass with (the swiftness) of lightning. He (the narrator) said: I said, O thou who art far dearer to me than my father and my mother I which thing is like the passing of lightning? He said: Have you not seen lightning, how it passes and then comes back within the twinkling of an eye? Then (they would pass) like the passing of the wind, then like the passing of a bird, and the

hastening of persons would be according to their deeds, and your
Apostle would be standing on the Path saying: Save, O my Lord,
save. (The people would go on passing) till the deeds of the
servants would be failing in strength, till a man would come who
would find it hard to go along (that Path) but crawlingly. He (the
narrator) said: And on the sides of the Path hooks would be
suspended ready to catch anyone whom these would be required (to
catch). There would be those who would somehow or other succeed
in traversing that Path and some would be piled up in Hell. By
Him in Whose Hand is the life of Abu Huraira it would take one
seventy years to fathom the depth of Hell.

Source: Sahih Muslim 195

Narrated Abu Sa'id Al-Khudri:

We said, "O Allah's Messenger! Shall we see our Lord on the Day
of Resurrection?" He said, "Do you have any difficulty in seeing
the sun and the moon when the sky is clear?" We said, "No." He
said, "So you will have no difficulty in seeing your Lord on that
Day as you have no difficulty in seeing the sun and the moon (in a
clear sky)." The Prophet then said, "Somebody will then announce,
'Let every nation follow what they used to worship.' So the
companions of the cross will go with their cross, and the idolators
(will go) with their idols, and the companions of every god (false
deities) (will go) with their god, till there remain those who used to
worship Allah, both the obedient ones and the mischievous ones,
and some of the people of the Scripture. Then Hell will be presented
to them as if it were a mirage. Then it will be said to the Jews,
"What did you use to worship?' They will reply, 'We used to
worship Ezra, the son of Allah.' It will be said to them, 'You are

liars, for Allah has neither a wife nor a son. What do you want (now)?' They will reply, 'We want You to provide us with water.' Then it will be said to them 'Drink,' and they will fall down in Hell (instead). Then it will be said to the Christians, 'What did you use to worship?'

They will reply, 'We used to worship Messiah, the son of Allah.' It will be said, 'You are liars, for Allah has neither a wife nor a son. What: do you want (now)?' They will say, 'We want You to provide us with water.' It will be said to them, 'Drink,' and they will fall down in Hell (instead). When there remain only those who used to worship Allah (Alone), both the obedient ones and the mischievous ones, it will be said to them, 'What keeps you here when all the people have gone?' They will say, 'We parted with them (in the world) when we were in greater need of them than we are today, we heard the call of one proclaiming, 'Let every nation follow what they used to worship,' and now we are waiting for our Lord.' Then the Almighty will come to them in a shape other than the one which they saw the first time, and He will say, 'I am your Lord,' and they will say, 'You are not our Lord.' And none will speak: to Him then but the Prophets, and then it will be said to them, 'Do you know any sign by which you can recognize Him?' They will say. 'The Shin,' and so Allah will then uncover His Shin whereupon every believer will prostrate before Him and there will remain those who used to prostrate before Him just for showing off and for gaining good reputation. These people will try to prostrate but their backs will be rigid like one piece of a wood (and they will not be able to prostrate). Then the bridge will be laid across Hell." We, the companions of the Prophet said, "O Allah's Messenger! What is the bridge?'

He said, "It is a slippery (bridge) on which there are clamps and (Hooks like) a thorny seed that is wide at one side and narrow at the other and has thorns with bent ends. Such a thorny seed is found in Najd and is called As-Sa'dan. Some of the believers will cross the bridge as quickly as the wink of an eye, some others as quick as lightning, a strong wind, fast horses or she-camels. So some will be safe without any harm; some will be safe after receiving some scratches, and some will fall down into Hell (Fire). The last person will cross by being dragged (over the bridge)." The Prophet said, "You (Muslims) cannot be more pressing in claiming from me a right that has been clearly proved to be yours than the believers in interceding with Almighty for their (Muslim) brothers on that Day, when they see themselves safe.

They will say, 'O Allah! (Save) our brothers (for they) used to pray with us, fast with us and also do good deeds with us.' Allah will say, 'Go and take out (of Hell) anyone in whose heart you find faith equal to the weight of one (gold) Dinar.' Allah will forbid the Fire to burn the faces of those sinners. They will go to them and find some of them in Hell (Fire) up to their feet, and some up to the middle of their legs. So they will take out those whom they will recognize and then they will return, and Allah will say (to them), 'Go and take out (of Hell) anyone in whose heart you find faith equal to the weight of one half Dinar.' They will take out whomever they will recognize and return, and then Allah will say, 'Go and take out (of Hell) anyone in whose heart you find faith equal to the weight of an atom (or a smallest ant), and so they will take out all those whom they will recognize." Abu Sa'id said: If you do not believe me then read the Verse:--

'Surely! Allah wrongs not even of the weight of an atom (or a smallest ant) but if there is any good (done) He doubles it.' (4.40) The Prophet added, "Then the prophets and Angels and the believers will intercede, and (last of all) the Almighty (Allah) will say, 'Now remains My Intercession. He will then hold a handful of the Fire from which He will take out some people whose bodies have been burnt, and they will be thrown into a river at the entrance of Paradise, called the water of life.

They will grow on its banks, as a seed carried by the torrent grows. You have noticed how it grows beside a rock or beside a tree, and how the side facing the sun is usually green while the side facing the shade is white. Those people will come out (of the River of Life) like pearls, and they will have (golden) necklaces, and then they will enter Paradise whereupon the people of Paradise will say, 'These are the people emancipated by the Beneficent. He has admitted them into Paradise without them having done any good deeds and without sending forth any good (for themselves).' Then it will be said to them, 'For you is what you have seen and its equivalent as well.'"

Source: Sahih al-Bukhari 7439

Narrated Abu Sa`id Al-Khudri:

Allah's Messenger said, "When the believers pass safely over (the bridge across) Hell, they will be stopped at a bridge in between Hell and Paradise where they will retaliate upon each other for the injustices done among them in the world, and when they get purified of all their sins, they will be admitted into Paradise. By Him in Whose Hands the life of Muhammad is everybody will recognize his dwelling in Paradise better than he recognizes his dwelling in this world."

Source: Sahih al-Bukhari 2440

Data on Paradise

Quran 2:25

And give glad tidings to those who believe and do righteous good deeds, that for them will be Gardens under which rivers flow (Paradise). Every time they will be provided with a fruit therefrom, they will say: "This is what we were provided with before," and they will be given things in resemblance (i.e. in the same form but different in taste) and they shall have therein Azwâjun Mutahharatun (purified mates or wives), and they will abide therein forever.

Quran 2:82

And those who believe (in the Oneness of Allâh swt- Islâmic Monotheism) and do righteous good deeds, they are dwellers of Paradise, they will dwell therein forever.

Quran 3:14-15

Beautified for men is the love of things they covet; women, children, much of gold and silver (wealth), branded beautiful horses, cattle and well-tilled land. This is the pleasure of the present world's life; but Allâh has the excellent return (Paradise with flowing rivers) with Him. (14) Say: "Shall I inform you of things far better than those? For Al-Muttaqûn (the pious) there are Gardens (Paradise) with their Lord, underneath which rivers flow. Therein (is their) eternal (home) and Azwâjun

Mutahharatun (purified mates or wives), And Allâh will be pleased with them. And Allâh is All-Seer of the (His) slaves"

Quran 3:134-136

Those who spend [in Allâh's Cause] in prosperity and in adversity, who repress anger, and who pardon men; verily, Allâh loves Al-Muhsinûn (the good - doers). (134) And those who, when they have committed Fahishah (illegal sexual intercourse) or wronged themselves with evil, remember Allâh and ask forgiveness for their sins; - and none can forgive sins but Allâh - And do not persist in what (wrong) they have done, while they know. (135) For such, the reward is Forgiveness from their Lord, and Gardens with rivers flowing underneath (Paradise), wherein they shall abide forever. How excellent is this reward for the doers (who do righteous deeds according to Allâh's Orders).

Quran 3:198

But, for those who fear their Lord, are Gardens under which rivers flow (in Paradise); therein are they to dwell (for ever), an entertainment from Allâh; and that which is with Allâh is the Best for Al-Abrâr (the pious believers of Islamic Monotheism).

Quran 4:13

These are the limits (set by) Allâh, and whosoever obeys Allâh and His Messenger (Muhammad) will be admitted to Gardens under which rivers flow (in Paradise), to abide therein, and that will be the great success.

Quran 4:31

If you avoid the great sins which you are forbidden to do, We shall expiate from you your (small) sins, and admit you to a Noble Entrance (i.e. Paradise).

Quran 4:57

But those who believe (in the Oneness of Allâh - Islâmic Monotheism) and do deeds of righteousness, We shall admit them to Gardens under which rivers flow (Paradise), abiding therein forever. Therein they shall have Azwâjun Mutahharatun [purified mates or wives] and We shall admit them to shades wide and ever deepening (Paradise).

Quran 4:69

And whoso obeys Allâh and the Messenger (Muhammad), then they will be in the company of those on whom Allâh has bestowed His Grace, of the Prophets, the Siddiqûn (those followers of the Prophets who were first and foremost to believe in them, like Abu Bakr As¬Siddiq), the martyrs, and the righteous. And how excellent these companions are!

Quran 4:122

But those who believe (in the Oneness of Allâh - Islâmic Monotheism) and do deeds of righteousness, We shall admit them to the Gardens under which rivers flow (i.e. in Paradise) to dwell therein forever. Allâh's Promise is the Truth, and whose words can be truer than those of Allâh?

Quran 4:124

And whoever does righteous good deeds, male or female, and is a (true) believer [in the Oneness of Allâh (Muslim)], such will enter Paradise and not the least injustice, even to the size of a speck on the back of a date-stone, will be done to them.

Quran 5:9

Allâh has promised those who believe (in the Oneness of Allâh - Islâmic Monotheism) and do deeds of righteousness, that for them there is forgiveness and a great reward (i.e. Paradise)

Quran 5:65

And if only the people of the Scripture (Jews and Christians) had believed (in Muhammad) and warded off evil (sin, ascribing partners to Allâh) and had become Al¬Muttaqûn (the pious) We would indeed have expiated from them their sins and admitted them to Gardens of pleasure (in Paradise).

Quran 5:85

So because of what they said, Allâh rewarded them Gardens under which rivers flow (in Paradise), they will abide therein forever. Such is the reward of Al-Muhsinûn (the good-doers).

Quran 6:126-127

And this is the Path of your Lord (the Qur'ân and Islâm) leading Straight. We have detailed Our Revelations for a people who take heed. (126) For them will be the home of peace (Paradise) with their Lord. And He will be their Walî (Helper and Protector) because of what they used to do.

Quran 7:42-44

But those who believed (in the Oneness of Allâh - Islâmic Monotheism), and worked righteousness - We tax not any person beyond his scope, — such are the dwellers of Paradise. They will abide therein. (42) And We shall remove from their breasts any (mutual) hatred or sense of injury (which they had, if at all, in the life of this world); rivers flowing under them, and they will say: "All the praises and thanks be to Allâh, Who has guided us to this, and never could we have found guidance, were it not that Allâh had guided us! Indeed, the Messengers of our Lord did come with the truth." And it will be cried out to them: "This is the Paradise which you have inherited for what you used to do." (43) And the dwellers of Paradise will call out to the dwellers of the Fire (saying): "We have indeed found true what our Lord had promised us; have you also found true, what your Lord promised (warnings)?" They shall say: "Yes." Then a crier will proclaim between them: "The Curse of Allâh is on the Zâlimûn (polytheists and wrong-doers),"

Quran 9:72

Allâh has promised the believers -men and women, - Gardens under which rivers flow to dwell therein forever, and beautiful mansions in Gardens of 'Adn (Eden Paradise). But the greatest bliss is the Good Pleasure of Allâh. That is the supreme success.

Quran 9:88-89

But the Messenger (Muhammad) and those who believed with him (in Islâmic Monotheism) strove hard and fought with their wealth and their lives (in Allâh's Cause). Such are they for whom are the good things, and it is they who will be successful. (88) For them

Allâh has got ready Gardens (Paradise) under which rivers flow, to dwell therein forever. That is the supreme success.

Quran 9:111

Verily, Allâh has purchased of the believers their lives and their properties for (the price) that theirs shall be the Paradise. They fight in Allâh's Cause, so they kill (others) and are killed. It is a promise in truth which is binding on Him in the Taurât (Torah) and the Injeel and the Qur'ân. And who is truer to his covenant than Allâh? Then rejoice in the bargain which you have concluded. That is the supreme success.

Quran 10:9-10

Verily, those who believe and do deeds of righteousness, their Lord will guide them through their Faith; under them will flow rivers in the Gardens of Delight (Paradise). (9) Their way of request therein will be Subhânaka Allâhumma (Glory to You, O Allâh!) and Salâm (peace, safety from evil) will be their greetings therein (Paradise)! and the close of their request will be: Al-Hamdu Lillâhi Rabbil-'Alamîn [All the praises and thanks are to Allâh, the Lord of 'Alamîn (mankind, jinn and all that exists)].

Quran 10:26

For those who have done good is the best (reward, i.e. Paradise) and even more (i.e. having the honour of glancing at the Countenance of Allâh) Neither darkness nor dust nor any humiliating disgrace shall cover their faces. They are the dwellers of Paradise, they will abide therein forever.

Quran 11:23

Verily, those who believe (in the Oneness of Allâh - Islâmic Monotheism) and do righteous good deeds, and humble themselves (in repentance and obedience) before their Lord, - they will be dwellers of Paradise to dwell therein forever.

Quran 11:108

And those who are blessed, they will be in Paradise, abiding therein for all the time that the heavens and the earth endure, except as your Lord wills, a gift without an end.

Quran 13:20-24

Those who fulfil the Covenant of Allâh and break not the Mîthâq (bond, treaty, covenant); (20) And those who join that which Allâh has commanded to be joined (i.e. they are good to their relatives and do not sever the bond of kinship), and fear their Lord, and dread the terrible reckoning (i.e. abstain from all kinds of sins and evil deeds which Allâh has forbidden and perform all kinds of good deeds which Allâh has ordained). (21) And those who remain patient, seeking their Lord's Countenance, perform As-Salât (Iqâmat-as-Salât), and spend out of that which We have bestowed on them, secretly and openly, and defend evil with good, for such there is a good end; (22) 'Adn (Eden) Paradise (everlasting Gardens), which they shall enter and (also) those who acted righteously from among their fathers, and their wives, and their offspring. And angels shall enter unto them from every gate (saying): (23) "Salâmun 'Alaikum (peace be upon you) for that you persevered in patience! Excellent indeed is the final home!"

Quran 13:29

Those who believed (in the Oneness of Allâh - Islâmic Monotheism), and work righteousness, Tûbâ (all kinds of happiness or name of a tree in Paradise) is for them and a beautiful place of (final) return.

Quran 13:35

The description of the Paradise which the Muttaqûn (pious): have been promised! -Underneath it rivers flow, its provision is eternal and so is its shade, this is the end (final destination) of the Muttaqûn (pious), and the end (final destination) of the disbelievers is Fire.

Quran 14:23

And those who believed (in the Oneness of Allâh and His Messengers and whatever they brought) and did righteous deeds, will be made to enter Gardens under which rivers flow, - to dwell therein forever (i.e.in Paradise), with the permission of their Lord. Their greeting therein will be: Salâm (peace!)

Quran 14:45-48

"Truly! The Muttaqûn (pious and righteous persons) will be amidst Gardens and water-springs (Paradise). (45) "(It will be said to them): 'Enter therein (Paradise), in peace and security.' (46) "And We shall remove from their breasts any deep feeling of bitterness (that they may have), (So they will be like) brothers facing each other on thrones. (47) "No sense of fatigue shall touch them, nor shall they (ever) be asked to leave it."

Quran 16:30-31

*And (when) it is said to those who are the Muttaqûn (pious)
"What is it that your Lord has sent down?" They say: "That which
is good." For those who do good in this world, there is good, and
the home of the Hereafter will be better. And excellent indeed will
be the home (i.e. Paradise) of the Muttaqûn (pious). (30) 'Adn
(Eden) Paradise (Gardens of Eternity) which they will enter, under
which rivers flow, they will have therein all that they wish. Thus
Allâh rewards the Muttaqûn (pious).*

Quran 16:96-97

*Whatever is with you, will be exhausted, and whatever is with
Allâh (of good deeds) will remain. And those who are patient, We
will certainly pay them a reward in proportion to the best of what
they used to do. (96) Whoever works righteousness, whether male
or female, while he (or she) is a true believer (of Islâmic
Monotheism) verily, to him We will give a good life (in this world
with respect, contentment and lawful provision), and We shall pay
them certainly a reward in proportion to the best of what they used
to do (i.e. Paradise in the Hereafter).*

Quran 17:9

*Verily, this Qur'ân guides to that which is most just and right and
gives glad tidings to the believers (in the Oneness of Allâh and His
Messenger, Muhammad). who work deeds of righteousness, that
they shall have a great reward (Paradise).*

Quran 17:19-21

*And whoever desires the Hereafter and strives for it, with the
necessary effort due for it (i.e. do righteous deeds of Allâh's*

Obedience) while he is a believer (in the Oneness of Allâh –
Islâmic Monotheism), then such are the ones whose striving shall
be appreciated, (thanked and rewarded by Allâh). (19) On - each
these as well as those - We bestow from the Bounties of your Lord.
And the Bounties of your Lord can never be forbidden. (20) See
how We prefer one above another (in this world) and verily, the
Hereafter will be greater in degrees and greater in preference

Quran 18:1-3

All the praises and thanks are to Allâh, Who has sent down to His
slave (Muhammad) the Book (the Qur'ân), and has not placed
therein any crookedness. (1) Straight to give warning (to the
disbelievers) of a severe punishment from Him, and to give glad
tidings to the believers (in the Oneness of Allâh Islâmic
Monotheism), who do righteous - deeds, that they shall have a fair
reward (i.e. Paradise). (2) They shall abide therein forever.

Quran 18:30-31

Verily As for those who believed and did righteous deeds, certainly
We shall not make to be lost the reward of anyone who does his
(righteous) deeds in the most perfect manner. (30) These! For them
will be 'Adn (Eden) Paradise (everlasting Gardens); wherein rivers
flow underneath them, therein they will be adorned with bracelets
of gold, and they will wear green garments of fine and thick silk.
They will recline therein on raised thrones. How good is the
reward, and what an excellent Murtafaq (dwelling, resting place)!

Quran 18:107-108

Verily! those who believe (in the Oneness of Allâh - Islâmic Monotheism) and do righteous deeds, shall have the Gardens of Al-Firdaus (the Paradise) for their entertainment. (107) "Wherein they shall dwell (forever). No desire will they have for removal therefrom."

Quran 19:60-63

Except those who repent and believe (in the Oneness of Allâh and His Messenger Muhammad), and work righteousness. Such will enter Paradise and they will not be wronged in aught. (60) (They will enter) 'Adn (Eden) Paradise (everlasting Gardens), which the Most Gracious (Allâh) has promised to His slaves in the unseen: Verily! His Promise must come to pass. (61) They shall not hear therein (in Paradise) any Laghw (dirty, false, evil vain talk), but only Salâm (salutations of peace). And they will have therein their sustenance, morning and afternoon. (62) Such is the Paradise which We shall give as an inheritance to those of Our slaves who have been Al-Muttaqûn (pious and righteous persons).

Quran 20:75-76

But whoever comes to Him (Allâh) as a believer (in the Oneness of Allâh), and has done righteous good deeds, for such are the high ranks (in the Hereafter), — (75)'Adn (Eden) Paradise (everlasting Gardens), under which rivers flow, wherein they will abide forever: such is the reward of those who purify themselves (by abstaining from all kinds of sins and evil deeds which Allâh has forbidden and by doing all that which Allâh has ordained).

Quran 22:14

Truly, Allâh will admit those who believe (in Islâmic Monotheism) and do righteous good deeds (according to the Qur'ân and the Sunnah) to Gardens underneath which rivers flow (in Paradise). Verily, Allâh does what He wills.

Quran 22:23

Truly, Allâh will admit those who believe (in the Oneness of Allâh - Islâmic Monotheism) and do righteous good deeds, to Gardens underneath which rivers flow (in Paradise), wherein they will be adorned with bracelets of gold and pearls and their garments therein will be of silk.

Quran 22:50

So those who believe (in the Oneness of Allâh - Islâmic Monotheism) and do righteous good deeds, for them is forgiveness and Rizqûn Karîm (generous provision, i.e. Paradise).

Quran 23:1-11

Successful indeed are the believers. (1) Those who offer their Salât (prayers) with all solemnity and full submissiveness. (2) And those who turn away from Al-Laghw (dirty, false, evil vain talk, falsehood, and all that Allâh has forbidden). (3) And those who pay the Zakât. (4) And those who guard their chastity (i.e. private parts, from illegal sexual acts). (5) Except from their wives or (slaves) that their right hands possess, - for then, they are free from blame; (6) But whoever seeks beyond that, then those are the transgressors; (7) Those who are faithfully true to their Amanât (all the duties which Allâh has ordained, honesty, moral responsibility and trusts) and to their covenants; (8) And those who strictly guard their (five compulsory congregational) Salawât (prayers) (at their fixed stated hours). (9) These are indeed the inheritors. (10) Who shall inherit the Firdaus (Paradise). They shall dwell therein forever.

Quran 25:10

Blessed is He Who, if He wills, will assign you better than (all) that, - Gardens under which rivers flow (Paradise) and will assign you palaces (i.e. in Paradise).

Quran 25:15-16

Say: (O Muhammad) "Is that (torment) better or the Paradise of Eternity which is promised to the Muttaqûn (pious and righteous persons)?" It will be theirs as a reward and as a final destination. (15) For them there will be therein all that they desire, and they will abide (there forever). It is a promise binding upon your Lord that must be fulfilled.

Quran 25:63-76

And the (faithful) slaves of the Most Gracious (Allâh) are those who walk on the earth in humility and sedateness, and when the foolish address them (with bad words) they reply back with mild words of gentleness. (63) And those who spend the night in worship of their Lord, prostrate and standing (64) And those who say: "Our Lord! Avert from us the torment of Hell. Verily! Its torment is ever an inseparable, permanent punishment." (65) Evil indeed it (Hell) is as an abode and as a place to rest in. (66) And those, who, when they spend, are neither extravagant nor niggardly, but hold a medium (way) between those (extremes).

(67) And those who invoke not any other ilâh (god) along with Allâh, nor kill such person as Allâh has forbidden, except for just cause, nor commit illegal sexual intercourse - and whoever does this shall receive the punishment (68) The torment will be doubled to him on the Day of Resurrection, and he will abide therein in disgrace; (69) Except those who repent and believe (in Islâmic Monotheism), and do righteous deeds, for those, Allâh will change their sins into good deeds, and Allâh is Oft-Forgiving, Most Merciful (70) And whosoever repents and does righteous good deeds, then verily, he repents towards Allâh with true repentance. (71) And those who do not witness to falsehood, and if they pass by some evil play or evil talk, they pass by it with dignity. (72) And those who, when they are reminded of the Ayât (proofs, evidences, verses, lessons, signs, revelations, etc.) of their Lord, fall not deaf and blind thereat. (73) And those who say: "Our Lord! Bestow on us from our wives and our offspring the comfort of our eyes, and make us leaders for the Muttaqûn" (pious)." (74) Those will be rewarded with the highest place (in Paradise) because of their patience. Therein they shall be met with greetings and the word of peace and respect. (75) Abiding therein; — excellent it is as an abode, and as a place to dwell.

Quran 29:9

And for those who believe (in the Oneness of Allâh and other articles of Faith) and do righteous good deeds, surely, We shall make them enter with (in the entrance of) the righteous (in Paradise).

Quran 29:58-59

And those who believe (in the Oneness of Allâh Islâmic Monotheism) and do righteous good deeds, to them We shall surely give lofty dwellings in Paradise, underneath which rivers flow, to live therein forever. Excellent is the reward of the workers. (58) Those who are patient, and put their trust (only) in their Lord (Allâh).

Quran 31:8-9

Verily, those who believe (in Islâmic Monotheism) and do righteous good deeds, for them are Gardens of Delight (Paradise). (8) To abide therein. It is a Promise of Allâh in truth. And He is the All¬Mighty, the All¬Wise.

Quran 32:19

As for those who believe (in the Oneness of Allâh Islâmic Monotheism) and do righteous good deeds, for them are Gardens (Paradise) as an entertainment, for what they used to do

Quran 33:35

Verily, the Muslims (those who submit to Allâh in Islâm) men and women, the believers men and women (who believe in Islâmic Monotheism), the men and the women who are obedient (to Allâh), the men and women who are truthful (in their speech and deeds), the men and the women who are patient (in performing all the duties which Allâh has ordered and in abstaining from all that Allâh has forbidden), the men and the women who are humble (before their Lord Allâh), the men and the women who give Sadaqât (i.e. Zakât, and alms), the men and the women who observe Saum (fast) (the obligatory fasting during the month of

Ramadân, and the optional Nawâfil fasting), the men and the women who guard their chastity (from illegal sexual acts) and the men and the women who remember Allâh much with their hearts and tongues. Allâh has prepared for them forgiveness and a great reward (i.e. Paradise)

Quran 34:37

And it is not your wealth, nor your children that bring you nearer to Us (i.e. pleases Allâh), but only he who believes (in the Islâmic Monotheism), and does righteous deeds (will please us); as for such, there will be twofold reward for what they did, and they will reside in the high dwellings (Paradise) in peace and security.

Quran 35:32-35

Then We gave the Book (the Qur'ân) as inheritance to such of Our slaves whom We chose (the followers of Muhammad). Then of them are some who wrong their ownselves, and of them are some who follow a middle course, and of them are some who are, by Allâh's Leave, foremost in good deeds. That (inheritance of the Qur'ân), that is indeed a great grace. (32) 'Adn (Eden) Paradise (everlasting Gardens) will they enter, therein will they be adorned with bracelets of gold and pearls, and their garments there will be of silk. (33) And they will say: "All the praises and thanks are to Allâh, Who has removed from us (all) grief. Verily, our Lord is indeed Oft¬Forgiving, Most Ready to appreciate (good deeds and to recompense). (34) Who, out of His Grace, has lodged us in a home that will last forever; where, toil will touch us not, nor weariness will touch us."

Quran 37:40-60

Save the chosen slaves of Allâh (i.e. the true believers of Islâmic Monotheism). (40) For them there will be a known provision (in Paradise), (41) Fruits; and they shall be honoured, (42) In the Gardens of delight (Paradise), (43) Facing one another on thrones, (44) Round them will be passed a cup of pure wine, − (45) White, delicious to the drinkers, (46) Neither will they have Ghoul (any kind of hurt, abdominal pain, headache, a sin) from that, nor will they suffer intoxication therefrom. (47) And beside them will be Qâsirât-at-Tarf [chaste females (wives), restraining their glances (desiring none except their husbands)], with wide and beautiful eyes. (48) (Delicate and pure) as if they were (hidden) eggs (well) preserved. (49) Then they will turn to one another, mutually questioning. (50) A speaker of them will say: "Verily, I had a companion (in the world), (51) Who used to say: "Are you among those who believe (in resurrection after death). (52) "(That) when we die and become dust and bones, shall we indeed (be raised up) to receive reward or punishment (according to our deeds)?" (53) (The speaker) said: "Will you look down?" (54) So he looked down and saw him in the midst of the Fire. (55) He said: "By Allâh! You have nearly ruined me. (56) "Had it not been for the Grace of my Lord, I would certainly have been among those brought forth (to Hell)." (57) (The dwellers of Paradise will say): "Are we then not to die (any more)? (58) "Except our first death, and we shall not be punished? (after we have entered Paradise)." (59) Truly, this is the supreme success!

Quran 38:49-54

This is a Reminder, and verily, for the Muttaqûn (pious and righteous persons) is a good final return (Paradise), -, (49) 'Adn (Edn) Paradise (everlasting Gardens), whose doors will be opened for them. (50) Therein they will recline; therein they will call for fruits in abundance and drinks; (51) And beside them will be Qasirat-at-Tarf chaste females (wives) restraining their glances (desiring none except their husbands)], (and) of equal ages. (52) This it is what you (Al-Muttaqûn - the pious.) are promised for the Day of Reckoning! (53) (It will be said to them)! Verily, this is Our Provision which will never finish;

Quran 39:20

But those who fear their Lord (Allâh) and keep their duty to Him, for them are built lofty rooms; one above another under which rivers flow (i.e. Paradise). (This is) the Promise of Allâh: and Allâh does not fail in (His) Promise.

Quran 41:8

Truly, those who believe (in the Oneness of Allâh and in His Messenger Muhammad — Islâmic Monotheism) and do righteous good deeds, for them will be an endless reward that will never stop (i.e. Paradise).

Quran 43:71-73

Trays of gold and cups will be passed round them, (there will be) therein all that the inner-selves could desire, and all that the eyes could delight in, and you will abide therein forever. (71) This is the Paradise which you have been made to inherit because of your deeds which you used to do (in the life of the world). (72) Therein for you will be fruits in plenty, of which you will eat (as you desire).

Quran 44:51-57

Verily! The Muttaqûn (pious), will be in place of Security (Paradise) (51) Among Gardens and Springs; (52) Dressed in fine silk and (also) in thick silk, facing each other, (53) So (it will be), and We shall marry them to Hur (fair females) with wide, lovely eyes. (54) They will call therein for every kind of fruit in peace and security; (55) They will never taste death therein except the first death (of this world), and He will save them from the torment of the blazing Fire, (56) As a Bounty from your Lord! That will be the supreme success!

Quran 46:13-14

Verily, those who say: "Our Lord is (only) Allâh," and thereafter stand firm (on the Islâmic Faith of Monotheism) on them shall be no fear, nor shall they grieve. (13) Such shall be the dwellers of Paradise, abiding therein (forever) — a reward for what they used to do.

Quran 47:15

The description of Paradise which the Muttaqûn (pious) have been promised (is that) in it are rivers of water the taste and smell of which are not changed, rivers of milk of which the taste never changes, rivers of wine delicious to those who drink; and rivers of clarified honey (clear and pure) therein for them is every kind of fruit; and forgiveness from their Lord. (Are these) like those who shall dwell forever in the Fire, and be given, to drink, boiling water, so that it cuts up their bowels?

Quran 48:5

That He may admit the believing men and the believing women to Gardens under which rivers flow (i.e. Paradise), to abide therein forever, and He may expiate from them their sins, and that is with Allâh, a supreme success

Quran 55:46-76

But for him who fears the standing before his Lord, there will be two Gardens (i.e. in Paradise). (46) Then which of the Blessings of your Lord will you both (jinn and men) deny? (47) With spreading branches. (48) Then which of the Blessings of your Lord will you both (jinn and men) deny? (49) In them (both) will be two springs flowing (free). (50) Then which of the Blessings of your Lord will you both (jinn and men) deny? (51) In them (both) will be every kind of fruit in pairs. (52) Then which of the Blessings of your Lord will you both (jinn and men) deny? (53) Reclining upon the couches lined with silk brocade, and the fruits of the two Gardens will be near at hand. (54) Then which of the Blessings of your Lord will you both (jinn and men) deny? (55) Wherein both will be Qasirat-ut-Tarf [chaste fmales (wives) restraining their glances, desiring none except their husbands], with whom no man or jinni has had Tameth before them. (56) Then which of the Blessings of your Lord will you both (jinn and men) deny? (57) (In beauty) they are like rubies and coral. (58) Then which of the Blessings of your Lord will you both (jinn and men) deny? (59) Is there any reward for good other than good? (60) Then which of the Blessings of your Lord will you both (jinn and men) deny? (61) And besides these two, there are two other Gardens (i.e. in Paradise). (62) Then which of the Blessings of your Lord will you both (jinn and men) deny? (63) Dark green (in colour). (64) Then which of the Blessings of your Lord will you both (jinn and men) deny? (65) In them (both) will be two springs gushing forth. (66) Then which of the Blessings of your Lord will you both (jinn and men) deny? (67) In them (both) will be fruits, and date- palms and pomegranates. (68) Then which of the Blessings of your Lord will you both (jinn and men) deny? (69) Therein (Gardens) will be Khairâtun-Hisân [fair (wives) good and beautiful]. (70) Then which of the Blessings of your Lord will you both (jinn and men) deny? (71) Hûr (beautiful, fair females) guarded in pavilions; (72) Then which of the Blessings of your Lord will you both (jinn and men) deny? (73) With Whom no man or jinni has had Tameth before them. (74) Then which of the Blessings of your Lord will you both (jinn and men) deny? (75) Reclining on green cushions and rich beautiful mattresses.

Quran 57:21

Race with one another in hastening towards forgiveness from your Lord (Allâh), and Paradise the width whereof is as the width of the heaven and the earth, prepared for those who believe in Allâh and His Messengers. That is the Grace of Allâh which He bestows on whom He is pleased with. And Allâh is the Owner of Great Bounty.

Quran 58:22

You will not find any people who believe in Allâh and the Last Day, making friendship with those who oppose Allâh and His Messenger (Muhammad), even though they were their fathers or their sons or their brothers or their kindred (people). For such He has written Faith in their hearts, and strengthened them with Rûh (proofs, light and true guidance) from Himself. And He will admit them to Gardens (Paradise) under which rivers flow to dwell therein (forever). Allâh is pleased with them, and they with Him. They are the Party of Allâh. Verily, it is the Party of Allâh that will be the successful.

Quran 61:10-12

O You who believe! Shall I guide you to a trade that will save you from a painful torment? (10) That you believe in Allâh and His Messenger (Muhammad), and that you strive hard and fight in the Cause of Allâh with your wealth and your lives, that will be better for you, if you but know! (11) (If you do so) He will forgive you your sins, and admit you into Gardens under which rivers flow, and pleasant dwellings in Adn (Edn) Paradise; that is indeed the great success.

Quran 65:11

(And has also sent to you) a Messenger (Muhammad), who recites to you the Verses of Allâh (the Qur'ân) containing clear explanations, that He may take out, those who believe and do righteous good deeds from the darkness (of polytheism and disbelief) to the light (of Islamic Monotheism). And whosoever believes in Allâh and performs righteous good deeds, He will admit him into Gardens under which rivers flow (Paradise), to dwell therein forever. Allâh has indeed granted for him an excellent provision.

Quran 68:34

Verily, for the Muttaqûn (pious and righteous persons) are Gardens of delight (Paradise) with their Lord.

Quran 70:23-35

Those who remain constant in their Salât (prayers); (23) And those in whose wealth there is a recognized right, (24) For the beggar who asks, and for the unlucky who has lost his property and wealth, (and his means of living has been straitened); (25) And those who believe in the Day of Recompense, (26) And those who fear the torment of their Lord, (27) Verily, the torment of their Lord is that before which none can feel secure — (28) And those who guard their chastity (i.e. private parts from illegal sexual acts). (29) Except with their wives and the (women slaves) whom their right hands possess — for (then) they are not blameworthy, (30) But whosoever seeks beyond that, then it is those who are trespassers. (31) And those who keep their trusts and covenants; (32) And those who stand firm in their testimonies; (33) And those who guard their Salât (prayers) well , (34) Such shall dwell in the Gardens (i.e. Paradise) honored.

Quran 74:38-48

Every person is a pledge for what he has earned, (38) Except those on the Right, (i.e. the pious true believers of Islâmic Monotheism); (39) In Gardens (Paradise) they will ask one another, (40) About Al-Mujrimûn (polytheists, criminals, disbelievers), (And they will say to them): (41) "What has caused you to enter Hell?" (42) They will say: "We were not of those who used to offer the Salât (prayers) (43) "Nor we used to feed Al-Miskin (the poor); (44) "And we used to talk falsehood (all that which Allâh hated) with vain talkers (45) "And we used to belie the Day of Recompense (46) "Until there came to us (the death) that is certain." (47) So no intercession of intercessors will be of any use to them

Quran 76:5-22

Verily, the Abrâr (the pious and righteous) shall drink of a cup (of wine) mixed with (water from a spring in Paradise called) Kâfûr. (5) A spring wherefrom the slaves of Allâh will drink, causing it to gush forth abundantly. (6) They (are those who) fulfill (their) vows, and they fear a Day whose evil will be wide-spreading. (7) And they give food, inspite of their love for it (or for the love of Him), to Miskin (the poor), the orphan, and the captive, (8) (Saying): "We feed you seeking Allâh's Countenance only. We wish for no reward, nor thanks from you. (9) "Verily, We fear from our Lord a Day, hard and distressful, that will make the faces look horrible (from extreme dislike to it)." (10) So Allâh saved them from the evil of that Day, and gave them Nadhrah (a light of beauty) and joy. (11) And their recompense shall be Paradise, and silken garments, because they were patient. (12) Reclining therein on raised thrones, they will see there neither the excessive heat of the sun, nor the excessive bitter cold, (as in Paradise there is no sun and no moon). (13) And the shade thereof is close upon them, and the bunches of fruit thereof will hang low within their reach. (14) And amongst them will be passed round vessels of silver and cups of crystal — (15) Crystal-clear, made of silver. They will determine the measure thereof (according to their wishes). (16) And they will be given to drink there of a cup (of wine) mixed with Zanjabîl (ginger). (17) A spring there, called Salsabîl. (18) And round about them will (serve) boys of everlasting youth. If you see them, you would think them scattered pearls. (19) And when you look there (in Paradise), you will see a delight (that cannot be imagined), and a great dominion. (20) Their garments will be of fine green silk, and gold embroidery. They will be adorned with bracelets of silver, and their Lord will give them a pure drink. (21)

(And it will be said to them): "Verily, this is a reward for you, and your endeavor has been accepted."

Quran 84:25

Save those who believe and do righteous good deeds, for them is a reward that will never come to an end (i.e. Paradise)

Quran 85:11

Verily, those who believe and do righteous good deeds, for them will be Gardens under which rivers flow (Paradise). That is the great success.

Quran 95:6

Save those who believe and do righteous deeds, Then they shall have a reward without end (Paradise).

Quran 98:7-8

Verily, those who believe [in the Oneness of Allâh, and in His Messenger Muhammad including all obligations ordered by Islâm] and do righteous good deeds, they are the best of creatures (7) Their reward with their Lord is 'Adn (Eden) Paradise (Gardens of Eternity), underneath which rivers flow, They will abide therein forever, Allâh will be pleased with them, and they with Him. That is for him who fears his Lord.

Quran 108:1

Verily, We have granted you (O Muhammad) Al-Kauthar (a river in Paradise)

It was narrated from Hudhaifah that the Messenger of Allah (ﷺ) said:

"My Cistern is wider than the distance between Ailah and 'Aden. By the One in Whose Hand is my soul, its vessels are more numerous than the number of stars, and it is whiter than milk and sweeter than honey. By the One in Whose Hand is my soul, I will drive men away from it as a man drives strange camels away from his cistern." It was said: "O Messenger of Allah, will you recognize us?" He said: "Yes, you will come to me with radiant faces, hands and feet, because of the traces of ablution, and this is not for anyone but you."

Source: Sunan ibn Majah

English reference : Vol. 5, Book 37, Hadith 4302

Graded Sahih by Darussalam

Abu Dharr narrated:

"I said: 'O Messenger of Allah! What about the vessels of the Hawd?' He said: 'By the one in Whose Hand is my soul! Its vessels number more than the stars of the heavens and the planets on a clear dark night. (They are) among the vessels of Paradise, whoever drinks from them, he will never be thirsty again. Its longest breadth is the same as its length, like that which is between 'Amman to Aylah, its water is whiter than milk and sweeter than honey.'"

Source: Jami at-Tirhmidi

English reference : Vol. 4, Book 11, Hadith 2445

Graded Sahih by Darussalam

Narrated Sahl:

The Prophet said, "The people of Paradise will see the Ghuraf (special abodes) in Paradise as you see a star in the sky."

Source: Sahih al-Bukhari 6555

Narrated Hudhaifa:

I heard the Prophet saying, "A Qattat (backbiter or talebearer) will not enter Paradise."

Source: Sahih al-Bukhari 6056

Narrated `Abdullah bin Qais:

The Prophet said, "(There will be) two Paradises of silver and all the utensils and whatever is therein (will be of silver); and two Paradises of gold, and its utensils and whatever therein (will be of gold), and there will be nothing to prevent the people from seeing their Lord except the Cover of Majesty over His Face in the Paradise of Eden (eternal bliss).

Source: Sahih al-Bukhari 7444

Anas bin Malik narrated that the Messenger of Allah said:

"Whoever asks Allah Paradise three times, Paradise says: 'O Allah, admit him into Paradise', and whoever seeks refuge from the Fire three times, the Fire says: 'O Allah, save him from the Fire.'"

Source: Jami at-Tirmidhi

English reference : Vol. 4, Book 12, Hadith 2572

Graded Sahih by Darussalam

Jabir narrated that the Messenger of Allah said:

" *Some of the people of Tawhid will be punished in the Fire until they are coals. Then the Mercy (of Allah) will reach them, they will be taken out and tossed at the doors of Paradise.*" *He said: " The people of Paradise will pour water over them, and they will sprout as the debris carried by the flood sprouts, then they will enter Paradise.*"

Source: Jami at-Tirmidhi

English reference : Vol. 4, Book 13, Hadith 2597

Graded Sahih by Darussalam

It was narrated from Abu Hurairah that the Prophet said:

"There are no two Muslims, three of whose children die before reaching puberty, but Allah will admit them to Paradise by virtue of His mercy toward them. It will be said to them: 'Enter Paradise.' They will say: 'Not until our parents enter.' So it will be said: 'Enter Paradise, you and your parents.'"

Source: Sunan an-Nasa'i 1876 Graded Sahih by Darussalam

Narrated Abu Umamah:

The Prophet said: I guarantee a house in the surroundings of Paradise for a man who avoids quarrelling even if he were in the right, a house in the middle of Paradise for a man who avoids lying

*even if he were joking, and a house in the upper part of Paradise for
a man who made his character good.*

Source: Sunan Abi Dawud 4800 Graded Hasan by Albani

Mu'adh bin Jabal narrated that the Prophet said:

*"The people of Paradise shall enter Paradise without body hair,
Murd, with Kuhl on their eyes, thirty years of age or thirty-three
years."*

Source: Jami at-Tirmidhi

English reference : Vol. 4, Book 12, Hadith 2545

Graded Sahih by Darussalam

**Abu Hurairah narrated that the Messenger of Allah (ﷺ)
said:**

*"If the believer knew what is with Allah of punishment, none
would hope for Paradise, and if the disbeliever knew what is with
Allah of mercy, none would despair of (attaining) Paradise."*

Source: Jami` at-Tirmidhi 3542 Graded Sahih by Darussalam

Narrated `Abdullah bin Qais:

*Allah's Messenger said, "In Paradise there is a pavilion made of a
single hollow pearl sixty miles wide, in each corner of which there
are wives who will not see those in the other corners; and the
believers will visit and enjoy them. And there are two gardens, the
utensils and contents of which are made of silver; and two other
gardens, the utensils and contents of which are made of so-and-so*

(i.e. gold) and nothing will prevent the people staying in the Garden of Eden from seeing their Lord except the curtain of Majesty over His Face."

Source: Sahih Bukhari USC-MSA web (English) reference : Vol. 6, Book 60, Hadith 402

Narrated Jubair bin Mut`im:

That he heard the Prophet saying, "The person who severs the bond of kinship will not enter Paradise."

Source: Sahih al-Bukhari 5984

Abu Hurairah narrated that the Messenger of Allah said:

"The world is a prison for the believer and Paradise for the disbeliever."

Source: Jami` at-Tirmidhi 2324 Graded Sahih by Darussalam

Abu Hurairah narrated that the Messenger of Allah said:

"There is not a tree in Paradise except that its tree is of gold."

Source: Jami at-Tirmidhi

English reference : Vol. 4, Book 12, Hadith 2525

Graded Hasan by Darussalam

Anas narrated that the Messenger of Allah said:

"Paradise is surrounded by hardships, and the Fire is surrounded by desires."

Source: Jami at-Tirmidhi

English reference : Vol. 4, Book 12, Hadith 2559

Graded Sahih by Darussalam

Abu Bakrah said:

"The Messenger of Allah said: 'Whoever kills a Mu'ahad (non-Muslim under protection of a Muslim state) with no justification, Allah will forbid Paradise to him."

Source: Sunan an-Nasa'i 4747 Graded Sahih by Darussalam

Hudhaifah reported the Messenger of Allah as saying :

A mischief-maker will not enter paradise.

Source: Sunan Abi Dawud 4871 Graded Sahih by Albani

Narrated Mu'adh bin Jabal :

The Messenger of Allah as saying: If anyone's last words are "There is no god but Allah" he will enter Paradise.

Source: Sunan Abi Dawud 3116 Graded Sahih by Albani

It was narrated from Abu Darda' that the Prophet (ﷺ) said:

"No one who is addicted to wine will enter Paradise."

Source: Sunan ibn Majah

English reference : Vol. 4, Book 30, Hadith 3376

Graded Hasan by Darussalam

It was narrated from 'Amr bin Malik Al-Janbi that he heard Fadalah bin 'Ubaid say:

"I heard the Messenger of Allah say: 'I am a Za'im - and the Za'im is the guarantor - for the one who believes in me and accepts Islam, and emigrates: A house on the outskirts of Paradise and a house in the middle of Paradise. And I am a guarantor, for the one who believes in me and accepts Islam, and strives in the cause of Allah: A house on the outskirts of Paradise and a house in the middle of Paradise and a house in the highest chambers of Paradise. Whoever does that (believes and strives in Jihad) and seeks goodness wherever it is, and avoids evil wherever it is, may die wherever he wants to die.'"

Source: Sunan an-Nasa'i 3133 Graded Hasan by Darussalam

Abdullah reported Allah's Messenger (ﷺ) as saying:

Truth leads one to Paradise and virtue leads one to Paradise and the person tells the truth until he is recorded as truthful, and lie leads to obscenity and obscenity leads to Hell, and the person tells a lie until he is recorded as a liar.

Source: Sahih Muslim 2607 a

Abu Musa Ash'ari reported that Allah's Messenger (ﷺ) said to him:

Should I not direct you to the words from the treasures of Paradise, or he said: Like a treasure from the treasures of Paradise? I said: Of course, do that. Thereupon he said:" There is no might and no power but that of Allah."

Source: Sahih Muslim 2704 g

Narrated `Abdullah bin `Umar:

Allah's Messenger said, "When anyone of you dies, he will be shown his destination both in the morning and in the evening, and if he belongs to the people of Paradise, he will be shown his place in Paradise, and if he is from the people of Hell, he will be shown his place in Hell."

Source: Sahih al-Bukhari 3240

Narrated Sahl bin Sa`d:

The Prophet said, "Seventy-thousand or seven-hundred thousand of my followers (the narrator is in doubt as to the correct number) will enter Paradise holding each other till the first and the last of them enter Paradise at the same time, and their faces will have a glitter like that of the moon at night when it is full."

Source: Sahih al-Bukhari 6543

Narrated Anas bin Malik:

The Prophet said, "Some people will come out of the Fire after they have received a touch of the Fire, changing their color, and they will enter Paradise, and the people of Paradise will name them 'Al-Jahannamiyin' the (Hell) Fire people."

Source: Sahih al-Bukhari 6559

Narrated Abu Huraira:

Allah's Messenger said, "All my followers will enter Paradise except those who refuse." They said, "O Allah's Messenger! Who will refuse?" He said, "Whoever obeys me will enter Paradise, and whoever disobeys me is the one who refuses (to enter it)."

Source: Sahih al-Bukhari 7280

Narrated Abu Hurairah:

that the Messenger of Allah said: "Indeed the space in Paradise taken up by a whip, is better than the world and what is in it. Recite if you wish: 'And whoever is moved away from the Fire and admitted to Paradise, he indeed is successful. The life of this world is only the enjoyment of deception (3:185).'"

Source: Jami at-Tirmidhi

English reference : Vol. 5, Book 44, Hadith 3013

Graded Hasan by Darussalam

It has been reported on the authority of Abu Huraira that the Messenger of Allah (ﷺ) said:

God laughs at the two men one of whom kills the other; both of them will enter Paradise. They (the Companions) said: How, Messenger of Allah? He said: One is slain (in the way of Allah) and enters Paradise. Then God forgives the other and guides him to Islam; then he fights in the way of Allah and dies a martyr.

Source: Sahih Muslim 1890 c

Imran bin Husain reported that Allah's Messenger (ﷺ) said:

Amongst the inmates of Paradise the women would form a minority.

Source: Sahih Muslim 2738 a

Narrated Sahl bin Sa`d Al-Saidi:

Allah's Messenger said, "A place in Paradise equal to the size of a lash is better than the whole world and whatever is in it."

Source: Sahih al-Bukhari 3250

Narrated Sahl:

Allah's Messenger said, "I and the one who looks after an orphan will be like this in Paradise," showing his middle and index fingers and separating them.

Source: Sahih al-Bukhari 5304

Jabir bin 'Abdullah, may Allah be pleased with them, narrated that :

Allah's Messenger said: "The key to Paradise is Salat, and the key to Salat is Wudu'."

Source: Jami` at-Tirmidhi 4 Graded Hasan by Darussalam

Thawban narrated that :

The Messenger of Allah said: "Whichever woman seeks a Khul(divorce) from her husband without harm (cause), then the scent of Paradise will be unlawful for her."

Source: Jami` at-Tirmidhi 1187 Graded Sahih by Darussalam

Umm Salamah narrated that The Messenger of Allah said:

"Whichever woman dies while her husband is pleased with her, then she enters Paradise."

Source: Jami` at-Tirmidhi 1161

Graded Hasan by Darussalam

Abu Hurairah narrated that the Messenger of Allah said:

"Al-Haya (modesty) is from faith, and faith is in Paradise. Obscenity is from rudeness, and rudeness is in the Fire."

Source: Jami` at-Tirmidhi 2009

Graded Hasan by Darussalam

Abu Sa'eed narrated that the Messenger of Allah said:

"The poor Muhajirin will enter Paradise before the rich among them by five hundred years."

Source: Jami` at-Tirmidhi 2351 Graded Sahih by Darussalam

Abu Hurairah narrated that the Messenger of Allah said:

"The poor Muslims are admitted into Paradise before their rich by half a day. And that is five hundred years."

Source: Jami` at-Tirmidhi 2354

Graded Hasan by Darussalam

Abu Hurairah narrated that the Messenger of Allah said:

"Verily, in Paradise there is a tree, a rider will travel in it's shade for a hundred years."

Source: Jami at-Tirmidhi

English reference : Vol. 4, Book 12, Hadith 2523

Graded Sahih by Darussalam

Abu Hurairah narrated that the Messenger of Allah (s.a.w) said:

"In Paradise, there are a hundred levels, between every two levels is (the distance of) a hundred years."

Source: Jami at-Tirmidhi

English reference : Vol. 4, Book 12, Hadith 2529

Graded Sahih by Darussalam

Abdullah bin Mas'ud narrated:

"We were in a tent with the Messenger of Allah, about forty of us when the Messenger of Allah said to us: 'Would you be pleased to be a quarter of the people of Paradise?' They said:'Yes.' He said: 'Would you be pleased to be a third of the people of Paradise?' They said: 'Yes.' He said: 'Would you be pleased to be one half of the people of Paradise? Verily none shall enter Paradise except a Muslim soul. And you are not with relation to Shirk except like the white hair on the hide of a black bull or like the black hair on the hide of a red bull."

Source: Jami at-Tirmidhi

English reference : Vol. 4, Book 12, Hadith 2547

Graded Sahih by Darussalam

Abu Hurairah narrated that the Messenger of Allah said:

"Umrah to 'Umrah atones for the sins between them, and for Al-Hajj Al-Mabrur there is no reward except Paradise."

Source: Jami` at-Tirmidhi 933 Graded Sahih by Darussalam

Narrated Kathir ibn Qays:

Kathir ibn Qays said: I was sitting with Abu-Darda' in the mosque of Damascus.

A man came to him and said: Abu-Darda, I have come to you from the town of the Messenger of Allah for a tradition that I have heard you relate from the Messenger of Allah. I have come for no other purpose.

He said: I heard the Messenger of Allah say: If anyone travels on a road in search of knowledge, Allah will cause him to travel on one of the roads of Paradise. The angels will lower their wings in their great pleasure with one who seeks knowledge, the inhabitants of the heavens and the Earth and the fish in the deep waters will ask forgiveness for the learned man. The superiority of the learned man over the devout is like that of the moon, on the night when it is full, over the rest of the stars. The learned are the heirs of the Prophets, and the Prophets leave neither dinar nor dirham, leaving only knowledge, and he who takes it takes an abundant portion.

Source: Sunan Abi Dawud 3641 Graded Sahih by Albani

It was narrated from Umm Habibah that:

The Prophet said: "Whoever prays twelve rak'ahs during the day and night, a house will be built for him in Paradise."

Source: Sunan an-Nasa'i 1804 Graded Sahih by Darussalam

It was narrated from 'Abdullah bin 'Amr bin Al-'As that:

The Messenger of Allah said: "Whoever is killed defending his wealth and is killed unjustly, Paradise will be his."

Source: Sunan an-Nasa'i 4086 Graded Sahih by Darussalam

Jabir said:

I heard the Prophet say: Those who go to Paradise will eat in it and drink.

Source: Sunan Abi Dawud 4741 Graded Sahih by Albani

It was narrated that Suhaib said:

"The Messenger of Allah recited this Verse: 'For those who have done good is the best reward and even more.' Then he said: 'When the people of Paradise enter Paradise, and the people of the Fire enter the Fire, a caller will cry out: "O people of Paradise! You have a covenant with Allah and He wants to fulfill it." They will say: "What is it?" Has Allah not made the Balance (of our good deeds) heavy, and made our faces bright, and admitted us to Paradise and saved us from Hell?" Then the Veil will be lifted and they will look upon Him, and by Allah, Allah will not give them anything that is more beloved to them or delightful, than looking upon Him.'"

Source: Sunan ibn Majah English reference : Vol. 1, Book 1, Hadith 187

Graded Sahih by Darussalam

Uthman bin 'Affan narrated that the Messenger of Allah (ﷺ) said:

"Allah will admit to Paradise a man who was lenient when he sold and when he bought. "

Source: Sunan ibn Majah

English reference : Vol. 3, Book 12, Hadith 2202

Graded Sahih by Darussalam

Abu Hurayra reported that the Prophet said,

"The Garden and the Fire quarreled and the Fire said, 'The tyrants will enter me and the proud will enter me.' The Garden retorted, 'The weak will enter me and the poor will enter me.' Allah Almighty said to the Garden, 'You are My mercy and I show you to whomever I will.' Then He said to the Fire, 'You are My punishment with which I will punish whomever I will. Each of you will have your fill.'"

Source: Al-Adab Al-Mufrad 554 Graded Sahih by Albani

Narrated Abu Huraira:

The Prophet said, "Whoever believes in Allah and His Apostle offers prayers perfectly and fasts (the month of) Ramadan then it is incumbent upon Allah to admit him into Paradise, whether he emigrates for Allah's cause or stays in the land where he was born." They (the companions of the Prophet) said, "O Allah's Messenger! Should we not inform the people of that?" He said, "There are one-hundred degrees in Paradise which Allah has prepared for those who carry on Jihad in His Cause. The distance between every two degrees is like the distance between the sky and the Earth, so if you ask Allah for anything, ask Him for the Firdaus, for it is the last part of Paradise and the highest part of Paradise, and at its top there is the Throne of Beneficent, and from it gush forth the rivers of Paradise."

Source: Sahih al-Bukhari 7423

Narrated Anas:

Um (the mother of) Haritha came to Allah's Messenger after Haritha had been martyred on the Day (of the battle) of Badr by an arrow thrown by an unknown person. She said, "O Allah's Messenger! You know the position of Haritha in my heart (i.e. how dear to me he was), so if he is in Paradise, I will not weep for him, or otherwise, you will see what I will do." The Prophet said, "Are you mad? Is there only one Paradise? There are many Paradises, and he is in the highest Paradise of Firdaus." The Prophet added, "A forenoon journey or an afternoon journey in Allah's Cause is better than the whole world and whatever is in it; and a place equal to an arrow bow of anyone of you, or a place equal to a foot in Paradise is better than the whole world and whatever is in it; and if one of the women of Paradise looked at the earth, she would fill the whole space between them (the earth and the heaven) with light, and would fill whatever is in between them, with perfume, and the veil of her face is better than the whole world and whatever is in it."

Source: Sahih al-Bukhari 6567, 6568

Muhammad reported that some (persons) stated with a sense of pride and some discussed whether there would be more men in Paradise or more women. It was upon this that Abu Huraira reported that Abu'l Qasim (the Prophet) (ﷺ) said:

The (members) of the first group to get into Paradise would have their faces as bright as full moon during the night, and the next to this group would have their faces as bright as the shining stars in the sky, and every person would have two wives and the marrow of their shanks would glimmer beneath the flesh and there would be none without a wife in Paradise.

Source: Sahih Muslim 2834 a

Narrated 'Ubada:

The Prophet said, "If anyone testifies that None has the right to be worshipped but Allah Alone Who has no partners, and that Muhammad is His Slave and His Apostle, and that Jesus is Allah's Slave and His Apostle and His Word which He bestowed on Mary and a Spirit created by Him, and that Paradise is true, and Hell is true, Allah will admit him into Paradise with the deeds which he had done even if those deeds were few." (Junada, the sub-narrator said, " 'Ubada added, 'Such a person can enter Paradise through any of its eight gates he likes.")

Source: Sahih al-Bukhari 3435

It is narrated on the authority of Abu Huraira that the Messenger of Allah observed:

He will not enter Paradise whose neighbor is not secure from his wrongful conduct.

Source: Sahih Muslim 46

It is narrated on the authority of 'Abdullah that the Messenger of Allah (ﷺ) observed:

He who has in his heart the weight of a mustard seed of pride shall not enter Paradise.

Source: Sahih Muslim 91 c

Jabir reported that he had heard with his ears the Apostle (ﷺ) saying:

Allah will bring out people from the Fire and admit them into Paradise.

Source: Sahih Muslim 191 b

Narrated Abu Bakr bin Abi Musa:

My father said, "Allah's Messenger said, 'Whoever prays the two cool prayers (`Asr and Fajr) will go to Paradise.' "

Source: Sahih al-Bukhari 574

Anas reported Allah's Apostle (ﷺ) as saying:

There would be left some space in Paradise as Allah would like that to be left. Then Allah would create another creation as He would like.

Source: Sahih Muslim 2848 d

Abu Sa'id reported that Ibn Sayyad asked Allah's Messenger (ﷺ) about the earth of Paradise. Whereupon he said:

It is like white shining pure musk.

Source: Sahih Muslim 2928 b

Narrated `Abdullah:

Allah's Messenger said, "Anyone who dies worshipping others along with Allah will definitely enter the Fire." I said, "Anyone who dies worshipping none along with Allah will definitely enter Paradise."

Source: Sahih al-Bukhari 1238

Narrated Abu Huraira:

Allah's Messenger said, "Allah has ninety-nine names, i.e. one-hundred minus one, and whoever knows them will go to Paradise."

Source: Sahih al-Bukhari 2736

Narrated `Imran bin Husain:

The Prophet said, "I looked at Paradise and found poor people forming the majority of its inhabitants; and I looked at Hell and saw that the majority of its inhabitants were women."

Source: Sahih al-Bukhari 3241

Narrated Sahl bin Sa`d:

The Prophet said, "Paradise has eight gates, and one of them is called Ar-Raiyan through which none will enter but those who observe fasting."

Source: Sahih al-Bukhari 3257

Narrated Abu Huraira:

The Prophet said, "Paradise and the Fire (Hell) argued, and the Fire (Hell) said, "I have been given the privilege of receiving the arrogant and the tyrants.' Paradise said, 'What is the matter with me? Why do only the weak and the humble among the people enter me?' On that, Allah said to Paradise. 'You are My Mercy which I bestow on whoever I wish of my servants.' Then Allah said to the (Hell) Fire, 'You are my (means of) punishment by which I punish whoever I wish of my slaves. And each of you will have its fill.' As for the Fire (Hell), it will not be filled till Allah puts His Foot over it whereupon it will say, 'Qati! Qati!' At that time it will be filled, and its different parts will come closer to each other; and Allah will not wrong any of His created beings. As regards Paradise, Allah will create a new creation to fill it with."

Source: Sahih Bukhari USC-MSA web (English) reference : Vol. 6, Book 60, Hadith 373

Narrated `Aisha:

Allah's Messenger said, "Do good deeds properly, sincerely and moderately and know that your deeds will not make you enter

Paradise, and that the most beloved deed to Allah is the most regular and constant even if it were little."

Source: Sahih al-Bukhari 6464

Narrated Abu Huraira:

Allah's Messenger said, "The (Hell) Fire is surrounded by all kinds of desires and passions, while Paradise is surrounded by all kinds of disliked undesirable things."

Source: Sahih al-Bukhari 6487

Narrated `Imran bin Husain:

The Prophet said, "Some people will be taken out of the Fire through the intercession of Muhammad they will enter Paradise and will be called Al-Jahannamiyin (the Hell Fire people).

Source: Sahih al-Bukhari 6566

Narrated Ma'qil:

I heard the Prophet saying, "Any man whom Allah has given the authority of ruling some people and he does not look after them in an honest manner, will never feel even the smell of Paradise."

Source: Sahih al-Bukhari 7150

Narrated Ma'qil:

Allah's Messenger said, "If any ruler having the authority to rule Muslim subjects dies while he is deceiving them, Allah will forbid Paradise for him."

Source: Sahih al-Bukhari 7151

Uthman bin Affan narrated that :

he heard Allah's Messenger say: "Whoever builds a Masjid for (the sake of) Allah, then Allah will build a similar house for him in Paradise."

Source: Jami` at-Tirmidhi 318 Graded Sahih by Darussalam

Abdullah narrated that the Messenger of Allah said:

"Whoever has a mustard seed's weight of pride (arrogance) in his heart, shall not be admitted into Paradise. And whoever has a mustard seed's weight of faith in his heart, shall not be admitted into the Fire."

Source: Jami` at-Tirmidhi 1998 Graded Sahih by Darussalam

Abu Hurairah narrated that the Messenger of Allah said:

"For whomever Allah protects against the evil of what is between his jaws and the evil of what is between his legs, he shall enter Paradise."

Source: Jami` at-Tirmidhi 2409

 Graded Hasan by Darussalam

Abu Hurairah narrated from the Messenger of Allah that he said:

"The people of Paradise are without body hair, Murd, with Kuhl(on their eyelids), their youth does not come to an end, and their clothes do not wear out."

Source: Jami at-Tirmidhi

English reference : Vol. 4, Book 12, Hadith 2539

Graded Hasan by Darussalam

Anas narrated that the Prophet said:

"The believer shall be given in paradise such and such strength in intercourse ." it was said: "O Messenger of Allah! And will he able to do that?" He said: "He will be given the strength of a hundred."

Source: Jami at-Tirmidhi

English reference : Vol. 4, Book 12, Hadith 2536

Graded Hasan by Darussalam

Ibn Buraidah narrated from his father that the Messenger of Allah said:

"The people of Paradise are a hundred and twenty rows, eighty of them are from this nation, and forty are from the rest of the nations."

Source: Jami at-Tirmidhi

English reference : Vol. 4, Book 12, Hadith 2546

Graded Hasan by Darussalam

Abu Sa'eed Al-Khudri narrated that the Messenger of Allah said:

"The believer, when he desires a child in Paradise, he shall be carried (in pregnancy), born, and complete his aging in an hour as he desires."

Source: Jami at-Tirmidhi

English reference : Vol. 4, Book 12, Hadith 2563

Graded Hasan by Darussalam

Hakim bin Mu'awiyah narrated from his father, that the Prophet said:

"Indeed in Paradise there is a sea of water, and a sea of honey, and a sea of milk, and a sea of wine, then the rivers shall split off afterwards."

Source: Jami at-Tirmidhi

English reference : Vol. 4, Book 12, Hadith 2571

Graded Hasan by Darussalam

It was narrated that Umm Habibah said:

"The Messenger of Allah said: 'Whoever prays twelve rak'ahs in a day apart from the obligatory prayers, Allah will build for him, or there will be built for him, a house in Paradise.'"

Source: Sunan an-Nasa'i 1808 Graded Sahih by Darussalam

It was narrated that Thawban said:

"The Messenger of Allah said: 'Whoever can promise me one thing. Paradise will be his." (One of the narrators) Yahya said:

"Here a statement which means: That he will not ask the people for anything."

Source: Sunan an-Nasa'i 2590 Graded Sahih by Darussalam

It was narrated that Ibn 'Abbas, who attributed it to the Prophet, said:

"Some people will dye their hair black like the breasts of pigeons at the end of time, but they will not even smell the fragrance of Paradise."

Source: Sunan an-Nasa'i 5075 Graded Sahih by Darussalam

'Uqbah bin 'Amir narrated that:

The Messenger of Allah used to tell his wives not to wear jewelry and silk. He said: "If you want the jewelry and silk of Paradise, then do not wear them in this world."

Source: Sunan an-Nasa'i 5136 Graded Sahih by Darussalam

It was narrated from 'Abdullah bin 'Amr that:

The Prophet said: "No one who reminds others of his favors, no one who is disobedient to his parents and no drunkard, will enter Paradise."

Source: Sunan an-Nasa'i 5672 Graded Hasan by Darussalam

It was narrated from Abu Hurairah that the prophet (ﷺ) said:

"Whoever spends on a pair (of things) in the cause of Allah will be called in Paradise: 'O slave of Allah, here is prosperity.' Whoever

is one of the people of Salah, he will be called from the gate of Paradise, Whoever is one of the people of jihad, he will be called from the gate of paradise. Whoever is one of the people of charity, he will be called from the gate of Paradise. Whoever is one of the people who fast, he will be called from the gate of Ar-Rayyan." Abu Bakr, may Allah be pleased with him, said: "O Messenger of Allah, no distress or need will befall the one who is called from those gates. Will there be anyone who will be called from all these gates?" The Messenger of Allah said: "Yes, and I hope that you will be one of them."

Source: Sunan an-Nasa'i 3183 Graded Sahih by Darussalam

Narrated Abu Hurayrah:

The Prophet said: If anyone acquires knowledge that should be sought seeking the Face of Allah, but he acquires it only to get some worldly advantage, he will not experience the arf, i.e. the fragrance, of Paradise.

Source: Sunan Abi Dawud 3664 Graded Sahih by Albani

It was narrated from Ibn Abbas that the Messenger of Allah(☀) said:

"There is no man whose two daughters reach the age of puberty and he treats them kindly for the time they are together, but they will gain him admittance to Paradise."

Source: Sunan Ibn Majah 3670 Graded Sahih by Darussalam

It was narrated from Abu Sa'eed Al-Khudri that the Messenger of Allah (☀) said:

"When the believer wants a child in Paradise, he will be conceived and born and grown up, in a short while, according to his desire."

Source: Sunan ibn Majah

English reference : Vol. 5, Book 37, Hadith 4338

Graded Hasan by Darussalam

Sahl b. Sa'd reported Allah's Messenger (ﷺ) as saying:

The inmates of Paradise will look to the upper apartment of Paradise as you see the planets in the sky. I narrated this hadith to Nu'man b. Abi 'Ayyash and he said: I heard Abu Sa'id al-Khudri as saying: As you see the shining planets in the eastern and western (sides of) horizon.

Source: Sahih Muslim 2830, 2831 a

Narrated Abu Aiyub:

A man said to the Prophet "Tell me of such a deed as will make me enter Paradise." The people said, "What is the matter with him? What is the matter with him?" The Prophet said, "He has something to ask. (What he needs greatly) The Prophet said: (In order to enter Paradise) you should worship Allah and do not ascribe any partners to Him, offer prayer perfectly, pay the Zakat and keep good relations with your Kith and kin."

Source: Sahih al-Bukhari 1396

Narrated Abu Sa`id Al-Khudri:

The Prophet said, "The people of Paradise will look at the dwellers of the lofty mansions (i.e. a superior place in Paradise) in the same way as one looks at a brilliant star far away in the East or in the West on the horizon; all that is because of their superiority over one another (in rewards)." On that the people said, "O Allah's Messenger! Are these lofty mansions for the prophets which nobody else can reach? The Prophet replied," No! "By Allah in whose Hands my life is, these are for the men who believed in Allah and also believed in the Prophets."

Source: Sahih al-Bukhari 3256

Narrated Abu Huraira:

The Prophet said, "None will enter Paradise but will be shown the place he would have occupied in the (Hell) Fire if he had rejected faith, so that he may be more thankful; and none will enter the (Hell) Fire but will be shown the place he would have occupied in Paradise if he had faith, so that may be a cause of sorrow for him."

Source: Sahih al-Bukhari 6569

Ubadah bin As-Samit narrated that the Messenger of Allah said:

"In Paradise, there are a hundred levels, what is between every two levels is like what is between the heavens and the earth. Al-Firdaus is its highest level, and from it the four rivers of Paradise are made to flow forth. So when you ask Allah, ask Him for Al-Firdaus."

Source: Jami at-Tirmidhi

English reference : Vol. 4, Book 12, Hadith 2531

Graded Sahih by Darussalam

Dawud bin Amir bin Sa'd bin Abi Waqqas narrated from his father, from his grandfather that the Prophet said:

"If as little as what can be placed on a fingernail of what is in Paradise were to become apparent, it would have beautified all the far corners of the heavens and the earth. And if a man among the people of Paradise were to appear and his bracelets were to become apparent, it would have blotted out the light of the sun, as the sun blots out the light of the stars."

Source: Jami at-Tirmidhi

English reference : Vol. 4, Book 12, Hadith 2538

Graded Hasan by Darussalam

Abu Ayyub narrated that a Bedouin came to the Prophet and said:

"O Messenger of Allah, indeed, I love horses. Are there horses in Paradise?" The Messenger of Allah said: "If you are admitted into Paradise, you shall be brought a horse of rubies with two wings, then you shall be carried on it, then it will fly with you wherever you want."

Source: Jami at-Tirmidhi

English reference : Vol. 4, Book 12, Hadith 2544

Graded Hasan by Darussalam

It was narrated that Rifa'ah Al-Juhani said:

"We came back (from a campaign) with the Messenger of Allah and he said: 'By the One in Whose Hand is the soul of Muhammad, there is no person who believes then stands firm, but he will be caused to enter Paradise. I hope that they will not enter it until you and those who are righteous among your offspring will enter it and take up your dwelling places therein. And my Lord has promised me that seventy thousand of my nation will enter Paradise without being brought to account.'"

Source: Sunan ibn Majah

English reference : Vol. 5, Book 37, Hadith 4285

Graded Sahih by Darussalam

Sa'd and Abu Bakra each one of them said:

My ears heard and my hearing preserved it that Muhammad observed: He who claimed for another one his fatherhood besides his own father knowingly that he was not his father-to him Paradise is forbidden.

Source: Sahih Muslim 63 b

Narrated Abu Huraira:

The Prophet said, "Allah will prepare for him who goes to the mosque (every) morning and in the afternoon (for the congregational prayer) an honorable place in Paradise with good hospitality for (what he has done) every morning and afternoon goings.

Source: Sahih al-Bukhari 662

Abu Huraira reported Allah's Messenger (ﷺ) as saying:

Let him be humbled, let him be humbled. It was said: Allah's Messenger, who is he? He said. He who finds his parents in old age, either one or both of them, and does not enter Paradise.

Source: Sahih Muslim 2551 b

Abu Huraira reported Allah's Messenger (ﷺ) as saying:

A person while walking along the path saw the branches of a tree lying there. He said: By Allah, I shall remove these from this so that these may not do harm to the Muslims, and he was admitted to Paradise.

Source: Sahih Muslim 1914 c

Abdullah (b. Mas'ud) reported that Allah's Messenger (ﷺ) who is the most truthful (of the human beings) and his being truthful (is a fact) said:

Verily your creation is on this wise. The constituents of one of you are collected for forty days in his mother's womb in the form of blood, after which it becomes a clot of blood in another period of forty days. Then it becomes a lump of flesh and forty days later Allah sends His angel to it with instructions concerning four things, so the angel writes down his livelihood, his death, his deeds, his fortune and misfortune. By Him, besides Whom there is no god, that one amongst you acts like the people deserving Paradise until between him and Paradise there remains but the distance of a cubit, when suddenly the writing of destiny overcomes him and he begins to act like the denizens of Hell and thus enters Hell, and another one acts in the way of the denizens of Hell, until there remains between him and Hell a distance of a cubit that the writing of destiny overcomes him and then he begins to act like the people of Paradise and enters Paradise.

Source: Sahih Muslim 2643 a

Jabir reported:

I heard Allah's Apostle as saying: None of you would get into Paradise because of his good deeds alone, and he would not be rescued from Fire, not even I, but because of the Mercy of Allah.

Source: Sahih Muslim 2817 c

Abu Huraira reported Allah's Apostle (ﷺ) as saying:

He who would get into Paradise (would be made to enjoy such an everlasting) bliss that he would neither become destitute, nor would his clothes wear out, nor his youth would decline.

Source: Sahih Muslim 2836

Narrated `Abdullah bin Qais Al-Ash`ari:

The Prophet said, "A tent (in Paradise) is like a hollow pearl which is thirty miles in height and on every corner of the tent the believer will have a family that cannot be seen by the others." (Narrated Abu `Imran in another narration, "The tent is sixty miles in height.")

Source: Sahih al-Bukhari 3243

Narrated `Abdullah:

The Prophet said one statement and I said another. The Prophet said "Whoever dies while still invoking anything other than Allah as a rival to Allah, will enter Hell (Fire)." And I said, "Whoever dies without invoking anything as a rival to Allah, will enter Paradise."

Source: Sahih Bukhari USC-MSA web (English) reference : Vol. 6, Book 60, Hadith 24

Narrated Anas bin Malik:

I heard Allah's Messenger saying, "Allah said, 'If I deprive my slave of his two beloved things (i.e., his eyes) and he remains patient, I will let him enter Paradise in compensation for them.'"

Source: Sahih al-Bukhari 5653

Narrated Abu Huraira:

Allah's Messenger said, "Allah says, 'I have nothing to give but Paradise as a reward to my believer slave, who, if I cause his dear friend (or relative) to die, remains patient (and hopes for Allah's Reward).

Source: Sahih al-Bukhari 6424

'Imran b. Husain reported:

Verily the Messenger of Allah said: Seventy thousand men of my Ummah would enter Paradise without rendering account. They (the companions of the Prophet) said: Who would be those, Messenger of Allah? He (the Prophet) said: They would be those who neither practice charm, not take omens, nor do they cauterise, but they repose their trust in their Lord.

Source: Sahih Muslim 218 b

Narrated Abu Huraira:

The Prophet said, "A man saw a dog eating mud from (the severity of) thirst. So, that man took a shoe (and filled it) with water and kept on pouring the water for the dog till it quenched its thirst. So Allah approved of his deed and made him to enter Paradise."

Source: Sahih al-Bukhari 173

Narrated Anas bin Malik:

The Prophet said, "Nobody who enters Paradise likes to go back to the world even if he got everything on the earth, except a Mujahid who wishes to return to the world so that he may be martyred ten times because of the dignity he receives (from Allah)."

Source: Sahih al-Bukhari 2817

Abu Sa'eed Al-Khudri narrated that :

the Messenger of Allah said: "Whoever has three daughters, or three sisters, or two daughters, or two sisters and he keeps good company with them and fears Allah regarding them, then Paradise is for him.

Source: Jami` at-Tirmidhi 1916

Graded Hasan by Darussalam

Narrated Abu Hurairah:

That the Messenger of Allah said, "I was shown the first of (every) three to enter Paradise: A martyr, an 'Atif, who is a Muta'affif, and a slave who perfected his worship of Allah, and was sincere to his masters."

Source: Jami` at-Tirmidhi 1642

Graded Hasan by Darussalam

Narrated 'Abdullah bin 'Amr:

That the Messenger of Allah said: "(All of you) worship Ar-Rahman, feed others, spread the (greeting of) Salam, then you will enter Paradise in security."

Source: Jami` at-Tirmidhi 1855 Graded Sahih by Darussalam

Abdullah bin `Umar narrated that :

the Messenger of Allah said: "Al-Kauthar is a river in Paradise, whose banks are of gold, and it flows over pearls and corundum. Its dirt is purer than musk, and its water is sweeter than honey and whiter than milk."

Source: Jami at-Tirmidhi

English reference : Vol. 5, Book 44, Hadith 3361

Graded Hasan by Darussalam

Narrated Abu Dharr:

I came to the Prophet while he was wearing white clothes and sleeping. Then I went back to him again after he had got up from his sleep. He said, "Nobody says: 'None has the right to be worshipped but Allah' and then later on he dies while believing in that, except that he will enter Paradise." I said, "Even if he had committed illegal sexual intercourse and theft?" He said. 'Even if he had committed illegal sexual intercourse and theft." I said, "Even if he had committed illegal sexual intercourse and theft?" He said. 'Even if he had committed illegal sexual intercourse and theft." I said, 'Even if he had committed illegal sexual intercourse and theft?' He said, "Even if he had committed illegal sexual intercourse and theft, inspite of Abu Dharr's dislike. Abu `Abdullah said, "This is at the time of death or before it if one repents and regrets and says "None has the right to be worshipped but Allah. He will be forgiven his sins."

Source: Sahih al-Bukhari 5827

It was narrated from Sahi bin Sad that the Prophet said:

"For those who fast there is a gate in Paradise called Ar-Rayyan, through which no one but they will enter. When the last of them has entered it, it will be closed. Whoever enters through it will drink, and whoever drinks will never thirst again."

Source: Sunan an-Nasa'i 2236 Graded Sahih by Darussalam

It was narrated that 'Uqbah bin 'Amir Al-Juhani said:

"The Messenger of Allah said: 'Whoever performs Wudu' and does it well, then prays two Rak'ahs in which his heart and face are focused, Paradise will be his."

Source: Sunan an-Nasai

English reference: Vol. 1, Book 1, Hadith 151

Graded Sahih by Darussalam

It was narrated from 'Uqbah bin 'Amir that the Prophet (ﷺ) said:

"Allah, the Mighty and Sublime, will admit three people into Paradise for one arrow: The one who makes it, intending it to be used for a good cause, the one who shoots it, and one who passes it to him."

Source: Sunan an-Nasa'i 3146 Graded Hasan by Darussalam

Narrated Abu Qatadah ibn Rib'iyy:

Allah , the Exalted said: I made five times' prayers obligatory on your people, and I took a guarantee that if anyone observes them regularly at their times, I shall admit him to Paradise; if anyone does not offer them regularly, there is no such guarantee of Mine for him.

Source: Sunan Abi Dawud 430 Graded Hasan by Albani

Narrated Samurah ibn Jundub:

The Prophet said: Attend the sermon (on Friday) and sit near the imam, for a man keeps himself away until he will be left behind at the time of entering Paradise though he enters it.

Source: Sunan Abi Dawud 1108 Graded Hasan by Albani

Thawban, the client of the Messenger of Allah, reported him as saying :

If anyone guarantees me that he will not beg from people, I will guarantee him Paradise. Thawban said : I (will not beg). He never asked anyone for anything.

Source: Sunan Abi Dawud 1643 Graded Sahih by Albani

It was narrated from Abu Sa`eed Al-Khudri that the Messenger of Allah (ﷺ) said:

"It will be said to the companion of the Qur'an, when he enters Paradise: 'Recite and rise one degree for every Verse,' until he recites the last thing that he knows."

Source: Sunan Ibn Majah 3780

Graded Hasan by Darussalam

It was narrated from Thawban, the freed slave of the Messenger of Allah (ﷺ), that the Messenger of Allah (ﷺ) said:

"Anyone whose soul leaves his body and he is free of three things, will enter Paradise: Arrogance, stealing from the spoils of war, and debt."

Source: Sunan ibn Majah

English reference : Vol. 3, Book 15, Hadith 2412

Graded Sahih by Darussalam

It was narrated from Abu Umamah that the Prophet (ﷺ) said:

"Allah says: 'O son of Adam! If you are patient and seek reward at the moment of first shock, I will not approve of any reward for you less than Paradise.'"

Source: Sunan ibn Majah

English reference : Vol. 1, Book 6, Hadith 1597

Graded Hasan by Darussalam

Harithah bin Wahb narrated that the Messenger of Allah (ﷺ) said:

"Shall I not tell you about the people of Paradise? Every weak and oppressed one. Shall I not tell you about the people of Hell? Every harsh, haughty and arrogant one."

Source: Sunan ibn Majah

English reference : Vol. 5, Book 37, Hadith 4116

Graded Sahih by Darussalam

It was narrated from Ibn 'Abbas that the Messenger of Allah (ﷺ) said:

"The people of Paradise are those whose ears Allah fills with the praise of people when they are listening, and the people of Hell- fire are those whom He fills their ears with condemnation when they are listening."

Source: Sunan ibn Majah

English reference : Vol. 5, Book 37, Hadith 4224

Graded Hasan by Darussalam

It was narrated that Abu Hurairah said:

"The Prophet was asked: 'What most admits people to Paradise?'
He said: 'Piety and good manners.' And he was asked: 'What most
leads people to Hell?' He said: 'The two hollow ones: The mouth
and the private part.'"

Source: Sunan ibn Majah

English reference : Vol. 5, Book 37, Hadith 4246

Graded Sahih by Darussalam

It is narrated on the authority of Abu Ayyub that a man
came to the Prophet (ﷺ) and said:

Direct me to a deed which draws me near to Paradise and takes me
away from the Fire (of Hell). Upon this he (the Prophet) said: You
worship Allah and never associate anything with Him, establish
prayer, and pay Zakat, and do good to your kin. When he turned
his back, the Messenger of Allah remarked: If he adheres to what
he has been ordered to do, he would enter Paradise.

Source: Sahih Muslim 14 a

It is narrated on the authority of Ubadah b. Samit that the
messenger of Allah (ﷺ) observed:

He who said:" There is no god but Allah, He is One and there is no
associate with Him, that Muhammad is his servant and His
messenger, that Christ is servant and the son of His slave-girl and
he (Christ) His word which He communicated to Mary and is His

Spirit, that Paradise is a fact and Hell is a fact," Allah would make him (he who affirms these truths) enter Paradise through any one of its eight doors which he would like.

Source: Sahih Muslim 28 a

Abu Sa'id al-Khudri reported:

Verily the Messenger of Allah said: Allah will admit into Paradise those deserving of Paradise, and He will admit whom He wishes out of His Mercy, and admit those condemned to Hell into the Fire (of Hell). He would then say: See, he whom you find having as much faith in his heart as a grain of mustard, bring him out. They will then be brought out burned and turned to charcoal, and would be cast into the river of life, and they would sprout as does a seed in the silt carried away by flood. Have you not seen that it comes out yellow (fresh) and intertwined?

Source: Sahih Muslim 184 a

Abu Dharr said:

Allah's Messenger, what about the vessels of that Cistern? He said: By Him in Whose Hand is the life of Muhammad, the vessels would outnumber the stars in the sky and its planets shining on a dark cloudless night. These would be the vessels of Paradise. He who drinks out of it (the Cistern) would never feel thirsty. There would flow in it two spouts from Paradise and he who would drink out of it would not feel thirsty; and the distance between its (two corners) is that between 'Amman and Aila, and its water is whiter than milk and sweeter than honey.

Source: Sahih Muslim 2300

'A'isha, the mother of the believers, said that Allah's Messenger (ﷺ) was called to lead the funeral prayer of a child of the Ansar. I said:

Allah's Messenger, there is happiness for this child who is a bird from the birds of Paradise for it committed no sin nor has he reached the age when one can commit sin. He said: 'A'isha, per adventure, it may be otherwise, because God created for Paradise those who are fit for it while they were yet in their father's loins and created for Hell those who are to go to Hell. He created them for Hell while they were yet in their father's loins.

Source: Sahih Muslim 2662 c

Narrated Abu Huraira:

Allah's Messenger said, "The first group (of people) who will enter Paradise will be (glittering) like the moon when it is full. They will not spit or blow their noses or relieve nature. Their utensils will be of gold and their combs of gold and silver; in their centers the aloe wood will be used, and their sweat will smell like musk. Everyone of them will have two wives; the marrow of the bones of the wives' legs will be seen through the flesh out of excessive beauty. They (i.e. the people of Paradise) will neither have differences nor hatred amongst themselves; their hearts will be as if one heart and they will be glorifying Allah in the morning and in the evening."

Source: Sahih al-Bukhari 3245

Narrated Abu Huraira:

I heard Allah's Messenger saying, "The good deeds of any person will not make him enter Paradise." (i.e., None can enter Paradise through his good deeds.) They (the Prophet's companions) said, 'Not even you, O Allah's Messenger?' He said, "Not even myself, unless Allah bestows His favor and mercy on me." So be moderate in your religious deeds and do the deeds that are within your ability: and none of you should wish for death, for if he is a good doer, he may increase his good deeds, and if he is an evil doer, he may repent to Allah."

Source: Sahih al-Bukhari 5673

Narrated Abu Sa`id Al-Khudri:

Allah's Messenger said, "Allah will say to the people of Paradise, 'O the people of Paradise!' They will say, 'Labbaik, O our Lord, and Sa`daik!' Allah will say, 'Are you pleased?" They will say, 'Why should we not be pleased since You have given us what You have not given to anyone of Your creation?' Allah will say, 'I will give you something better than that.' They will reply, 'O our Lord! And what is better than that?' Allah will say, 'I will bestow My pleasure and contentment upon you so that I will never be angry with you after for-ever.' "

Source: Sahih al-Bukhari 6549

Narrated Abu Huraira:

A Bedouin came to the Prophet and said, "Tell me of such a deed as will make me enter Paradise, if I do it." The Prophet said, "Worship Allah, and worship none along with Him, offer the (five) prescribed compulsory prayers perfectly, pay the compulsory

Zakat, and fast the month of Ramadan." The Bedouin said, "By Him, in Whose Hands my life is, I will not do more than this." When he (the Bedouin) left, the Prophet said, "Whoever likes to see a man of Paradise, then he may look at this man."

Source: Sahih al-Bukhari 1397

Narrated Buraydah ibn al-Hasib:

The Prophet said: Judges are of three types, one of whom will go to Paradise and two to Hell. The one who will go to Paradise is a man who knows what is right and gives judgment accordingly; but a man who knows what is right and acts tyrannically in his judgment will go to Hell; and a man who gives judgment for people when he is ignorant will go to Hell.

Abu Dawud said: On this subject this is the soundest tradition, that is, the tradition of Ibn Buraidah: Judges are of three types.

Source: Sunan Abi Dawud 3573 Graded Sahih by Albani

Abu al-Darda' reported the Messenger of Allah (ﷺ) as saying:

There are five thing, if anyone observe them with faith, he will enter Paradise. He who prays the five times prayer regularly, with the ablution for them, with their bowing, with their prostration and their (right) times ; keeps fast during Ramadan ; performs Hajj (pilgrimage) to the House (Ka'bah), provided he has the ability for its passage; pays Zakat happily ; and fulfills the trust (he will enter Paradise). People said: Abu al-Darda', what is fulfilling the trust ? He replied: Washing because of sexual defilement.

Source: Sunan Abi Dawud 429 Graded Hasan by Albani

It is reported on the authority of al-Mughira b. Shu'ba that the Messenger of Allah (ﷺ) said:

Moses asked his Lord: Who amongst the inhabitants of Paradise is the lowest to rank? He (Allah) said: The person who would be admitted into Paradise last of all among those deserving of Paradise who are admitted to it. It would be said to him: Enter Paradise. He would say: O my Lord! how (should I enter) while the people have settled in their apartments and taken the shares (portions)? It would be said to him: Would you be pleased if there be for you like the kingdom of a king amongst the kings of the world? He would say: I am pleased my Lord. He (Allah) would say: For you is that, and like that, and like that, and like that, and that. He would say at the fifth (point): I am well pleased. My Lord. He (Allah) would say: It is for you and, ten times like it, and for you is what your self desires and your eye enjoys. He would say: I am well pleased, my Lord. He (Moses) said: (Which is) the highest of their (inhabitants of Paradise) ranks? He (Allah) said: They are those whom I choose. I establish their honour with My own hand and then set a seal over it (and they would be blessed with Bounties) which no eye has seen, no ear has heard and no human mind has perceived: and this is substantiated by the Book of Allah, Exalted and Great:" So no soul knows what delight of the eye is hidden for them; a reward for what they did" (xxxii. 17).

Source: Sahih Muslim 189 b

It has been narrated on the authority of Abu Sa`id al-Khudri that the Messenger of Allah (ﷺ) said (to him):

~ 280 ~

Abu Sa`id, whoever cheerfully accepts Allah as his Lord, Islam as his religion and Muhammad as his Apostle is necessarily entitled to enter Paradise. He (Abu Sa`id) wondered at it and said: Messenger of Allah, repeat it for me. He (the Messenger of Allah) did that and said: There is another act which elevates the position of a man in Paradise to a grade one hundred (higher), and the elevation between one grade and the other is equal to the height of the heaven from the earth. He (Abu Sa`id) said: What is that act? He replied: Jihad in the way of Allah! Jihad in the way of Allah!

Source: Sahih Muslim 1884

It is narrated on the authority of Jabir that a man once said to the Messenger of Allah (ﷺ):

Shall I enter Paradise in case I say the obligatory prayers, observe the (fasts) of Ramadan and treat that as lawful which has been made permissible (by the Shari'ah) and deny myself that what is forbidden, and make no addition to it? He (the Prophet) replied in the affirmative. He (the inquirer) said: By Allah, I would add nothing to it.

Source: Sahih Muslim 15 c

Abdullah b. Mas'ud reported:

I said: Messenger of Allah, which of the deeds (takes one) nearer to Paradise? He (the Prophet) replied: Prayer at its proper time, I said: What next, Messenger of Allah? He replied: Kindness to the parents. I said: What next? He replied: Jihad in the cause of Allah.

Source: Sahih Muslim 85 b

It has been narrated on the authority of Abu Malik that Ubaidullah b. Ziyad visited Ma'qil b. Yaser in the latter's illness. Ma'qil said to him:

I am narrating to you a tradition. If I were not at death's door, I would not narrate it to you. I heard the Messenger of Allah (may peace he upon him) say: A ruler who, having obtained control over the affairs of the Muslims, does not strive for their betterment and does not serve them sincerely shall not enter Paradise with them.

Source: Sahih Muslim 142 g

Abdullah reported Allah's Messenger (ﷺ) as saying:

It is obligatory for you to tell the truth, for truth leads to virtue and virtue leads to Paradise, and the man who continues to speak the truth and endeavors to tell the truth is eventually recorded as truthful with Allah, and beware of telling of a lie for telling of a lie leads to obscenity and obscenity leads to Hell-Fire, and the person who keeps telling lies and endeavors to tell a lie is recorded as a liar with Allah.

Source: Sahih Muslim 2607 c

Imran b. Husain reported that it was said to Allah's Messenger (ﷺ):

Has there been drawn a distinction between the people of Paradise and the denizens of hell? He said: Yes. It was again said: (If it is so), then What is the use of doing good deeds? Thereupon he said: Everyone is facilitated in what has been created for him.

Source: Sahih Muslim 2649 a

Jabir reported:

I heard Allah's Apostle as saying that the inmates of Paradise would eat and drink but would neither spit, nor pass water, nor void excrement, nor suffer catarrah. It was said: Then, what would happen with food? Thereupon he said: They would belch and sweat (and it would be over with their food), and their sweat would be that of musk and they would glorify and praise Allah as easily as you breathe.

Source: Sahih Muslim 2835 a

Narrated Abu Huraira:

Allah's Messenger said, "The first group of people who will enter Paradise, will be glittering like the full moon and those who will follow them, will glitter like the most brilliant star in the sky. They will not urinate, relieve nature, spit, or have any nasal secretions. Their combs will be of gold, and their sweat will smell like musk. The aloes-wood will be used in their centers. Their wives will be houris. All of them will look alike and will resemble their father Adam (in stature), sixty cubits tall."

Source: Sahih al-Bukhari 3327

Abdullah narrated:

"The Messenger of Allah said: 'Whoever has a speck of pride (arrogance) in his heart, shall not be admitted into Paradise. And whoever has a speck of faith in his heart, shall not be admitted in to the Fire.'" He said: "So a man said to him: 'I like for my clothes to be nice, and my sandals to be nice?' So he said: 'Indeed Allah loves beauty. But pride is refusing the truth and belittling the people.'"

Source: Jami` at-Tirmidhi 1999 Graded Sahih by Darussalam

Abu Sa'eed Al-Khudri narrated that the Messenger of Allah said:

"Whoever eats the Tayyib and acts in accordance with the Sunnah, and the people are safe from his harm, he will enter Paradise." So a man said: "O Messenger of Allah! This is the case with many people today." So he said: "It shall be so in the generation after me."

Source: Jami at-Tirmidhi

English reference : Vol. 4, Book 11, Hadith 2520

Graded Hasan by Darussalam

Ali narrated that the Messenger of Allah said:

"Indeed in Paradise there are chambers whose outside can be seen from their inside, and their inside can be seen fom their outside." A Bedouin stood and said: "Who are they for O Prophet of Allah?" he said: "For those who speak well, feed others, fast regularly, and perform Salat for Allah during the night while the people sleep."

Source: Jami at-Tirmidhi

English reference : Vol. 4, Book 12, Hadith 2527

Graded Hasan by Darussalam

Narrated Abu Hurairah:

that the Messenger of Allah said: "By the One in Whose Hand is my soul! You will not enter Paradise until you believe, and you will not believe until you love one another. Shall I inform you about a matter which if you do it, then you will love one another? Spread the Salam among each other."

Source: Jami` at-Tirmidhi 2688 Graded Sahih by Darussalam

It was narrated that Ubaid bin Hunain, the freed slave of the family of Zaib bin Al-Khattab, said:

"I heard Abu Hurairah say: 'I came back (from a journey) with the Messenger of Allah and he heard a man reciting 'Say: He is Allah, (the) One, Allah-us-Samad (the Self-Sufficient Master). He begets not, nor was He begotten. And there is none equal or comparable unto Him.' The Messenger of Allah said: 'It is guaranteed.' We asked him: 'What, O Messenger of Allah?' He said: 'Paradise.'"

Source: Sunan an-Nasa'i 994 Graded Hasan by Darussalam

Rabi'ah bin Ka'b Al-Aslami said:

"I used to bring to the Messenger of Allah water for wudu and serve him. He said: 'Ask of me.' I said: 'I want to be with you in Paradise.' He said: 'Is there anything else?' I said: 'That is all.' He said: 'Help me to fulfill your wish by prostrating a great deal.'"

Source: Sunan an-Nasa'i 1138 Graded Sahih by Darussalam

It was narrated from Salim bin 'Abdullah that his father said:

"The Messenger of Allah said: "There are three at whom Allah will not look on the Day of Resurrection: The one who disobeys his parents, the woman who imitates men in her outward appearance, and the cuckold. And there are three who will not enter Paradise: The one who disobeys his parents, the drunkard, and the one who reminds people of what he has given them.""

Source: Sunan an-Nasa'i 2562 Graded Hasan by Darussalam

It was narrated that Anas said:

"A funeral passed by and the deceased was praised." The Prophet said: "It is granted." Another funeral passed by and the deceased was criticized. The Prophet said: "It is granted." 'Umar said: "May my father and mother be ransomed for you. One funeral passed by and the deceased was praised, and you said, 'It is granted?"' He said: "Whoever is praised will be granted Paradise, and whoever is criticized will be granted Hell, You are the witnesses of Allah on Earth."

Source: Sunan an-Nasa'i 1932 Graded Sahih by Darussalam

It was narrated that Abu Hurairah said:

"A man came to the Messenger of Allah and said: 'O Messenger of Allah, what do you think if someone comes to steal my wealth?' He said: 'Urge him by Allah.' He said: 'What if he persists?' He said: 'Urge him by Allah.' He said: 'What if he persists?' He said: 'Urge him by Allah.' He said: 'What if he persists?' He said: 'Then fight. If you are killed you will be in Paradise, and if you kill him, he will be in the Fire.'"

Source: Sunan an-Nasa'i 4082 Graded Sahih by Darussalam

It was narrated that 'Uqbah bin 'Amir said:

"I heard the Messenger of Allah say: 'Your Lord is pleased with a shepherd high in the mountains who calls the Adhan for the prayer and prays. Allah says: 'Look at this slave of Mine; he calls the Adhan and Iqamah for the prayer and fears Me. I have forgiven My slave and admitted him to Paradise.'"

Source: Sunan an-Nasai

English reference : Vol. 1, Book 7, Hadith 667

Graded Sahih by Darussalam

An-Nasr bin Sufyan narrated he heard Abu Hurairah say:

"We were with the Messenger of Allah and Bilal stood up and gave the call. When he fell silent the Messenger of Allah said: 'Whoever says the same as this (what the Mu'adhdhin) with certainty, he will enter Paradise.

Source: Sunan an-Nasai

English reference : Vol. 1, Book 7, Hadith 675

Graded Hasan by Darussalam

It was narrated that 'Umar bin Al-Khattab said:

"The Messenger of Allah said: 'Whoever performs Wudu' and does it well, then says: "Ashhadu an la ilaha ill-Allah was ashhadu anna Muhammadan 'abduhu wa rasuluh (I bear witness that there is none worthy of worship except Allah, and I bear witness that Muhammad is his slave and Messenger)," eight gates of Paradise

will be opened for him, and he may enter through whichever one he wishes.'"

Source: Sunan an-Nasai

English reference : Vol. 1, Book 1, Hadith 148

Graded Sahih by Darussalam

It was narrated from Mu'awiyah bin Jahimah As-Sulami, that Jahimah came to the Prophet (ﷺ) and said:

"O Messenger of Allah! I want to go out and fight (in Jihad) and I have come to ask your advice." He said: "Do you have a mother?" He said: "Yes." He said: "Then stay with her, for Paradise is beneath her feet."

Source: Sunan an-Nasa'i 3104 Graded Sahih by Darussalam

It was narrated that Sabrah bin Abi Fakih said:

"I heard the Messenger of Allah say: 'the Shaitan sits in the paths of the son of Adam. He sits waiting for him, in the path to Islam, and he says: Will you accept Islam, and leave your religion, and the religion of your forefathers? But he disobeys him and accepts Islam. Then he sits waiting for him, on the path to emigration, and he says: Will you emigrate and leave behind your land and sky? The one who emigrates is like a horse tethered to a peg. But he disobeys him and emigrates. Then he sits, waiting for him, on the path to Jihad, and he says: Will you fight in Jihad when it will cost you your life and your wealth? You will fight and be killed, and your wife will remarry, and your wealth will be divided. But he disobeys him and fights in Jihad.' The Messenger of Allah said:

~ 288 ~

'Whoever does that, then he had a right from Allah, the Mighty and Sublime, that He will admit him to paradise. Whoever is killed, he has a right from Allah, the Mighty and Sublime, that He will admit him to Paradise. If he is drowned, he has a right from Allah that He will admit him to paradise, or whoever is thrown by his mount and his neck is broken, he had a right from Allah that he will admit him to Paradise.'"

Source: Sunan an-Nasa'i 3134 Graded Hasan by Darussalam

It was narrated that Abu Najih As-Sulami said:

"I heard the Messenger of Allah say: 'Whoever shoots an arrow in the cause of Allah and it hits the target, it will raise him one level in Paradise.' That day I shot sixteen arrows that hit their targets." He said: "And I heard the Messenger of Allah say: 'Whoever shoots an arrow in the cause of Allah, it is equal to the reward of freeing a slave.'"

Source: Sunan an-Nasa'i 3143 Graded Sahih by Darussalam

Abu Hurairah narrated that:

Allah's Messenger said: "Qintar is twelve thousand 'Uqiyah, each 'Uqiyah of which is better than what is between heaven and earth." And the Messenger of Allah said: "A man will be raised in status in Paradise and will say: 'Where did this come from?' And it will be said: 'From your son's praying for forgiveness for you.'"

Source: Sunan Ibn Majah 3660 Graded Hasan by Darussalam

It was narrated from Abu Hurairah that the Messenger of Allah (ﷺ) said:

"When the first night of Ramadan comes, the satans and mischievous jinns are chained up, and the gates of the Fire are closed, and none of its gates are opened. The gates of Paradise are opened and none of its gates are closed. And a caller cried out: 'O seeker of good, proceed, O seeker of evil, stop.' And Allah has necks (people) whom He frees (from the Fire), and that happens every day."

Source: Sunan ibn Majah

English reference : Vol. 1, Book 7, Hadith 1642

Graded Hasan by Darussalam

It was narrated that 'Ali said:

"I heard the Messenger of Allah say: 'Whoever comes to his Muslim brother and visits him (when he is sick), he is walking among the harvest of Paradise until he sits down, and when he sits down he is covered with mercy. If it is morning, seventy thousand angels will send blessing upon him until evening, and if it is evening, seventy thousand angels will send blessing upon him until morning.'"

Source: Sunan ibn Majah

English reference : Vol. 1, Book 6, Hadith 1442

Graded Hasan by Darussalam

Narrated Abu Sa`id Al-Khudri:

The Prophet said, "The (planet of) earth will be a bread on the Day of Resurrection, and The resistible (Allah) will topple turn it with

~ 290 ~

His Hand like anyone of you topple turns a bread with his hands while (preparing the bread) for a journey, and that bread will be the entertainment for the people of Paradise." A man from the Jews came (to the Prophet) and said, "May The Beneficent (Allah) bless you, O Abul Qasim! Shall I tell you of the entertainment of the people of Paradise on the Day of Resurrection?" The Prophet said, "Yes." The Jew said, "The earth will be a bread," as the Prophet had said. Thereupon the Prophet looked at us and smiled till his premolar tooth became visible. Then the Jew further said, "Shall I tell you of the udm (additional food taken with bread) they will have with the bread?" He added, "That will be Balam and Nun." The people asked, "What is that?" He said, "It is an ox and a fish, and seventy thousand people will eat of the caudate lobe (i.e. extra lobe) of their livers."

Source: Sahih al-Bukhari 6520

Abu Hurairah narrated that the Messenger of Allah said:

"When Allah created Paradise and the Fire, He sent Jibril to Paradise , saying: 'Look at it and at what I have prepared in it for its inhabitants.'" He said: "So he came to it and looked at it, and at what Allah had prepared in it. He (Jibril) said: 'Indeed, by your Might, none shall hear of it except that he shall enter it.' Then He gave the order for it to be surrounded with hardships. He said: 'Return to it and look at it, and at what I have prepared in it for its inhabitants.'" He said: "So he returned to it and found it surrounded with hardships. He returned to Him and said: 'Indeed, by your Might, I fear that none shall enter it.' He said: 'Go to the Fire and look at it and at what I have prepared in it for its inhabitants.' So he found it, one part of it riding the other. So he

returned to Him and said: 'Indeed, by your Might, none shall hear of it and then enter it.' So He gave the order for it to be surrounded with desires, then He said: 'Return to it.,' so he (Jibril) returned to it, then he said: 'Indeed, by Your Might, I fear that none shall be saved from it except that he shall enter it.'"

Source: Jami at-Tirmidhi

English reference : Vol. 4, Book 12, Hadith 2560

Graded Hasan by Darussalam

Shaddad bin Aws narrated that:

The Prophet said to him: "Should I not direct you to the chief of supplications for forgiveness? 'O Allah, You are my Lord, there is none worthy of worship except You, You created me and I am Your slave. I am adhering to Your covenant and Your promise as much as I am able to, I seek refuge in You from the evil of what I have done. I admit to You your blessings upon me, and I admit to my sins. So forgive me, for there is none who can forgive sins except You (Allāhumma anta rabbī lā ilāha illā anta, khalaqtanī wa ana `abduka, wa ana `alā `ahdika wa wa`dika ma-stata`tu. A`ūdhu bika min sharri ma sana`tu, wa abū'u ilayka bini`matika `alayya wa a`tarifu bidhunūbī faghfirlī dhunūbī innahu lā yaghfirudh-dhunūba illā ant).' None of you says it when he reaches the evening, and a decree comes upon him before he reaches morning, except that Paradise becomes obligatory upon him. And none says it when he reaches the morning, and a decree comes upon him before he reaches evening, except that Paradise becomes obligatory for him."

Source: Jami` at-Tirmidhi 3393 Graded Sahih by Darussalam

Narrated Abu Hurayrah:

I heard the Messenger of Allah say: There were two men among Banu Isra'il, who were striving for the same goal. One of them would commit sin and the other would strive to do his best in the world. The man who exerted himself in worship continued to see the other in sin.

He would say: Refrain from it. One day he found him in sin and said to him: Refrain from it.

He said: Leave me alone with my Lord. Have you been sent as a watchman over me? He said: I swear by Allah, Allah will not forgive you, nor will he admit you to Paradise. Then their souls were taken back (by Allah), and they met together with the Lord of the worlds.

He (Allah) said to this man who had striven hard in worship; Had you knowledge about Me or had you power over that which I had in My hand? He said to the man who sinned: Go and enter Paradise by My mercy. He said about the other: Take him to Hell.

Abu Hurayrah said: By Him in Whose hand my soul is, he spoke a word by which this world and the next world of his were destroyed.

Source: Sunan Abi Dawud 4901 Graded Sahih by Albani

Abdullah b. Amr b. al-As reported Allah's Messenger (ﷺ) as saying:

When you hear the Mu'adhdhin, repeat what he says, then invoke a blessing on me, for everyone who invokes a blessing on me will receive ten blessings from Allah; then beg from Allah al-Wasila for me, which is a rank in Paradise fitting for only one of Allah's servants, and I hope that I may be that one. If anyone who asks that I be given the Wasila, he will be assured of my intercession.

Source: Sahih Muslim 384

Hudhaifa reported Allah's Apostle (ﷺ) as saying:

A person died and he entered Paradise. It was said to him What (act) did you do? (Either he recalled it himself or he was made to recall), he said I used to enter into transactions with people and I gave respite to the insolvent and did not show any strictness in case of accepting a coin or demanding cash payment. (For these acts of his) he was granted pardon. Abu Mas'ud said: I heard this from Allah's Messenger.

Source: Sahih Muslim 1560 c

Abu Huraira reported Allah's Messenger (ﷺ) as saying:

The gates of Paradise are not opened but on two days, Monday and Thursday. and then every servant (of Allah) is granted pardon who does not associate anything with Allah except the person in whose (heart) there is rancour against his brother. And it would be said: Look towards both of them until there is reconciliation; look toward both of them until there is reconciliation; look towards both of them until there is reconciliation. This hadith has been narrated on the authority of Suhail who narrated it on the authority of his father with the chain of transmitters of Malik, but with this variation of wording:, (Those would not be granted pardon) who boycott each other."

Source: Sahih Muslim 2565 a, b

Anas b. Malik reported that Allah's Messenger (ﷺ) said:

In Paradise there is a street to which they would come every Friday. The north wind will blow and would scatter fragrance on their faces and on their clothes and would add to their beauty and loveliness, and then they would go back to their family after having an added luster to their beauty and loveliness, and their family would say to them: By Allah, you have been increased in beauty and loveliness after leaving us, and they would say: By Allah, you have also increased in beauty and loveliness after us.

Source: Sahih Muslim 2833

Narrated Abu Huraira:

That heard Allah's Messenger saying, "We are the last but will be the foremost to enter Paradise." The Prophet added, "He who obeys me, obeys Allah, and he who disobeys me, disobeys Allah. He who obeys the chief, obeys me, and he who disobeys the chief, disobeys me. The Imam is like a shelter for whose safety the Muslims should fight and where they should seek protection. If the Imam orders people with righteousness and rules justly, then he will be rewarded for that, and if he does the opposite, he will be responsible for that."

Source: Sahih al-Bukhari 2956, 2957

Narrated Abu Huraira:

Allah's Messenger said, "The first batch (of people) who will enter Paradise will be (glittering) like a full moon; and those who will enter next will be (glittering) like the brightest star. Their hearts will be as if the heart of a single man, for they will have no enmity amongst themselves, and everyone of them shall have two wives, each of whom will be so beautiful, pure and transparent that the marrow of the bones of their legs will be seen through the flesh. They will be glorifying Allah in the morning and evening, and will never fall ill, and they will neither blow their noses, nor spit. Their utensils will be of gold and silver, and their combs will be of gold, and the fuel used in their centers will be the aloeswood, and their sweat will smell like musk."

Source: Sahih al-Bukhari 3246

Narrated Abu Huraira:

The Prophet said, " Let the slave of Dinar and Dirham, of Quantify and Khamisa perish as he is pleased if these things are given to him, and if not, he is displeased. Let such a person perish and relapse, and if he is pierced with a thorn, let him not find anyone to take it out for him. Paradise is for him who holds the reins of his horse to strive in Allah's Cause, with his hair unkempt and feet covered with dust: if he is appointed in the vanguard, he is perfectly satisfied with his post of guarding, and if he is appointed in the rearward, he accepts his post with satisfaction; (he is so simple and unambiguous that) if he asks for permission he is not permitted, and if he intercedes, his intercession is not accepted."

Source: Sahih al-Bukhari 2887

It was narrated that Abu Aswad Ad-Dili said:

"I came to Al-Madinah and sat with 'Umar bin Al-Khattab. A funeral passed by and the deceased was praised, and 'Umar said: 'It is granted.' Then another passed by and the deceased was praised, and 'Umar Said: 'It is granted.' Then a third passed by, and the deceased was criticized, and 'Umar said: 'It is granted.' I said: What is granted, O commander of the believers?' He said: 'I said what the Messenger of Allah said: Any Muslim for whom four people bear witness and say good things, Allah will admit him to Paradise.' We said: 'Or three?' He said: 'Or three.' We said: 'Or two?' He said: 'Or two.'"

Source: Sunan an-Nasa'i 1934 Graded Sahih by Darussalam

It was narrated that Muhammad bin Jahsh said:

"We were sitting with the Messenger of Allah when he raised his head toward the sky, and put his palm on his forehead, then he said: 'Subhan Allah, what a stern warning has been revealed! We fell silent and were scared. The following day I asked him: 'O Messenger of Allah, what is this stern warning that has been revealed? He said: 'By the One in Whose hand is my soul, if a man were to be killed in the cause of Allah then brought back to life, then killed, but he owed a debt, he would not enter paradise until his debt was paid off,"

Source: Sunan an-Nasa'i 4684 Graded Sahih by Darussalam

Abu Huraira reported that the Messenger of Allah (ﷺ) said:

Who fasted among you today? Abu Bakr replied: I did. He (the Prophet again) said: Who among you followed a bier today? Abu Bakr replied: I did. He (the Prophet again) said: Who among you fed a poor man today? Abu Bakr replied: I did. He (again) said: Who among you visited an invalid today? Abu Bakr said: I did. Upon this the Messenger of Allah said: Anyone in whom (these good deeds) are combined will certainly enter paradise.

Source: Sahih Muslim 1028

Abdurabbih bin Bariq Al-Hanafi said:

"I heard my grandfather, the father of my mother, Simak bin Al-Walid Al-Hanadi narrating, that he heard Ibn Abbas narrated, that he heard the Messenger of Allah saying: "Whoever has two predecessors (in death) among my Ummah, then Allah will admit them into Paradise." So Aishah said to him: "What about one from your Umma who has one predecessor?" He said: "And whoever has one predecessor O Muwaffaqqah!" So she said: "What about one who does not have a predecessor from your Ummah?" He said: "I am the predecessor for my Ummah: you will never suffer (in grief) for (the loss of) anyone similar to me."

Source: Jami` at-Tirmidhi 1062

Graded Hasan by Darussalam

Ma'dan bin Talha Al-Ya'muri said:

"I met Thawban, the freed slave of the Messenger of Allah and said: "Tell me of an action that will benefit me or gain me admittance to Paradise.' He remained silent for a while, then he turned to me and said: 'You should prostrate, because I heard the Messenger of Allah say: "There is no one who prostrated once to Allah, the Mighty and Sublime, except that Allah will raise him one degree in status thereby, and erase one sin thereby." Ma'dan

said: "Then I met Abu Ad-Darda' and asked him the same question I had asked Thawban." He said to me: "You should prostrate, for I heard the Messenger of Allah say: "There is no one who prostrates once to Allah, but Allah will raise him one degree thereby and erase one sin thereby."

Source: Sunan an-Nasa'i 1139 Graded Sahih by Darussalam

Narrated Anas:

When the news of the arrival of the Prophet at Medina reached `Abdullah bin Salam, he went to him to ask him about certain things, He said, "I am going to ask you about three things which only a Prophet can answer: What is the first sign of The Hour? What is the first food which the people of Paradise will eat? Why does a child attract the similarity to his father or to his mother?" The Prophet replied, "Gabriel has just now informed me of that." Ibn Salam said, "He (i.e. Gabriel) is the enemy of the Jews amongst the angels. The Prophet said, "As for the first sign of The Hour, it will be a fire that will collect the people from the East to the West. As for the first meal which the people of Paradise will eat, it will be the caudate (extra) lobe of the fish-liver. As for the child, if the man's discharge proceeds the woman's discharge, the child attracts the similarity to the man, and if the woman's discharge proceeds the man's, then the child attracts the similarity to the woman." On this, `Abdullah bin Salam said, "I testify that None has the right to be worshipped except Allah, and that you are the Messenger of Allah." and added, "O Allah's Messenger! Jews invent such lies as make one astonished, so please ask them about me before they know about my conversion to Islam . " The Jews came, and the Prophet said, "What kind of man is `Abdullah bin Salam among you?"

They replied, "The best of us and the son of the best of us and the most superior among us, and the son of the most superior among us. "The Prophet said, "What would you think if `Abdullah bin Salam should embrace Islam?" They said, "May Allah protect him from that." The Prophet repeated his question and they gave the same answer. Then `Abdullah came out to them and said, "I testify that None has the right to be worshipped except Allah and that Muhammad is the Messenger of Allah!" On this, the Jews said, "He is the most wicked among us and the son of the most wicked among us." So they degraded him. On this, he (i.e. `Abdullah bin Salam) said, "It is this that I was afraid of, O Allah's Messenger.

Source: Sahih al-Bukhari 3938

Narrated Abu Sa'eed Al-Khudri:

that the Messenger of Allah said: "I am the chief of the children of Adam on the Day of Judgement and I am not boasting, and in my hand is the banner of praise and I am not boasting, and there has been no Prophet since Adam or other than him, except that he is under my banner. And I am the first for whom the earth will split open, and I am not boasting." He said: "The people will be frightened by three frights. So they will come to Adam saying: 'You are our father Adam, so intercede for us with your Lord.' So he says: 'I committed a sin for which I was expelled to the earth, so go to Nuh.' So they will come to Nuh and he will say: 'I supplicated against the people of the earth, so they were destroyed. So go to Ibrahim.' So they will go to Ibrahim, and he says: 'I lied three times.'" Then the Messenger of Allah said: "He did not lie except defending Allah's religion." "So go to Musa.' So they will come to Musa, and he will say: 'I took a life. So go to 'Eisa(Jesus).

So they go to 'Eisa(Jesus) and he says: 'I was worshiped besides Allah. So go to Muhammad.'" He said: "So they will come to me, and I will go to them." (One of the narrators) Ibn Ju'dan said: "Anas said: 'It is as if I am looking at the Messenger of Allah , and he is saying: "So I will take hold of a ring of a gate of Paradise to rattle it, and it will be said: 'Who is there?' It will be said: 'Muhammad.' They will open it for me, and welcome me saying, 'Welcome.' I will fall prostrate and Allah will inspire me with statements of gratitude and praise and it will be said to me: 'Raise your head, ask and you shall be given, intercede, and your intercession shall be accepted, speak, and your saying shall be heard.' And that is Al-Maqam Al-Mahmud about which Allah said: It may be that your Lord will raise you to Maqaman-Mahmud (17:79)." Sufyan said: "None of it is from Anas except this sentence: 'I will take hold of a ring of a gate of Paradise to rattle it.'"

Source: Jami at-Tirmidhi

English reference : Vol. 5, Book 44, Hadith 3148

Graded Hasan by Darussalam

Narrated Jabir bin `Abdullah:

Some angels came to the Prophet while he was sleeping. Some of them said, "He is sleeping." Others said, "His eyes are sleeping but his heart is awake." Then they said, "There is an example for this companion of yours." One of them said, "Then set forth an example for him." Some of them said, "He is sleeping." The others said, "His eyes are sleeping but his heart is awake." Then they said, "His example is that of a man who has built a house and then offered therein a banquet and sent an inviter (messenger) to invite the people. So whoever accepted the invitation of the inviter, entered the house and ate of the banquet, and whoever did not accept the invitation of the inviter, did not enter the house, nor did he eat of the banquet." Then the angels said, "Interpret this example to him so that he may understand it." Some of them said, "He is sleeping.'' The others said, "His eyes are sleeping but his heart is awake." And then they said, "The houses stands for Paradise and the call maker is Muhammad; and whoever obeys Muhammad, obeys Allah; and whoever disobeys Muhammad, disobeys Allah. Muhammad separated the people (i.e., through his message, the good is distinguished from the bad, and the believers from the disbelievers).

Source: Sahih al-Bukhari 7281

Narrated Abdullah ibn Amr:

The Prophet said: There are two qualities or characteristics which will not be returned by any Muslim without his entering Paradise. While they are easy, those who act upon them are few. One should say: "Glory be to Allah" ten times after every prayer, "Praise be to Allah" ten times and "Allah is Most Great" ten times. That is a hundred and fifty on the tongue, but one thousand and five hundred on the scale. When he goes to bed, he should say: "Allah is Most Great" thirty-four times, "Praise be to Allah" thirty-three times, and Glory be to Allah thirty-three times, for that is a hundred on the tongue and a thousand on the scale. (He said:) I saw the Messenger of Allah counting them on his hand.

The people asked: Messenger of Allah! How is it that while they are easy, those who act upon them are few?

He replied: The Devil comes to one of you when he goes to bed and he makes him sleep, before he utters them, and he comes to him while he is engaged in prayer and calls a need to his mind before he utters them.

Source: Sunan Abi Dawud 5065 Graded Sahih by Albani

Narrated Mu'adh bin Jabal:

*"I accompanied the Prophet on a journey. One day I was near him while we were moving so I said: 'O Messenger of Allah! Inform me about an action by which I will be admitted into Paradise, and which will keep me far from the Fire.' He said: 'You have asked me about something great, but it is easy for whomever Allah makes it easy: Worship Allah and do not associate any partners with Him, establish the Salat, give the Zakat, fast Ramadan and perform Hajj to the House.' Then he said: 'Shall I not guide you to the doors of good? Fasting is a shield, and charity extinguishes sins like water extinguishes fire - and a man's praying in depths of the night.'"
He said: "Then he recited: 'Their sides forsake their beds to call upon their Lord.' Until he reached: 'What they used to do.' [32:16-17] Then he said: 'Shall I not inform you about the head of the entire matter, and its pillar, and its hump?' I said: 'Of course O Messenger of Allah! He said: 'The head of the matter is Islam, and its pillar is the Salat, and its hump is Jihad.' Then he said: 'Shall I not inform you about what governs all of that?' I said: 'Of course O Messenger of Allah!'" He said: "So he grabbed his tongue. He said 'Restrain this.' I said: 'O Prophet of Allah! Will we be taken*

to account for what we say?' He said: 'May your mother grieve your loss O Mu'adh! Are the people tossed into the Fire upon their faces, or upon their noses, except because of what their tongues have wrought'"

Source: Jami` at-Tirmidhi 2616

Graded Hasan by Darussalam

Iyad b. Him-ar reported that Allah's Messenger (ﷺ), while delivering a sermon one day, said:

Behold, my Lord commanded me that I should teach you which you do not know and which He has taught me today. (He has instructed thus): The property which I have conferred upon them is lawful for them. I have created My servants as one having a natural inclination to the worship of Allah but it is Satan who turns them away from the right religion and he makes unlawful what has been declared lawful for them and he commands them to ascribe partnership with Me, although he has no justification for that. And verily, Allah looked towards the people of the world and He showed hatred for the Arabs and the non-Arabs, but with the exception of some remnants from the People of the Book. And He (further) said: I have sent thee (the Prophet) in order to put you to test and put (those to test) through you. And I sent the Book to you which cannot be washed away by water, so that you may recite it while in the state of wakefulness or sleep. Verily, Allah commanded me to burn (kill) the Quraish. I said: My Lord, they would break my head (like the tearing) of bread, and Allah said: You turn them out as they turned you out, you fight against them and We shall help you in this, you should spend and you would be conferred upon. You send an army and I would send an army five times greater than that. Fight against those who disobey you along with those who obey you. The inmates of Paradise are three: One who wields authority and is just and fair, one who Is truthful and has been endowed with power to do good deeds. And the person who is merciful and kind hearted towards his relatives and to every pious Muslim, and one who does not stretch his hand in spite of having a large family to support. And He said: The inmates of Hell are five: the weak who lack power to (avoid evil), the (carefree) who pursue (everything irrespective of the fact that it is good or evil) and who do not have any care for their family or for their wealth. And those dishonest whose greed cannot be concealed even in the case of minor things. And the third. who betray you. morning and evening, in regard to your family and your property. He also made a mention of the miser and the liar and those who are in the habit of abusing people and using obscene and foul language. Abu Ghassan in his narration did not make mention of" Spend and there would be spent for you."

Source: Sahih Muslim 2865 a

Data on Hellfire

Quran 2:39

But those who disbelieve and belie Our Ayât (proofs, evidences, verses, lessons, signs, revelations, etc.)- such are the dwellers of the Fire, They shall abide therein forever.

Quran 2:80-81

And they (Jews) say, "The Fire (i.e. Hell-fire on the Day of Resurrection) shall not touch us but for a few numbered days." Say (O Muhammad to them): "Have you taken a covenant from Allâh, so that Allâh will not break His Covenant? Or is it that you say of Allâh what you know not?" (80) Yes! Whosoever earns evil and his sin has surrounded him, they are dwellers of the Fire (i.e. Hell); they will dwell therein forever.

Quran 2:119

Verily, We have sent you (O Muhammad) with the truth (Islâm), a bringer of glad tidings (for those who believe in what you brought, that they will enter Paradise) and a warner (for those who disbelieve in what you brought, they will enter the Hell-fire). And you will not be asked about the dwellers of the blazing Fire.

Quran 2:126

And (remember) when Ibrâhim (Abraham) said, "My Lord, make this city (Makkah) a place of security and provide its people with fruits, such of them as believe in Allâh and the Last Day." He

(Allâh) answered: "As for him who disbelieves, I shall leave him in contentment for a while, then I shall compel him to the torment of the Fire, and worst indeed is that destination!"

Quran 2:161-162

Verily, those who disbelieve, and die while they are disbelievers, it is they on whom is the Curse of Allâh and of the angels and of mankind, combined. (161) They will abide therein (under the curse in Hell), their punishment will neither be lightened, nor will they be reprieved.

Quran 2:166-167

When those who were followed, disown (declare themselves innocent of) those who followed (them), and they see the torment, then all their relations will be cut off from them. (166) And those who followed will say: "If only we had one more chance to return (to the worldly life), we would disown (declare ourselves as innocent from) them as they have disowned (declared themselves as innocent from) us." Thus Allâh will show them their deeds as regrets for them. And they will never get out of the Fire.

Quran 2:257

Allâh is the Walî (Protector or Guardian) of those who believe. He brings them out from darkness into light. But as for those who disbelieve, their Auliyâ (supporters and helpers) are Tâghût [false deities and false leaders], they bring them out from light into darkness. Those are the dwellers of the Fire, and they will abide therein forever.

Quran 3:10

Verily, those who disbelieve, neither their properties nor their offspring will avail them whatsoever against Allâh; and it is they who will be fuel of the Fire.

Quran 3:12

Say to those who disbelieve: "You will be defeated and gathered together to Hell, and worst indeed is that place to rest."

Quran 3:21-22

Verily! Those who disbelieve in the Ayât (proofs, evidences, verses, lessons, signs, revelations, etc.) of Allâh and kill the Prophets without right, and kill those men who order just dealings, ... then announce to them a painful torment. (21) They are those whose works will be lost in this world and in the Hereafter, and they will have no helpers.

Quran 3:116

Surely, those who reject Faith, neither their properties, nor their offspring will avail them aught against Allâh. They are the dwellers of the Fire, therein they will abide.

Quran 3:151

We shall cast terror into the hearts of those who disbelieve, because they joined others in worship with Allâh, for which He had sent no authority; their abode will be the Fire and how evil is the abode of the Zâlimûn (polytheists and wrong¬doers).

Quran 3:196-197

Let not the free disposal (and affluence) of the disbelievers throughout the land deceive you. (196) A brief enjoyment; then, their ultimate abode is Hell; and worst indeed is that place for rest.

Quran 4:14

And whosoever disobeys Allâh and His Messenger (Muhammad), and transgresses His limits, He will cast him into the Fire, to abide therein; and he shall have a disgraceful torment.

Quran 4:29-30

O you who believe! Eat not up your property among yourselves unjustly except it be a trade amongst you, by mutual consent. And do not kill yourselves (nor kill one another). Surely, Allâh is Most Merciful to you. (29) And whoever commits that through aggression and injustice, We shall cast him into the Fire, and that is easy for Allâh.

Quran 4:56

Surely! Those who disbelieved in Our Ayât (proofs, evidences, verses, lessons, signs, revelations, etc.) We shall burn them in Fire. As often as their skins are roasted through, We shall change them for other skins that they may taste the punishment. Truly, Allâh is Ever Most Powerful, All¬Wise.

Quran 4:93

And whoever kills a believer intentionally, his recompense is Hell to abide therein, and the Wrath and the Curse of Allâh are upon him, and a great punishment is prepared for him.

Quran 4:97

Verily! As for those whom the angels take (in death) while they are wronging themselves (as they stayed among the disbelievers even though emigration was obligatory for them), they (angels) say (to them): "In what (condition) were you?" They reply: "We were weak and oppressed on earth." They (angels) say: "Was not the earth of Allâh spacious enough for you to emigrate therein?" Such men will find their abode in Hell - What an evil destination!

Quran 4:115

And whoever contradicts and opposes the Messenger (Muhammad) after the right path has been shown clearly to him, and follows other than the believers' way. We shall keep him in the path he has chosen, and burn him in Hell - what an evil destination.

Quran 4:140

And it has already been revealed to you in the Book (this Qur'ân) that when you hear the Verses of Allâh being denied and mocked at, then sit not with them, until they engage in a talk other than that; (but if you stayed with them) certainly in that case you would be like them. Surely, Allâh will collect the hypocrites and disbelievers all together in Hell,

Quran 4:145

Verily, the hypocrites will be in the lowest depths (grade) of the Fire; no helper will you find for them.

Quran 4:168-169

Verily, those who disbelieve and did wrong [by concealing the truth about Prophet Muhammad and his message of true Islâmic Monotheism written in the Taurât (Torah) and the Injeel], Allâh will not forgive them, nor will He guide them to any way, . (168) Except the way of Hell, to dwell therein forever, and this is ever easy for Allâh.

Quran 5:10

And those who disbelieve and deny our Ayât (proofs, evidences, verses, lessons, signs, revelations, etc.) are those who will be the dwellers of the Hell-fire.

Quran 5:33

The recompense of those who wage war against Allâh and His Messenger and do mischief in the land is only that they shall be killed or crucified or their hands and their feet be cut off from the opposite sides, or be exiled from the land. That is their disgrace in this world, and a great torment is theirs in the Hereafter.

Quran 5:36-37

Verily, those who disbelieve, if they had all that is in the earth, and as much again therewith to ransom themselves thereby from the torment on the Day of Resurrection, it would never be accepted of them, and theirs would be a painful torment.(36) They will long to get out of the Fire, but never will they get out therefrom, and theirs will be a lasting torment.

Quran 5:86

But those who disbelieved and belied Our Ayât (proofs, evidences, verses, lessons, signs, revelations, etc.), they shall be the dwellers of the (Hell) Fire.

Quran 6:27

If you could but see when they will be held over the (Hell) Fire! They will say: "Would that we were but sent back (to the world)! Then we would not deny the Ayât (proofs, evidences, verses, lessons, revelations, etc.) of our Lord, and we would be of the believers!"

Quran 6:70

And leave alone those who take their religion as play and amusement, and whom the life of this world has deceived. But remind (them) with it (the Qur'ân) lest a person be given up to destruction for that which he has earned, when he will find for himself no protector or intercessor besides Allâh, and even if he offers every ransom, it will not be accepted from him. Such are they who are given up to destruction because of that which they have earned. For them will be a drink of boiling water and a painful torment because they used to disbelieve.

Quran 7:38-41

(Allâh) will say: "Enter you in the company of nations who passed away before you, of men and jinn, into the Fire." Every time a new nation enters, it curses its sister nation (that went before), until they will be gathered all together in the Fire. The last of them will say to the first of them: "Our Lord! These misled us, so give them a double torment of the Fire." He will say: "For each one there is double (torment), but you know not." (38) The first of them will say to the last of them: "You were not better than us, so taste the torment for what you used to earn." (39) Verily, those who belie Our Ayât (proofs, evidences, verses, lessons, signs, revelations) and treat them with arrogance, for them the gates of heaven will not be opened, and they will not enter Paradise until the camel goes through the eye of the needle (which is impossible). Thus do We recompense the Mujrimûn (criminals, polytheists, and sinners). (40) Theirs will be a bed of Hell (Fire), and over them coverings (of Hell-fire). Thus do We recompense the Zâlimûn (polytheists and wrong-doers).

Quran 7:50-51

And the dwellers of the Fire will call to the dwellers of Paradise: "Pour on us some water or anything that Allâh has provided you with." They will say: "Both (water and provision) Allâh has forbidden to the disbelievers." (50) "Who took their religion as an amusement and play, and the life of the world deceived them." So this Day We shall forget them as they forgot their meeting of this Day, and as they used to reject Our Ayât (proofs, evidences, verses, lessons, signs, revelations).

Quran 7:179

And surely, We have created many of the jinn and mankind for Hell. They have hearts wherewith they understand not, and they have eyes wherewith they see not, and they have ears wherewith they hear not (the truth). They are like cattle, nay even more astray; those! They are the heedless ones.

Quran 8:14

This is (the torment), so taste it, and surely for the disbelievers is the torment of the Fire.

Quran 8:16

And whoever turns his back to them on such a day - unless it be a stratagem of war, or to retreat to a troop (of his own), - he indeed has drawn upon himself wrath from Allâh. And his abode is Hell, and worst indeed is that destination!

Quran 8:36-37

Verily, those who disbelieve spend their wealth to hinder (men) from the Path of Allâh, and so will they continue to spend it; but in the end it will become an anguish for them. Then they will be overcome. And those who disbelieve will be gathered unto Hell (36) In order that Allâh may distinguish the wicked (disbelievers, polytheists and doers of evil deeds) from the good (believers of Islâmic Monotheism and doers of righteous deeds), and put the wicked (disbelievers, polytheists and doers of evil deeds) one over another, heap them together and cast them into Hell. Those! it is they who are the losers.

Quran 9:73

O Prophet (Muhammad)! Strive hard against the disbelievers and the hypocrites, and be harsh against them, their abode is Hell, - and worst indeed is that destination.

Quran 9:94-95

They (the hypocrites) will present their excuses to you (Muslims), when you return to them. Say "Present no excuses, we shall not believe you. Allâh has already informed us of the news concerning you. Allâh and His Messenger will observe your deeds. In the end you will be brought back to the All-Knower of the unseen and the seen, then He (Allâh) will inform you of what you used to do." (94) They will swear by Allâh to you (Muslims) when you return to them, that you may turn away from them. So turn away from them. Surely, they are Rijs [i.e. Najas (impure) because of their evil deeds], and Hell is their dwelling place, - a recompense for that which they used to earn.

Quran 9:109

Is it then he who laid the foundation of his building on piety to Allâh and His Good Pleasure better, or he who laid the foundation of his building on the brink of an undetermined precipice ready to crumble down, so that it crumbled to pieces with him into the Fire of Hell. And Allâh guides not the people who are the Zâlimûn (cruel, violent, proud, polytheist and wrong-doer).

Quran 9:113

It is not (proper) for the Prophet and those who believe to ask Allâh's Forgiveness for the Mushrikûn (polytheists, idolaters, pagans, disbelievers in the Oneness of Allâh) even though they be of kin, after it has become clear to them that they are the dwellers of the Fire (because they died in a state of disbelief).

Quran 10:7-8

Verily, those who hope not for their meeting with Us, but are pleased and satisfied with the life of the present world, and those who are heedless of Our Ayât (proofs, evidences, verses, lessons, signs, revelations, etc.), (7) Those, their abode will be the Fire, because of what they used to earn.

Quran 10:27

And those who have earned evil deeds, the recompense of an evil deed is the like thereof, and humiliating disgrace will cover them (their faces). No defender will they have from Allâh. Their faces will be covered, as it were with pieces from the darkness of night. They are dwellers of the Fire, they will abide therein forever.

Quran 11:15-16

Whosoever desires the life of the world and its glitter; to them We shall pay in full (the wages of) their deeds therein, and they will have no diminution therein. (15) They are those for whom there is nothing in the Hereafter but Fire; and vain are the deeds they did therein. And of no effect is that which they used to do

Quran 11:19-22

Those who hinder (others) from the Path of Allâh (Islâmic Monotheism), and seek a crookedness therein, while they are disbelievers in the Hereafter. (19) By no means will they escape (from Allâh's Torment) on earth, nor have they protectors besides Allâh! Their torment will be doubled! They could not bear to hear (the preachers of the truth) and they used not to see (the truth because of their severe aversion, inspite of the fact that they had the sense of hearing and sight). (20) They are those who have lost their ownselves, and their invented false deities will vanish from them. (21) Certainly, they are those who will be the greatest losers in the Hereafter.

Quran 11:106-107

As for those who are wretched, they will be in the Fire, sighing in a high and low tone. (106) They will dwell therein for all the time that the heavens and the earth endure, except as your Lord wills. Verily, your Lord is the Doer of whatsoever He intends (or wills).

Quran 11:118-119

And if your Lord had so willed, He could surely have made mankind one Ummah [nation or community (following one religion only i.e. Islâm)], but they will not cease to disagree, – (118) Except him on whom your Lord has bestowed His Mercy (the follower of truth - Islâmic Monotheism) and for that did He create them. And the Word of your Lord has been fulfilled (i.e. His Saying): "Surely, I shall fill Hell with jinn and men all together."

Quran 13:5

And if you wonder (at these polytheists who deny your message of Islâmic Monotheism and have taken besides Allâh others for worship who can neither harm nor benefit), then wondrous is their saying: "When we are dust, shall we indeed then be (raised) in a new creation?" They are those who disbelieved in their Lord! They are those who will have iron chains tying their hands to their necks. They will be dwellers of the Fire to abide therein.

Quran 13:25

And those who break the Covenant of Allâh, after its ratification, and sever that which Allâh has commanded to be joined (i.e. they sever the bond of kinship and are not good to their relatives), and work mischief in the land, on them is the curse (i.e. they will be far

*away from Allâh's Mercy); and for them is the unhappy (evil)
home (i.e. Hell)*

Quran 13:16-17

*In front of him (every obstinate, arrogant dictator) is Hell, and he
will be made to drink boiling, festering water. (16) He will sip it
unwillingly, and he will find a great difficulty to swallow it down
his throat, and death will come to him from every side, yet he will
not die and in front of him, will be a great torment.*

Quran 14:28-30

*Have you not seen those who have changed the Blessings of Allâh
into disbelief (by denying Prophet Muhammad and his Message of
Islâm), and caused their people to dwell in the house of
destruction? (28) Hell, in which they will burn, - and what an evil
place to settle in! (29) And they set up rivals to Allâh, to mislead
(men) from His Path! Say: "Enjoy (your brief life)! But certainly,
your destination is the (Hell) Fire!"*

Quran 15:39-44

*[Iblîs (Satan)] said: "O my Lord! Because you misled me, I shall
indeed adorn the path of error for them (mankind) on the earth,
and I shall mislead them all. (39) "Except Your chosen, (guided)
slaves among them." (40) (Allâh) said: "This is the Way which
will lead straight to Me." (41) "Certainly, you shall have no
authority over My slaves, except those who follow you of the
Ghâwun (Mushrikûn and those who go astray, criminals,
polytheists, and evil-doers) (42) "And surely, Hell is the promised*

place for them all. (43) "It (Hell) has seven gates, for each of those gates is a (special) class (of sinners) assigned.

Quran 16:62

They assign to Allâh that which they dislike (for themselves), and their tongues assert the falsehood that the better things will be theirs. No doubt for them is the Fire, and they will be the first to be hastened on into it, and left there neglected.

Quran 17:8

[And We said in the Taurât (Torah)]: "It may be that your Lord may show mercy unto you, but if you return (to sins), We shall return (to Our Punishment). And We have made Hell a prison for the disbelievers.

Quran 17:10

And that those who believe not in the Hereafter, for them We have prepared a painful torment (Hell).

Quran 17:18

Whoever desires the quick-passing (transitory enjoyment of this world), We readily grant him what We will for whom We like. Then, afterwards, We have appointed for him Hell, he will burn therein disgraced and rejected, - (far away from Allâhs Mercy).

Quran 17:22

Set not up with Allâh any other ilâh (god), or you will sit down reproved, forsaken (in the Hell-fire).

Quran 17:39

This is (part) of Al-Hikmah (wisdom, good manners and high character) which your Lord has revealed to you (O Muhammad). And set not up with Allâh any other ilâh (god) lest you should be thrown into Hell, blameworthy and rejected, (from Allâh's Mercy).

Quran 17:60

And (remember) when We told you: "Verily! Your Lord has encompassed mankind (i.e. they are in His Grip)." And We made not the vision which we showed you (O Muhammad as an actual eye-witness and not as a dream on the night of Al-Isrâ') but a trial for mankind, and (likewise) the accursed tree (Zaqqûm, mentioned) in the Qur'ân. We warn and make them afraid but it only increases them in naught save great disbelief, oppression and disobedience to Allâh.

Quran 17:62-63

[Iblîs (Satan)] said: "See this one whom You have honored above me, if You give me respite (keep me alive) to the Day of Resurrection, I will surely seize and mislead his offspring (by sending them astray) all but a few!" (62) (Allâh) said: "Go, and whosoever of them follows you, surely! Hell will be the recompense of you (all) - an ample recompense.

Quran 18:29

And say: "The truth is from your Lord." Then whosoever wills, let him believe, and whosoever wills, let him disbelieve. Verily, We have prepared for the Zâlimûn (polytheists and wrong-doers), a Fire whose walls will be surrounding them (disbelievers in the

Oneness of Allâh). And if they ask for help (relief, water) they will be granted water like boiling oil, that will scald their faces. Terrible is the drink, and an evil Murtafaq (dwelling, resting place)!

Quran 18:106

"That shall be their recompense, Hell; because they disbelieved and took My Ayât (proofs, evidences, verses, lessons, signs, revelations, etc.) and My Messengers by way of jest and mockery.

Quran 19:59

Then, there has succeeded them a posterity who have given up As-Salât (the prayers) [i.e. made their Salât (prayers) to be lost, either by not offering them or by not offering them perfectly or by not offering them in their proper fixed times] and have followed lusts. So they will be thrown in Hell.

Quran 19:68-70

So by your Lord, surely, We shall gather them together, and (also) the Shayâtin (devils) (with them), then We shall bring them round Hell on their knees. (68) Then indeed We shall drag out from every sect all those who were worst in obstinate rebellion against the Most Gracious (Allâh). (69) Then, verily, We know best those who are most worthy of being burnt therein.

Quran 20:74

Verily! whoever comes to his Lord as a Mujrim (criminal, polytheist, disbeliever in the Oneness of Allâh and His Messengers), then surely, for him is Hell, wherein he will neither die nor live

Quran 21:29

And if any of them should say: "Verily, I am an ilâh (a god) besides Him (Allâh)," such a one We should recompense with Hell. Thus We recompense the Zâlimûn (polytheists and wrong-doers).

Quran 21:39-40

If only those who disbelieved knew (the time) when they will not be able to ward off the Fire from their faces, nor from their backs; and they will not be helped. (39) Nay, it will come upon them all of a sudden and will perplex them, and they will have no power to avert it, nor will they get respite.

Quran 22:3-4

And among mankind is he who disputes concerning Allâh, without knowledge, and follows every rebellious (disobedient to Allâh) Shaitân (devil) (devoid of every kind of good). (3) For him (the devil) it is decreed that whosoever follows him, he will mislead him, and will drive him to the torment of the Fire.

Quran 22:19-22

These two opponents (believers and disbelievers) dispute with each other about their Lord; then as for those who disbelieved, garments of fire will be cut out for them, boiling water will be poured down over their heads. (19) With it will melt (or vanish away) what is within their bellies, as well as (their) skins. (20) And for them are hooked rods of iron (to punish them). (21) Every time they seek to get away therefrom, from anguish, they will be driven back therein, and (it will be) said to them: "Taste the torment of burning!"

Quran 22:25

Verily! those who disbelieved and hinder (men) from the Path of Allâh, and from Al-Masjid-al-Harâm (at Makkah) which We have made (open) to (all) men, the dweller in it and the visitor from the country are equal there [as regards its sanctity and pilgrimage (Hajj and 'Umrah)]. And whoever inclines to evil actions therein or to do wrong (i.e. practice polytheism and leave Islâmic Monotheism), him We shall cause to taste from a painful torment.

Quran 22:51

But those who strive against Our Ayât (proofs, evidences, verses, lessons, signs, revelations, etc.), to frustrate them, they will be dwellers of the Hell-fire.

Quran 22:72

And when Our Clear Verses are recited to them, you will notice a denial on the faces of the disbelievers! They are nearly ready to attack with violence those who recite Our Verses to them. Say: "Shall I tell you of something worse than that? The Fire (of Hell) which Allâh has promised to those who disbelieved, and worst indeed is that destination!"

Quran 23:104-115

The Fire will burn their faces, and therein they will grin, with displaced lips (disfigured). (104) "Were not My Verses (this Qur'ân) recited to you, and then you used to deny them?" (105) They will say: "Our Lord! Our wretchedness overcame us, and we were (an) erring people. (106) "Our Lord! Bring us out of this; if ever we return (to evil), then indeed we shall be Zâlimûn:

(polytheists, oppressors, unjust, and wrong-doers)." (107) He
(Allâh) will say: "Remain you in it with ignominy! And speak you
not to Me!" (108) Verily! there was a party of My slaves, who
used to say: "Our Lord! We believe, so forgive us, and have mercy
on us, for You are the Best of all who show mercy!" (109) But you
took them for a laughingstock, so much so that they made you
forget My Remembrance while you used to laugh at them! (110)
Verily! I have rewarded them this Day for their patience, they are
indeed the ones that are successful. (111) He (Allâh) will say:
"What number of years did you stay on earth?" (112) They will
say: "We stayed a day or part of a day. Ask of those who keep
account." (113) He (Allâh) will say: "You stayed not but a little, if
you had only known! (114) "Did you think that We had created
you in play (without any purpose), and that you would not be
brought back to Us?"

Quran 25:11-14

Nay, they deny the Hour (the Day of Resurrection), and for those
who deny the Hour, We have prepared a flaming Fire (i.e. Hell).
(11) When it (Hell) sees them from a far place, they will hear its
raging and its roaring. (12) And when they shall be thrown into a
narrow place thereof, chained together, they will exclaim therein
for destruction. (13) Exclaim not today for one destruction, but
exclaim for many destructions.

Quran 25:34

Those who will be gathered to Hell (prone) on their faces, such will
be in an evil state, and most astray from the (Straight) Path.

Quran 29:54-55

They ask you to hasten on the torment. And verily! Hell, of a surety, will encompass the disbelievers. (54) On the Day when the torment shall cover them from above them and from underneath their feet, and it will be said: "Taste what you used to do."

Quran 29:68

And who does more wrong than he who invents a lie against Allâh or denies the truth (Muhammad and his doctrine of Islâmic Monotheism and this Qur'ân), when it comes to him? Is there not a dwelling in Hell for disbelievers?

Quran 31:6-7

And of mankind is he who purchases idle talks (i.e. music, singing, etc.) to mislead (men) from the Path of Allâh without knowledge, and takes it (the Path of Allâh, or the Verses of the Qur'ân) by way of mockery. For such there will be a humiliating torment (in the Hell-fire). (6) And when Our Verses (of Qurân) are recited to such a one, he turns away in pride, as if he heard them not, — as if there were deafness in his ear. So announce to him a painful torment

Quran 32:12-14

And if you only could see when the Mujrimûn (criminals, disbelievers, polytheists, sinners, etc.) shall hang their heads before their Lord (saying): "Our Lord! We have now seen and heard, so send us back (to the world), that we will do righteous good deeds. Verily! We now believe with certainty." (12) And if We had willed, surely! We would have given every person his guidance, but the Word from Me took effect (about evil¬doers), that I will fill Hell with jinn and mankind together (13) Then taste you (the torment of the Fire) because of your forgetting the Meeting of this Day of yours, surely! We too will forget you, so taste you the abiding torment for what you used to do

Quran 32:20-22

And as for those who are Fâsiqûn (disbelievers and disobedient to Allâh), their abode will be the Fire, everytime they wish to get away therefrom, they will be put back thereto, and it will be said to them: "Taste you the torment of the Fire which you used to deny." (20) And verily, We will make them taste of the near torment (i.e. the torment in the life of this world, i.e. disasters, calamities, etc.) prior to the supreme torment (in the Hereafter), in order that they may (repent and) return (i.e. accept Islâm). (21) And who does more wrong than he who is reminded of the Ayât (proofs, evidences, verses, lessons, signs, revelations, etc.) of his Lord, then turns aside therefrom? Verily, We shall exact retribution from the Mujrimûn (criminals, disbelievers, polytheists, sinners, etc.)

Quran 33:57

Verily, those who annoy Allâh and His Messenger Allâh has cursed them in this world, and in the Hereafter, and has prepared for them a humiliating torment

Quran 33:64-68

Verily, Allâh has cursed the disbelievers, and has prepared for them a flaming Fire (Hell). (64) Wherein they will abide forever, and they will find neither a Walî (a protector) nor a helper. (65) On the Day when their faces will be turned over in the Fire, they will say: "Oh, would that we had obeyed Allâh and obeyed the

Messenger (Muhammad)." (66) And they will say: "Our Lord! Verily, we obeyed our chiefs and our great ones, and they misled us from the (Right) Way. (67) Our Lord! Give them double torment and curse them with a mighty curse!"

Quran 34:38

And those who strive against Our Ayât (proofs, evidences, verses, lessons, signs, revelations, etc.), to frustrate them, will be brought to the torment.

Quran 35:6-7

Surely, Shaitân (Satan) is an enemy to you, so take (treat) him as an enemy. He only invites his Hizb (followers) that they may become the dwellers of the blazing Fire. (6) Those who disbelieve, theirs will be a severe torment; and those who believe (in the Oneness of Allâh Islâmic Monotheism) and do righteous good deeds, theirs will be forgiveness and a great reward (i.e. Paradise).

Quran 35:36-37

But those who disbelieve, (in the Oneness of Allâh - Islâmic Monotheism) for them will be the Fire of Hell. Neither will it have a complete killing effect on them so that they die, nor shall its torment be lightened for them. Thus do We requite every disbeliever! (36) Therein they will cry: "Our Lord! Bring us out, we shall do righteous good deeds, not (the evil deeds) that we used to do." (Allâh will reply): "Did We not give you lives long enough, so that whosoever would receive admonition, could receive it? And the warner came to you. So taste you (the evil of your deeds). For the Zâlimûn (polytheists and wrong¬doers) there is no helper."

Quran 37:62-68

Is that (Paradise) better entertainment or the tree of Zaqqûm (a horrible tree in Hell)? (62) Truly We have made it (as) a trial for the Zâlimûn (polytheists, disbelievers, wrong-doers). (63) Verily, it is a tree that springs out of the bottom of Hell-fire, (64)The shoots of its fruit-stalks are like the heads of Shayâtin (devils); (65) Truly, they will eat thereof and fill their bellies therewith. (66) Then on the top of that they will be given boiling water to drink so that it becomes a mixture (of boiling water and Zaqqûm in their bellies). (67) Then thereafter, verily, their return is to the flaming fire of Hell.

Quran 38:55-64

This is so! And for the Tâghûn (transgressors, disobedient to Allâh and His Messenger - disbelievers in the Oneness of Allâh, criminals), will be an evil final return (Fire), (55) Hell! Where they will burn, and worst (indeed) is that place to rest! (56) This is so! Then let them taste it, a boiling fluid and dirty wound discharges. (57) And other (torments) of similar kind — all together! (58) This is a troop entering with you (in Hell), no welcome for them! Verily, they shall burn in the Fire! (59) (The followers of the misleaders will say): "Nay, you (too)! No welcome for you! It is you (misleaders) who brought this upon us (because you misled us in the world), so evil is this place to stay in!" (60) They will say: "Our Lord! Whoever brought this upon us, add to him a double torment in the Fire!" (61) And they will say: "What is the matter with us that we see not men whom we used to count among the bad ones?" (62) Did we take them as an object of mockery, or have (our) eyes failed to perceive them?" (63) Verily, that is the very truth, the mutual dispute of the people of the Fire!

Quran 38:84-85

(Allâh) said: "The Truth is, – and the Truth I say, – (84) That I will fill Hell with you [Iblîs (Satan)] and those of them (mankind) that follow you, together."

Quran 39:8

And when some hurt touches man, he cries to his Lord (Allâh Alone), turning to Him in repentance, but when He bestows a favor upon him from Himself, he forgets that for which he cried for before, and he sets up rivals to Allâh, in order to mislead others from His Path. Say: "Take pleasure in your disbelief for a while: surely, you are (one) of the dwellers of the Fire!"

Quran 39:15-16

So worship what you like besides Him. Say: "The losers are those who will lose themselves and their families on the Day of Resurrection. Verily, that will be a manifest loss!" (15) They shall have coverings of Fire, above them and covering (of Fire) beneath them; with this Allâh does frighten His slaves: "O My slaves, therefore fear Me!"

Quran 40:6

Thus has the Word of your Lord been justified against those who disbelieved, that they will be the dwellers of the Fire

Quran 40:10-12

Those who disbelieve will be addressed (at the time of entering the Fire): "Allâh's aversion was greater towards you (in the worldly life when you used to reject the Faith) than your aversion towards one another (now in the Fire of Hell, as you are now enemies to one another), when you were called to the Faith but you used to refuse." (10) They will say: "Our Lord! You have made us to die twice (i.e. we were dead in the loins of our fathers and dead after our life in this world), and You have given us life twice (i.e. life when we were born and life when we are Resurrected)! Now we confess our sins, then is there any way to get out (of the Fire)?" (11) (It will be said): "This is because, when Allâh Alone was invoked (in worship) you disbelieved, but when partners were joined to Him, you believed (deneid)! So the judgement is only with Allâh, the Most High, the Most Great!"

Quran 40:46-50

The Fire; they are exposed to it, morning and afternoon, and on the Day when the Hour will be established (it will be said to the angels): "Cause Fir'aun's (Pharaoh) people to enter the severest torment!" (46) And, when they will dispute in the Fire, the weak will say to those who were arrogant: "Verily! We followed you, can you then take from us some portion of the Fire?" (47) Those who were arrogant will say: "We are all (together) in this (Fire)! Verily Allâh has judged between (His) slaves!" (48) And those in the Fire will say to the keepers (angels) of Hell: "Call upon your Lord to lighten for us the torment for a day!" (49) They will say: "Did there not come to you, your Messengers with (clear) evidences (and signs)? They will say: "Yes." They will reply: "Then call (as you like)! And the invocation of the disbelievers is nothing but in vain (as it will not be answered by Allah)!"

Quran 40:60

And your Lord said: "Invoke Me, [i.e. believe in My Oneness (Islâmic Monotheism)] (and ask Me for anything) I will respond to your (invocation). Verily! Those who scorn My worship [i.e. do not invoke Me, and do not believe in My Oneness, (Islâmic Monotheism)] they will surely enter Hell in humiliation!"

Quran 40:70-76

Those who deny the Book (this Qur'ân), and that with which We sent Our Messengers (i.e. to worship none but Allâh Alone sincerely, and to reject all false deities and to confess resurrection after the death for recompense) they will come to know (when they will be cast into the Fire of Hell). (70) When iron collars will be rounded over their necks, and the chains, they shall be dragged along (71) In the boiling water, then they will be burned in the Fire. (72) Then it will be said to them: "Where are (all) those whom you used to join in worship as partners. (73) "Besides Allâh"? They will say: "They have vanished from us: Nay, we did not invoke (worship) anything before." Thus Allâh leads astray the disbelievers. (74) That was because you had been exulting in the earth without any right (by worshipping others instead of Allâh and by committing crimes), and that you used to rejoice extremely (in your error). (75) Enter the gates of Hell to abide therein, and (indeed) what an evil abode of the arrogant!

Quran 41:19-24

And (remember) the Day that the enemies of Allâh will be gathered to the Fire, then they will be driven [(to the fire), former ones being withheld till their later ones will join them]. (19) Till, when they reach it (Hell-fire), their hearing (ears) and their eyes, and their skins will testify against them as to what they used to do. (20) And they will say to their skins, "Why do you testify against us?" They will say: "Allâh has caused us to speak," — He causes all things to speak, and He created you the first time, and to Him you are made to return." (21) And you have not been hiding yourselves (in the world), lest your ears, and your eyes, and your skins should testify against you, but you thought that Allâh knew not much of what you were doing. (22) And that thought of yours which you thought about your Lord, has brought you to destruction, and you have become (this Day) of those utterly lost! (23) Then, if they bear the torment patiently, then the Fire is the home for them, and if they seek to please Allâh, yet they are not of those who will ever be allowed to please Allâh.

Quran 41:27-29

But surely, We shall cause those who disbelieve to taste a severe torment, and certainly, We shall requite them the worst of what they used to do. (27) That is the recompense of the enemies of Allâh: the Fire. Therein will be for them the eternal home, a (deserving) recompense for that they used to deny Our Ayât (proofs, evidences, verses, lessons, signs, revelations, etc.). (28) And those who disbelieve will say: "Our Lord! Show us those among jinn and men who led us astray, that we may crush them under our feet so that they become the lowest."

Quran 43:74-77

Verily, the Mujrimûn (criminals, sinners, disbelievers) will be in the torment of Hell to abide therein forever. (74) (The torment) will not be lightened for them, and they will be plunged into destruction with deep regrets, sorrows and in despair therein. (75) We wronged them not, but they were the Zâlimûn (polytheists, wrong-doers). (76) And they will cry: "O Malik (Keeper of Hell)! Let your Lord make an end of us." He will say: "Verily you shall abide forever."

Quran 44:43-50

Verily, the tree of Zaqqûm, (43) Will be the food of the sinners, (44) Like boiling oil, it will boil in the bellies, (45) Like the boiling of scalding water. (46) (It will be said) "Seize him and drag him into the midst of blazing Fire, (47) "Then pour over his head the torment of boiling water, (48) "Taste you (this)! Verily, you were (pretending to be) the mighty, the generous! (49) "Verily, this is that whereof you used to doubt!"

Quran 45:7-11

Woe to every sinful liar, (7) Who hears the Verses of Allâh (being) recited to him, yet persists with pride as if he heard them not. So announce to him a painful torment! (8) And when he learns something of Our Verses (this Qur'ân), he makes them a jest. For such there will be a humiliating torment. (9) In front of them there is Hell, and that which they have earned will be of no profit to them, nor (will be of any profit to them) those whom they have taken as Auliyâ' (protectors, helpers) besides Allâh. And theirs will be a great torment. (10) This (Qur'ân) is a guidance. And those who disbelieve in the Ayât (proofs, evidences, verses, lessons, signs, revelations) of their Lord, for them there is a painful torment of Rijz (a severe kind of punishment).

Quran 48:6

And that He may punish the Munâfiqûn (hypocrites), men and women, and also the Mushrikûn men and women, who think evil thoughts about Allâh, for them is a disgraceful torment, And the Anger of Allâh is upon them, and He has cursed them and prepared Hell for them — and worst indeed is that destination.

Quran 48:13

And whosoever does not believe in Allâh and His Messenger (Muhammad), then verily, We have prepared for the disbelievers a blazing Fire

Quran 53:26

And there are many angels in the heavens, whose intercession will avail nothing except after Allâh has given leave for whom He wills and is pleased with.

Quran 58:8

Have you not seen those who were forbidden to hold secret counsels, and afterwards returned to that which they had been forbidden, and conspired together for sin and wrong doing and disobedience to the Messenger (Muhammad). And when they come to you, they greet you with a greeting wherewith Allâh greets you not, and say within themselves: "Why should Allâh not punish us for what we say?" Hell will be sufficient for them, they will burn therein, and worst indeed is that destination!

Quran 58:14-20

Have you not seen those (hypocrites) who take as friends a people upon whom is the Wrath of Allâh ? They are neither of you

(Muslims) nor of them, and they swear to a lie while they know. (14) Allâh has prepared for them a severe torment. Evil indeed is that which they used to do. (15) They have made their oaths a screen (for their evil actions). Thus they hinder (men) from the Path of Allâh, so they shall have a humiliating torment. (16) Their children and their wealth will avail them nothing against Allâh. They will be the dwellers of the Fire, to dwell therein forever. (17) On the Day when Allâh will resurrect them all together (for their account), then they will swear to Him as they swear to you (O Muslims). And they think that they have something (to stand upon). Verily, they are liars! (18) Shaitân (Satan) has overpowered them. So he has made them forget the remembrance of Allâh. They are the party of Shaitân (Satan). Verily, it is the party of Shaitân (Satan) that will be the losers! (19) Those who oppose Allâh and His Messenger (Muhammad), they will be among the lowest (most humiliated).

Quran 59:16-17

(Their allies deceived them) like Shaitân (Satan), when he says to man: "Disbelieve in Allâh." But when (man) disbelieves in Allâh, Shaitân (Satan) says: "I am free of you, I fear Allâh, the Lord of the 'Alamîn (mankind, jinn and all that exists)!" (16) So the end of both will be that they will be in the Fire, abiding therein. Such is the recompense of the Zâlimûn (i.e. polytheists, wrong-doers, disbelievers in Allâh and in His Oneness).

Quran 66:6-7

O you who believe! Ward off from yourselves and your families against a Fire (Hell) whose fuel is men and stones, over which are (appointed) angels stern (and) severe, who disobey not, (from *executing) the Commands they receive from Allâh, but do that which they are commanded. (6) (It will be said in the Hereafter) O you who disbelieve (in the Oneness of Allâh - Islâmic Monotheism)! Make no excuses this Day! You are being requited only for what you used to do.*

Quran 66:9

O Prophet! Strive hard against the disbelievers and the hypocrites, and be severe against them; their abode will be Hell, and worst indeed is that destination.

Quran 67:6-11

And for those who disbelieve in their Lord (Allâh) is the torment of Hell, and worst indeed is that destination (6) When they are cast therein, they will hear the (terrible) drawing in of its breath as it blazes forth (7) It almost bursts up with fury. Every time a group is cast therein, its keeper will ask: "Did no warner come to you?" (8) They will say: "Yes indeed a warner did come to us, but we belied him and said: 'Allâh never sent down anything (of revelation), you are only in great error.'" (9) And they will say: "Had we but listened or used our intelligence, we would not have been among the dwellers of the blazing Fire!" (10) Then they will confess their sin. So, away with the dwellers of the blazing Fire

Quran 72:15

And as for the Qâsitûn (disbelievers who deviated from the Right Path), they shall be firewood for Hell

Quran 72:23

"(Mine is) but conveyance (of the truth) from Allâh and His Messages (of Islâmic Monotheism), and whosoever disobeys Allâh and His Messenger, then verily, for him is the Fire of Hell, he shall dwell therein forever."

Quran 73:11-13

And leave Me Alone to deal with the beliers (those who deny My Verses), those who are in possession of good things of life. And give them respite for a little while. (11) Verily, with Us are fetters (to bind them), and a raging Fire. (12) And a food that chokes, and a painful torment.

Quran 74:27-31

And what will make you know (exactly) what Hell-fire is? (27) It spares not (any sinner), nor does it leave (anything unburnt)! (28) Burning and blackening the skins! (29) Over it are nineteen (angels as guardians and keepers of Hell). (30) And We have set none but angels as guardians of the Fire, and We have fixed number only as a trial for the disbelievers, in order that the people of the Scripture (Jews and Christians) may arrive at a certainty [that this Qur'ân is the truth as it agrees with their Books regarding their number which is written in the Taurât (Torah) and the Injeel] and that the believers may increase in Faith (as this Qur'ân is the truth) and that no doubt may be left for the people of the Scripture and the believers, and that those in whose hearts is a disease (of hypocrisy) and the disbelievers may say: "What Allâh intends by this (curious) example ?" Thus Allâh leads astray whom He wills and guides whom He wills. And none can know the hosts of your Lord but He. And this (Hell) is nothing else than a (warning) reminder to mankind

Quran 76:4

Verily, We have prepared for the disbelievers iron chains, iron collars, and a blazing Fire.

Quran 85:10

Verily, those who put into trial the believing men and believing women, and then do not turn in repentance, (to Allâh), then they will have the torment of Hell, and they will have the punishment of the burning Fire.

Quran 87:10-13

The reminder will be received by him who fears (Allâh), (10) But it will be avoided by the wretched, (11) Who will enter the great Fire (and will be made to taste its burning). (12) There he will neither die (to be in rest) nor live (a good living).

Quran 90:19-20

But those who disbelieved in Our Ayât (proofs, evidences, verses, lessons, signs, revelations, etc.), they are those on the Left Hand (the dwellers of Hell) (19) The Fire will be shut over them (i.e. they will be enveloped by the Fire without opening, window or outlet.)

Quran 92:14-16

Therefore I have warned you of a blazing (Hell); (14) None shall enter it save the most wretched, (15) Who denies and turns away.

Quran 98:6

Verily, those who disbelieve (in the religion of Islâm, the Qur'ân and Prophet Muhammad) from among the people of the Scripture (Jews and Christians) and Al-Mushrikûn will abide in the Fire of Hell. They are the worst of creatures.

Quran 104:1-9

Woe to every slanderer and backbiter. (1) Who has gathered wealth and counted it, (2) He thinks that his wealth will make him last forever! (3) Nay! Verily, he will be thrown into the crushing Fire (4) And what will make you know what the crushing Fire is? (5) The fire of Allâh, kindled, (6) Which leaps up over the hearts, (7) Verily, it shall be closed upon them, (8) In pillars stretched forth (i.e. they will be punished in the Fire with pillars).

Quran 108:3

For he who hates you (O Muhammad), he will be cut off from every posterity (good thing in this world and in the Hereafter)

Quran 111:1-5

Perish the two hands of Abû Lahab (an uncle of the Prophet), and perish he! (1) His wealth and his children will not benefit him! (2) He will be burnt in a Fire of blazing flames! (3) And his wife too, who carries wood (thorns of Sadan which she used to put on the way of the Prophet , or use to slander him). (4) In her neck is a twisted rope of Masad (palm fibre).

Narrated Ibn `Umar:

The Prophet; said, "The people of Paradise will enter Paradise, and the people of the (Hell) Fire will enter the (Hell) Fire: then a call-

maker will get up (and make an announcement) among them, 'O the people of the (Hell) Fire! No death anymore ! And O people of Paradise! No death (anymore) but Eternity."

Source: Sahih al-Bukhari 6544

Narrated Abu Huraira:

Allah's Messenger said, "Your (ordinary) fire is one of 70 parts of the (Hell) Fire." Someone asked, "O Allah's Messenger This (ordinary) fire would have been sufficient (to torture the unbelievers)," Allah's Apostle said, "The (Hell) Fire has 69 parts more than the ordinary (worldly) fire, each part is as hot as this (worldly) fire."

Source: Sahih al-Bukhari 3265

This hadith proves the hotness of hell to the degree if you do the math calculating 70 times the hotness of this world's fire. The point being those who complain of a hot summer's day or anything else as being "As hot as hell" are wrong and in disbelief of the prophetic data about the actual heat of hell. To make such a statement of indirect disbelief and rejection of hell's hotness by diminishing it and comparing it to something experienced in this life actually qualifies one to enter the hell which is so much hotter than anything in this world. The lesson being, never say something in this world is comparable to hell or you may enter hell as a result.

Abu Huraira reported Allah's Messenger (ﷺ) as saying:

The servant speaks words that he does not understand its repercussions but he sinks down in Hell-Fire farther than the distance between the east and the west.

Source: Sahih Muslim 2988 b

Narrated Abu Huraira-:

The Prophet said, "He who commits suicide by throttling shall keep on throttling himself in the Hell Fire (forever) and he who commits suicide by stabbing himself shall keep on stabbing himself in the Hell-Fire."

Source: Sahih al-Bukhari 1365

It was narrated that Ibn Awfa said:

"The Messenger of Allah said: 'The Khawarij are the dogs of Hell.'"

Source: Sunan ibn Majah

English reference : Vol. 1, Book 1, Hadith 173

Graded Sahih by Darussalam

Narrated `Ali:

The Prophet said, "Do not tell a lie against me for whoever tells a lie against me then he will surely enter the Hell-fire."

Source: Sahih al-Bukhari 106

Narrated Abu `Abs:

I heard the Prophet saying, "Anyone whose feet are covered with dust in Allah's cause, shall be saved by Allah from the Hell-Fire."

Source: Sahih al-Bukhari 907

Narrated `Adi bin Hatim heard the Prophet (ﷺ) saying:

"Save yourself from Hell-fire even by giving half a date-fruit in charity."

Source: Sahih al-Bukhari 1417

Narrated Abu Huraira:

The Prophet said, "In very hot weather delay the Zuhr prayer till it becomes (a bit) cooler because the severity of heat is from the raging of the Hell-fire. The Hell-fire of Hell complained to its Lord saying: O Lord! My parts are eating (destroying) one another. So Allah allowed it to take two breaths, one in the winter and the other in the summer. The breath in the summer is at the time when you feel the severest heat and the breath in the winter is at the time when you feel the severest cold."

Source: Sahih al-Bukhari 536, 537

Abd al-Rahman reported on the authority of his mother's sister Umm Salama who said that Allah's Messenger (ﷺ) said:

He who drank in vessels of gold or silver he in fact drank down in his belly the fire of Hell.

Source: Sahih Muslim 2065 c

Narrated Abu Huraira:

The Prophet said, "Whoever purposely throws himself from a mountain and kills himself, will be in the (Hell) Fire falling down into it and abiding therein perpetually forever; and whoever drinks poison and kills himself with it, he will be carrying his poison in his hand and drinking it in the (Hell) Fire wherein he will abide eternally forever; and whoever kills himself with an iron weapon, will be carrying that weapon in his hand and stabbing his `Abdomen with it in the (Hell) Fire wherein he will abide eternally forever."

Source: Sahih al-Bukhari 5778

Samura b. Jundub reported Allah's Apostle as saying:

There will be some to whose ankles the fire will reach, some to whose knees, some to whose waist the fire will reach, and some to whose collar-bone the fire will reach.

Source: Sahih Muslim 2845 a

Anas bin Malik narrated that the Messenger of Allah said:

"Whoever asks Allah Paradise three times, Paradise says: 'O Allah, admit him into Paradise', and whoever seeks refuge from the Fire three times, the Fire says: 'O Allah, save him from the Fire.'"

Source: Jami at-Tirmidhi

English reference : Vol. 4, Book 12, Hadith 2572

Graded Sahih by Darussalam

Narrated `Adi bin Hatim:

The Prophet mentioned the (Hell) Fire and sought refuge (with Allah) from it, and turned his face to the other side. He mentioned the (Hell) Fire again and took refuge (with Allah) from it and turned his face to the other side. (Shu`ba, the sub-narrator, said, "I have no doubt that the Prophet repeated it twice.") The Prophet then said, "(O people!) Save yourselves from the (Hell) Fire even if with one half of a date fruit (given in charity), and if this is not available, then (save yourselves) by saying a good pleasant friendly word."

Source: Sahih al-Bukhari 6023

Abdullah bin 'Amr said:

"The Messenger of Allah saw some people performing ablution, and their heels were dry. He said: 'Woe to the heels because of Hell-fire, perform ablution properly!'"

Source: Sunan ibn Majah

English reference : Vol. 1, Book 1, Hadith 450

Graded Sahih by Darussalam

Abu Musa' reported that Allah's Messenger (ﷺ) said:

When it will be the Day of Resurrection Allah would deliver to every Muslim a Jew or a Christian and say: That is your rescue from Hell-Fire.

Source: Sahih Muslim 2767 a

Narrated Khaula Al-Ansariya:

I heard Allah's Messenger saying, "Some people spend Allah's Wealth (i.e. Muslim's wealth) in an unjust manner; such people will be put in the (Hell) Fire on the Day of Resurrection."

Source: Sahih al-Bukhari 3118

Abdullah bin Mas'ud narrated the Messenger of Allah said:

"Shall I not inform you of whom the Fire is unlawful and he is unlawful for the Fire? Every person who is near(to people), amicable, and easy(to deal with).'"

Source: Jami at-Tirmidhi

English reference : Vol. 4, Book 11, Hadith 2488

Graded Hasan by Darussalam

Narrated Ibn `Umar:

The Prophet said, "A woman entered the (Hell) Fire because of a cat which she had tied, neither giving it food nor setting it free to eat from the vermin of the earth. "

Source: Sahih al-Bukhari 3318

It was narrated that Abu Bakrah said:

"If two Muslim men bear weapons against each other, then they are both on the brink of Hell. And if one of them kills the other, they will both be in Hell."

Source: Sunan an-Nasa'i 4117 Graded Sahih by Darussalam

It was narrated that Abu Hurairah said:

"No man who weeps for fear of Allah will be touched by the Fire until the milk goes back into the udders. And the dust (of Jihad) in the cause of Allah and the smoke of Hell, will never be combined in the nostrils of a Muslim."

Source: Sunan an-Nasa'i 3107 Graded Sahih by Darussalam

Narrated Jabir ibn Abdullah:

The Prophet said: One should not take a false oath at this pulpit of mine even on a green tooth-stick; otherwise he will make his abode in Hell, or Hell will be certain for him.

Source: Sunan Abi Dawud 3246 Graded Sahih by Albani

It was narrated from Abu Hurairah that the Prophet (ﷺ) said:

"The Fire will consume all of the son of Adam except the mark of prostration. Allah has forbidden the Fire to consume the mark of prostration.'"

Source: Sunan ibn Majah

 English reference : Vol. 5, Book 37, Hadith 4326

Graded Sahih by Darussalam

Narrated Abu Huraira:

The Prophet said, "None will enter Paradise but will be shown the place he would have occupied in the (Hell) Fire if he had rejected faith, so that he may be more thankful; and none will enter the (Hell) Fire but will be shown the place he would have occupied in Paradise if he had faith, so that may be a cause of sorrow for him."

Source: Sahih al-Bukhari 6569

Amr bin Shu'aib narrated from his father, from his grandfather from the Prophet who said:

"The proud will be gathered on the Day of Judgement resembling tiny particles in the image of men. They will be covered with humiliation everywhere, they will be dragged into a prison in Hell called Bulas, submerged in the Fire of Fires, drinking the drippings of the people of the Fire, filled with derangement."

Source: Jami at-Tirmidhi

English reference : Vol. 4, Book 11, Hadith 2492

Graded Hasan by Darussalam

It was narrated from Abu Hurairah that The Messenger of Allah (ﷺ) said:

"Two will never be gathered together in the Fire: A Muslim who killed a disbeliever then tried his best and did not deviate. And two will never be gathered together in the lungs of a believer: Dust in the cause of Allah, and the odor of Hell. And two will never be gathered in the heart of a slave: Faith and envy."

Source: Sunan an-Nasa'i 3109 Graded Hasan by Darussalam

Nu'man b. Bashir reported:

The Messenger of Allah said: Verily the least suffering for the inhabitants of Fire would be for him who would have two shoes and two laces of Fire (on his feet), and with these would boil his brain as boils the cooking vessel, and he would think that he would not see anyone in a more grievous torment than him, whereas he would be in the least torment.

Source: Sahih Muslim 213 b

It was narrated from 'Uqbah bin 'Amir that the Messenger of Allah said:

"Whoever fasts one day in the cause of Allah, the mighty and sublime, Allah will separate him the distance of one hundred years from the fire."

Source: Sunan an-Nasa'i 2254 Graded Hasan by Darussalam

Narrated Abu Huraira:

The Prophet said, "None of you should point out towards his Muslim brother with a weapon, for he does not know, Satan may tempt him to hit him and thus he would fall into a pit of fire (Hell)"

Source: Sahih al-Bukhari 7072

It was narrated from Abu Hurairah that the Messenger of Allah (ﷺ) said:

"There is no one among you who does not have two abodes: An abode in Paradise and an abode in Hell. If he dies and enters Hell,

the people of Paradise inherit his abode. This is what Allah says: 'These are indeed the inheritors.'" [23:10]

Source: Sunan ibn Majah

English reference : Vol. 5, Book 37, Hadith 4341

Graded Sahih by Darussalam

Umm Habibah narrated that:

Allah's Messenger said: "Whoever prays four before Az-Zuhr and four after, Allah makes him prohibited for the Fire."

Source: Jami` at-Tirmidhi 427 Graded Sahih by Darussalam

Narrated Abu Hurairah:

that the Messenger of Allah said: "Whoever is asked about some knowledge that he knows, then he conceals it, he will be bridled with bridle of fire."

Source: Jami` at-Tirmidhi 2649

Graded Hasan by Darussalam

Abu Umamah, and other than him from the Companions of the Prophet (ﷺ), narrated that the Prophet (ﷺ) said:

"Any Muslim man who frees a Muslim man, then it is his salvation from the Fire - each of his limbs suffices for a limb of himself. And any Muslim man that frees two Muslim women, then are his salvation from the Fire - each of their limbs suffices for a limb of himself. And any Muslim woman that frees a Muslim

woman, then she is her salvation from the Fire - each of her limb suffices for a limb of herself."

Source: Jami` at-Tirmidhi 1547 Graded Sahih by Darussalam

Narrated Abu Hurayrah:

The Prophet said: If anyone wants to put a ring of fire on one he loves, let him put a gold ring on him: if anyone wants to put a necklace of fire on one he loves, let him put a gold necklace on him, and if anyone wants to put a bracelet of fire on one he loves let him put a gold bracelet on him. Keep to silver and amuse yourselves with it.

Source: Sunan Abi Dawud 4236 Graded Hasan by Albani

It was narrated from 'Awf bin Malik that the Messenger of Allah(ﷺ) said:

"The Jews split into seventy-one sects, one of which will be in Paradise and seventy in Hell. The Christians split into seventy-two sects, seventy-one of which will be in Hell and one in Paradise. I swear by the One Whose Hand is the soul of Muhammad, my nation will split into seventy-three sects, one of which will be in Paradise and seventy-two in Hell." It was said: *"O Messenger of Allah, who are they?"* He said: *"The main body."*

Source: Sunan Ibn Majah 3992 Graded Hasan by Darussalam

Abu Huraira reported directly from Allah's Messenger (ﷺ) that he said:

The distance of the two shoulders of the non-believer in Hell will be a three-day journey for a swift rider.

Source: Sahih Muslim 2852

Abdullah bin Mas'ud narrated that the Messenger of Allah said:

"Hell will be brought forth on that Day (of Resurrection) having seventy thousand bridles, and with every handle will be seventy thousand angels dragging it'".

Source: Jami at-Tirmidhi

English reference : Vol. 4, Book 13, Hadith 2573

Graded Sahih by Darussalam

Narrated Ibn 'Abbas:

The Prophet said: "I was shown the Hell-fire and that the majority of its dwellers were women who were ungrateful." It was asked, "Do they disbelieve in Allah?" (or are they ungrateful to Allah?) He replied, "They are ungrateful to their husbands and are ungrateful for the favors and the good (charitable deeds) done to them. If you have always been good (benevolent) to one of them and then she sees something in you (not of her liking), she will say, 'I have never received any good from you."

Source: Sahih al-Bukhari 29

It was narrated that Abu Hurairah said:

"*The Messenger of Allah said: 'The dust in the cause of Allah and the smoke of Hell will never be combined in the nostrils of a Muslim, and stinginess and faith will never be combined in a Muslim man's heart.'*"

Source: Sunan an-Nasa'i 3114 Graded Hasan by Darussalam

Abu 'Ali At-Tujibi (said) that he heard Abu Raihanah say:

"*I heard the Messenger of Allah say: 'The eye that stays awake in the cause of Allah will be forbidden to the Fire.'*"

Source: Sunan an-Nasa'i 3117 Graded Hasan by Darussalam

Narrated Imran ibn Husayn:

The Prophet said: If anyone swears a false oath in confinement, he should make his seat in Hell on account of his (act).

Source: Sunan Abi Dawud 3242 Graded Sahih by Albani

Narrated Abu Hurayrah:

The Prophet said: Allah Most High says: Pride is my cloak and majesty is my lower garment, and I shall throw him who vie with me regarding one of them into Hell.

Source: Sunan Abi Dawud 4090 Graded Sahih by Albani

Narrated Abu Hurayrah:

The Prophet said: It is not allowable for a Muslim to keep apart from his brother for more than three days, for one who does so and dies will enter Hell.

Source: Sunan Abi Dawud 4914 Graded Sahih by Albani

It was narrated that Abu Dharr said:

"The Prophet passed by me and I was lying on my stomach. He nudged me with his foot and said: 'O Junaidib! This is how the people of Hell lie.'"

Source: Sunan Ibn Majah 3724 Graded Sahih by Darussalam

Abu Hurairah narrated that:

the Messenger of Allah said: "Whoever begs from people so as to accumulate more riches, he is asking for a live coal from hell, so let him ask for a lot or a little."

Source: Sunan Ibn Majah 1838 Graded Sahih by Darussalam

It was narrated from Abu Dharr that he heard the Messenger of Allah (ﷺ) say:

"Whoever claims something that does not belong to him; he is not one of us, so let him take his place in Hell."

Source: Sunan Ibn Majah 2319 Graded Sahih by Darussalam

It was narrated from 'Abdullah bin 'Amr that the Messenger of Allah (ﷺ) said:

"Whoever drinks wine and gets drunk, his prayer will not be accepted for forty days, and if he dies he will enter Hell, but if he repents, Allah will accept his repentance. If he drinks wine again and gets drunk, his prayer will not be accepted for forty days, and if he dies he will enter Hell, but if he repents, Allah will accept his

repentance. If he drinks wine again and gets drunk, his prayer will not be accepted for forty days, and if he dies he will enter Hell, but if he repents Allah will accept his repentance. But if he does it again, then Allah will most certainly make him drink of the mire of the puss or sweat on the Day of Resurrection." They said: "O Messenger of Allah, what is the mire of the pus or sweat? He said: "The drippings of the people of Hell."

Source: Sunan ibn Majah

English reference : Vol. 4, Book 30, Hadith 3377

Graded Sahih by Darussalam

It was narrated from Abu Hurairah that the Messenger of Allah (ﷺ) said:

"A man may speak a word that angers Allah and not see anything wrong with it, but it will cause him to sink down in Hell the depth of seventy autumns."

Source: Sunan Ibn Majah 3970 Graded Sahih by Darussalam

It was narrated from Abu Hurairah that the Prophet (ﷺ) said:

"Wretched is the slave of the Dinar, the slave of the Dirham and the slave of the Khamisah. He is wretched and will be thrown (into Hell) on his face, and if he is pricked with a thorn may find no relief."

Source: Sunan ibn Majah

English reference : Vol. 5, Book 37, Hadith 4136

Graded Sahih by Darussalam

It is narrated on the authority of Jabir that a man came to the Messenger of Allah (ﷺ) and said:

Messenger of Allah, what are the two things quite unavoidable? He replied: He who dies without associating anyone with Allah would (necessarily) enter Paradise and he who dies associating anything with Allah would enter the (Fire of) Hell.

Source: Sahih Muslim 93 a

It is narrated on the authority of Abu Huraira that the Messenger of Allah (ﷺ) observed:

By Him in Whose hand is the life of Muhammad, he who amongst the community of Jews or Christians hears about me, but does not affirm his belief in that with which I have been sent and dies in this state (of disbelief), he shall be but one of the denizens of Hell-Fire.

Source: Sahih Muslim 153

Abu Hurairah narrated that the Messenger of Allah said:

"Some of the Fire (in the shape of a long neck) will come out of the Fire on the Day of judgment. It will have two eyes which can see, two ears which can hear, and a tongue which can speak. It will say: 'I have been left in charge of three: Every obstinate oppressor, everyone who called upon a deity besides Allah, and the image makers."

Source: Jami at-Tirmidhi

English reference : Vol. 4, Book 13, Hadith 2574

Graded Hasan by Darussalam

Narrated Al-Mustawrid:

The Prophet said: If anyone eats once at the cost of a Muslim's honour, Allah will give him a like amount of Hellfire to eat; if anyone clothes himself with a garment at the cost of a Muslim's honour, Allah will clothe him with like amount of Hellfire; and if anyone puts himself in a position of reputation and show Allah will disgrace him with a place of reputation and show on the Day of Resurrection.

Source: Sunan Abi Dawud 4881 Graded Sahih by Albani

Narrated Abdullah ibn Habashi:

The Prophet said: If anyone cuts the lote-tree, Allah brings him headlong into Hell.

Abu Dawud was asked about the meaning of this tradition. He said: This is a brief tradition. It means that if anyone cuts uselessly, unjustly and without any right a lote-tree under the shade of which travellers and beasts take shelter, Allah will bring him into Hell headlong.

Source: Sunan Abi Dawud 5239 Graded Sahih by Albani

Ahnaf b. Qais said:

I came out with the intention of (participating in) fighting. Abu Bakrah met me and said: Go back, for I heard the Messenger of Allah say: When two Muslims face each other with their swords, the killer and the slain will go to Hell. He asked: Messenger of

Allah, this is the killer (so naturally he should go to Hell), but what is the matter with the slain ? He replied: He intended to kill his companion.

Source: Sunan Abi Dawud 4268 Graded Sahih by Albani

Ali said:

"The Messenger of Allah sent an army and appointed a man as a commander for them and he commanded them to listen to him and obey. He kindled fire and ordered them to jump into it. A group refused to enter into it and said "We escaped from the fire"; a group intended to enter into it. When the Prophet was informed about it, he said "Had they entered into it, they would have remained into it. There is no obedience in matters involving disobedience to Allaah. Obedience is in matters which are good and universally recognized."

Source: Sunan Abi Dawud 2625 Graded Sahih by Albani

It was narrated that 'Adi bin Hatim said:

"The Messenger of Allah said: 'There is no one among you but his Lord will speak to him without any intermediary between them. He will look to his right and will not see anything but that which he sent forth. He will look to his left and will not see anything but that which he sent forth. Then he will look in front of him and will be faced with the Fire. So whoever among you can protect himself from fire, even by means of half a date, let him do so.'"

Source: Sunan ibn Majah

English reference : Vol. 1, Book 1, Hadith 185

Graded Sahih by Darussalam

It was narrated that Abu Sa'eed Khudri said:

"The Messenger of Allah said: 'When Allah has saved the believers from Hell and they are safe, none of you will dispute with his companion more vehemently for some right of his in this world than the believers will dispute with their Lord on behalf of their brothers in faith who have entered Hell. They will say: " Our Lord! They are our brothers, they used to pray with us, fast with us and perform Hajj with us, and you have admitted them to Hell." He will say: "Go and bring forth those whom you recognize among them." So they will come to them , and they will recognize them by their faces. The Fire will not consume their faces, although there will be some whom the Fire will seize halfway up their shins, and others whom it will seize up to their ankles. They will bring them forth, and will say. "Our Lord, we have brought forth those whom You commanded us to bring forth." Then He will say: "Bring forth those who have a Dinar's weight of faith in their hearts, then those who have half a Dinar's weight in their hearts, then those who have a mustard-seed's weight." Abu Sa'eed said. :"He who does not believe this, let him recite, 'Surely, Allah wrongs not even of the weight of an atom (or a small ant), but is there is any good (done), He doubles it, and gives from Him a great reward.'"

Source: Sunan ibn Majah

English reference : Vol. 1, Book 1, Hadith 60

Graded Sahih by Darussalam

Abu Hurairah narrated that the Messenger of Allah (s.a.w) said:

"The molar teeth of the disbeliever on the Day of Judgment will be like Uhud (mountain), his thigh will be like Al-Baida, and his seat in the Fire will be like the distance of three the likes of Ar-Rabadhah."

Source: Jami at-Tirmidhi

English reference : Vol. 4, Book 13, Hadith 2578

Graded Hasan by Darussalam

An-Nu`man bin Bashir narrated that:

The Prophet said: "The supplication, is worship." Then he recited: And Your Lord said: "Call upon me, I will respond to you. Verily, those who scorn My worship, they will surely enter Hell humiliated."

Source: Jami` at-Tirmidhi 3372 Graded Sahih by Darussalam

Narrated Abu Miljaz:

that Mu'awiyah came out and 'Abdullah bin Az-Zubair and Ibn Safwan stood for him when they saw him, so he said: "Sit, I heard the Messenger of Allah saying: 'Whoever wishes that he be received by men standing then, let him take his seat in the Fire.'"

Source: Jami at-Tirhmidi

English reference : Vol. 5, Book 41, Hadith 2755

Graded Hasan by Darussalam

Narrated Abdullah ibn Mas'ud:

I heard the Messenger of Allah say: He who lets his garment trail during prayer out of pride, Allah, the Almighty, has nothing to do with pardoning him and protecting him from Hell.

Source: Sunan Abi Dawud 637 Graded Sahih by Albani

It was narrated from 'Ali bin Abu Talib that:

The Prophet said: "Whoever leaves an area the size of a hair on his body and does not cleanse it from sexual impurity, such and such will be done to him in the Fire." 'Ali said: "Because of that I am hostile towards my hair," and he used to shave his head.

Source: Sunan ibn Majah

English reference : Vol. 1, Book 1, Hadith 599

Graded Hasan by Darussalam

It was narrated from Abu Malik Ash'ari that the Messenger of Allah (ﷺ) said:

'Wailing is one of the affairs of the Days of Ignorance, and if the woman who wails dies without having repented, Allah will cut a garment of pitch (tar) for her and a shirt of flaming fire.'"

Source: Sunan ibn Majah

English reference : Vol. 1, Book 6, Hadith 1581

Graded Hasan by Darussalam

Abu Hurayra reported that the Prophet, said:

"Disgrace! Disgrace! Disgrace!" They said, "Messenger of Allah, who?" He said, "The one who fails his parents or one of them when they are old will enter the Fire."

Source: Al-Adab Al-Mufrad 21 Graded Sahih by Albani

Abu Mas'ud al-Ansari reported:

When I was beating my servant, I heard a voice behind me (saying): Abu Mas'ud, bear in mind Allah has more dominance over you than you have upon him. I turned and (found him) to be Allah's Messenger. I said: Allah's Messenger, I set him free for the sake of Allah. Thereupon he said: Had you not done that, Hell would have opened for you, or the fire would have burnt you.

Source: Sahih Muslim 1659 c

It was narrated from Jabir that:

A man from (the tribe of) Jaishan, who are from Yemen, came and asked the Messenger of Allah about a drink that they drank in his homeland that was made of corn and called Al-Mizr (beer). The Prophet said to him: "Is it an intoxicant?" He said: "Yes." The Messenger of Allah said: "Every intoxicant is unlawful. Allah, the Mighty and Sublime, has promised the one who drinks intoxicants that He will give him to drink from the mud of Khibal." They said: "O Messenger of Allah, what is the mud of Khibal?" He said: "The sweat of the people of Hell," or he said: "The juice of the people of Hell."

Source: Sunan an-Nasa'i 5709 Graded Sahih by Darussalam

Narrated Abu Huraira:

When Khaibar was conquered, Allah's Messenger was presented with a poisoned (roasted) sheep. Allah's Apostle said, "Collect for me all the Jews present in this area." (When they were gathered) Allah's Apostle said to them, "I am going to ask you about something; will you tell me the truth?" They replied, "Yes, O Abal-Qasim!" Allah's Messenger said to them, "Who is your father?" They said, "Our father is so-and-so." Allah's Messenger said, "You have told a lie. for your father is so-and-so," They said, "No doubt, you have said the truth and done the correct thing." He again said to them, "If I ask you about something; will you tell me the truth?" They replied, "Yes, O Abal-Qasim! And if we should tell a lie you will know it as you have known it regarding our father," Allah's Messenger then asked, "Who are the people of the (Hell) Fire?" They replied, "We will remain in the (Hell) Fire for a while and then you (Muslims) will replace us in it" Allah's Messenger said to them. ''You will abide in it with ignominy. By Allah, we shall never replace you in it at all." Then he asked them again, "If I ask you something, will you tell me the truth?" They replied, "Yes." He asked. "Have you put the poison in this roasted sheep?" They replied, "Yes," He asked, "What made you do that?" They replied, "We intended to learn if you were a liar in which case we would be relieved from you, and if you were a prophet then it would not harm you."

Source: Sahih al-Bukhari 5777

Narrated Hudhaifa bin Al-Yaman:

The people used to ask Allah's Messenger about the good but I used to ask him about the evil lest I should be overtaken by them. So I said, "O Allah's Messenger! We were living in ignorance and in an (extremely) worst atmosphere, then Allah brought to us this good (i.e., Islam); will there be any evil after this good?" He said, "Yes." I said, 'Will there be any good after that evil?" He replied, "Yes, but it will be tainted (not pure.)'' I asked, "What will be its taint?" He replied, "(There will be) some people who will guide others not according to my tradition? You will approve of some of their deeds and disapprove of some others." I asked, "Will there be any evil after that good?" He replied, "Yes, (there will be) some people calling at the gates of the (Hell) Fire, and whoever will respond to their call, will be thrown by them into the (Hell) Fire." I said, "O Allah s Apostle! Will you describe them to us?" He said, "They will be from our own people and will speak our language." I said, "What do you order me to do if such a state should take place in my life?" He said, "Stick to the group of Muslims and their Imam (ruler)." I said, "If there is neither a group of Muslims nor an Imam (ruler)?" He said, "Then turn away from all those sects even if you were to bite (eat) the roots of a tree till death overtakes you while you are in that state."

Source: Sahih al-Bukhari 7084

Abu Hurairah narrated that the Messenger of Allah said:

"Indeed a man, and a woman, perform deeds in obedience to Allah for sixty years, then death presents itself to them, and they cause such harm in the will that the Fire becomes warranted for them." Then he recited: After payment of legacies he (or she) may have bequeathed or debts, without causing harm. This is a Commandment from Allah. up to His saying: That is the magnificent success.

Source: Jami` at-Tirmidhi 2117

Graded Hasan by Darussalam

Abdullah bin Buraidah narrated from his father that:

A man came to the Prophet and he was wearing an iron ring. He said: "Why do I see you wearing the jewelry of the people of Hell?" He threw it away, then he came and he was wearing a brass ring. He said: "Why do I notice the stench of idols from you?" So he threw it away, and said: "O Messenger of Allah, what should I use?" He said: "Silver, but it should not equal a Mithqal."

Source: Sunan an-Nasa'i 5195 Graded Hasan by Darussalam

It was narrated from Abu Hurairah that the Messenger of Allah said:

"Avoid the seven sins that doom one to Hell." It was said: "O Messenger of Allah, what are they?" He said: "Associating others with Allah (Shirk), magic, killing a soul whom Allah has forbidden killing, except in cases dictated by Islamic law, consuming Riba(usury / interest), consuming the property of orphans, fleeing on the day of the march (to battlefield), and slandering chaste women who never even think of anything touching their chastity and are good believers."

Source: Sunan an-Nasa'i 3671 Graded Sahih by Darussalam

Yazid bin Abi Mariam said:

"Abayah bin Rafi' met me when I was walking to Friday prayers, and he said: 'Rejoice, for these steps you are taking are in the cause

of Allah. I heard Abu 'Abs say: The Messenger of Allah said: Anyone whose feet become dusty in the cause of Allah, he will be forbidden to the Fire.'"

Source: Sunan an-Nasa'i 3116 Graded Sahih by Darussalam

Narrated Abu Huraira:

The Prophet said, "The part of an Izar (lower garment) which hangs below the ankles is in the Fire."

Source: Sahih al-Bukhari 5787

Narrated Abdur Rahman:

I asked Abu Sa'id al-Khudri about wearing lower garment. He said: You have come to the man who knows it very well. The Messenger of Allah said: The way for a believer to wear a lower garment is to have it halfway down his legs and he is guilty of no sin if it comes halfway between that and the ankles, but what comes lower than the ankles is in Hell. On the day of Resurrection. Allah will not look at him who trails his lower garment conceitedly.

Source: Sunan Abi Dawud 4093

Graded Sahih by Darussalam

The above two hadith about not letting the lower garment trail below the ankles is regarding males only. Other hadith explain this. It is part of a believing woman's modesty to be covered head to toe. Since this is an aqeedah book dealing with the Akhirah the fiqh of woman's clothing is not mentioned, aside from this explanation saying women should have clothing below their ankles when in public. Besides otherwise it'd be female imitation of males which is sinful as has been previously mentioned in other hadith.

It was narrated that 'Ubadah bin Samit said:

"I taught people from Ahlus-Suffah" Qur'an and how to write, and one of them gave me a bow. I said: 'It is not money, and I can shoot (with it) for the sake of Allah., I asked the Messenger of Allah about it and he said: 'If it would please you to have a necklace of fire placed around your neck, then accept it.'"

Source: Sunan ibn Majah

English reference : Vol. 3, Book 12, Hadith 2157

Graded Hasan by Darussalam

Abu Umamah Al-Harithi narrated that he heard the Messenger of Allah (ﷺ) say:

"No man seizes the wealth of a Muslim unlawfully by means of his (false) oath, but Allah will deny Paradise to him and will doom him to Hell." A man among the people said: "O Messenger of Allah, even if it is something small?" He said: "Even if it is a twig of an Arak tree."

Source: Sunan Ibn Majah 2324 Graded Sahih by Darussalam

Mutarrif, from the tribe of Banu 'Amir bin Sa'sa'ah narrated that 'Uthman bin Abul-'As Ath-Thaqafi invited

him to drink some milk that he poured for him. Mutarrif said:

"I am fasting." 'Uthman said: "I heard the Messenger of Allah say: 'Fasting is a shield against the Fire just like the shield of anyone of you against fighting.'"

Source: Sunan ibn Majah

English reference : Vol. 1, Book 7, Hadith 1639

Graded Sahih by Darussalam

It was narrated that 'Ubadah bin Samit said:

"The Messenger of Allah led us in prayer on the Day of Hunain, beside a camel that was part of the spoils of war. Then he took something from the camel, and extracted from it a hair, which he placed between two of his fingers. Then he said: 'O people, this is part of your spoils of war. Hand over a needle and thread and anything greater than that or less than that. For stealing from the spoils of war will be a source of shame for those who do it, and ignominy and Fire, on the Day of Resurrection.'"

Source: Sunan ibn Majah

English reference : Vol. 4, Book 24, Hadith 2850

Graded Hasan by Darussalam

Abu Huraira reported Allah's Messenger (ﷺ) having said this:

*Two are the types of the denizens of Hell whom I did not see:
people having flogs like the tails of the ox with them and they
would be beating people, and the women who would be dressed but
appear to be naked, who would be inclined (to evil) and make their
husbands incline towards it. Their heads would be like the humps
of the bukht camel inclined to one side. They will not enter
Paradise and they would not smell its odour whereas its odour
would be smelt from such and such distance.*

Source: Sahih Muslim 2128

Yahya ibn Rashid said:

*We were sitting waiting for Abdullah ibn Umar who came out to
us and sat. He then said: I heard the Messenger of Allah as saying:
If anyone's intercession intervenes as an obstacle to one of the
punishments prescribed by Allah, he has opposed Allah; if anyone
disputes knowingly about something which is false, he remains in
the displeasure of Allah till he desists, and if anyone makes an
untruthful accusation against a Muslim, he will be made by Allah
to dwell in the corrupt fluid flowing from the inhabitants of Hell
till he retracts his statement.*

Source: Sunan Abi Dawud 3597

Graded Sahih by Albani

**It was narrated from Abu Hurairah that the Messenger of
Allah (ﷺ) said:**

*"A man may do the deeds of the people of goodness for seventy
years, then when he makes his will, he is unjust in his will, so he
ends (his life) with evil deeds and enters Hell. And a man may do*

the people of evil for seventy years, then he is just in his will, so he ends (his life) with good deeds and enters Paradise."Abu Hurairah said: "Recite, if you wish: "These are the limits (set by) Allah up to His saying: 'a disgraceful torment'"

Source: Sunan ibn Majah

English reference : Vol. 3, Book 22, Hadith 2704

Graded Hasan by Darussalam

Shaqiq reported that it was said to Usama b. Zaid:

Why don't you visit 'Uthman and talk to him? Thereupon he said: Do you think that I have not talked to him but that I have made you hear? By Allah. I have talked to him (about things) concerning me and him and I did not like to divulge those things about which I had to take the initiative and I do not say to my ruler: "You are the best among people," after I heard Allah's Messenger as saying: A man will be brought on the Day of Resurrection and thrown in Hell-Fire and his intestines will pour forth in Hell and he will go round along with them, as an ass goes round the mill stone. The denizens of Hell would gather round him and say: O, so and so, what has happened to you? Were you not enjoining us to do what was reputable and forbid us to do what was disreputable? He will say: Of course, it is so; I used to enjoin (upon people) to do what was reputable but did not practice that myself. I had been forbidding people to do what was disreputable, but practiced it myself.

Source: Sahih Muslim 2989 a

Narrated Sa`d bin Sahl As-Sa`idi:

The Prophet looked at a man fighting against the pagans and he was one of the most competent persons fighting on behalf of the Muslims. The Prophet said, "Let him who wants to look at a man from the dwellers of the (Hell) Fire, look at this (man)." Another man followed him and kept on following him till he (the fighter) was injured and, seeking to die quickly, he placed the blade tip of his sword between his breasts and leaned over it till it passed through his shoulders (i.e., committed suicide)." The Prophet added, "A person may do deeds that seem to the people as the deeds of the people of Paradise while in fact, he is from the dwellers of the (Hell) Fire: and similarly a person may do deeds that seem to the people as the deeds of the people of the (Hell) Fire while in fact, he is from the dwellers of Paradise. Verily, the (results of) deeds done, depend upon the last actions."

Source: Sahih al-Bukhari 6493

A'isha reported Allah's Messenger (ﷺ) as saying:

Every one of the children of Adam has been created with three hundred and sixty joints; so he who declares the Glory of Allah, praises Allah, declares Allah to be One, Glorifies Allah, and seeks forgiveness from Allah, and removes stone, or thorn, or bone from people's path, and enjoins what is good and forbids from evil, to the number of those three hundred and sixty joints, will walk that day having saved himself from the Fire.

Source: Sahih Muslim 1007 a

Amazingly Muhammad pbuh was exactly right when saying there are 360 joints. The scientific disbelievers thousands of years later have counted them and count them as 360 exactly. By the modern scientific consensus of the medical community there are 86 skull joints, 6 throat joints, 66 thorax joints, 76 in your spine and pelvis with 32 in each upper limb and 31 in each lower limb. How could Muhammad pbuh have known they were 360 to such a degree of accuracy in the 600s CE? Counting the joints by scientific methods was impossible in his era. God the Creator of those joints told him. That's just 1 proof of the many proofs of true prophethood which no one can rightly deny. The same Muhammad pbuh has authentically reported all the preceding Quranic ayat and hadith in this book about the Akhirah. So be warned of the blazing hellfire prepared for the non-Muslims and the eventual paradise for those Muslims who submit to the Creator with sincerity. For the Akhirah awaits you, all 360 joints. Pray that we die upon the way of the prophets and the salaf and meet in paradise.

Lastly it is reported that 'Alī bin Abī Ṯālib said:

"Mention what you will of the greatness of Allāh, but Allāh is greater than anything you say. And mention what you will of the Fire, but it is more severe than anything you say. And mention what you will of Paradise, but it is better than anything you say."

Abū Bakr Al-Daynūrī, Al-Mujālasah wa Jawāhir Al-'Ilm article 853.